AMERICAN
INTOLERANCE

ALSO BY ROBERT E. BARTHOLOMEW AND PETER HASSALL

A Colorful History of Popular Delusions

ALSO BY ROBERT E. BARTHOLOMEW AND BENJAMIN RADFORD

Hoaxes, Myths, and Manias

ALSO BY ROBERT E. BARTHOLOMEW AND GEORGE S. HOWARD

UFOs & Alien Contact

AMERICAN
INTOLERANCE

OUR DARK HISTORY OF
DEMONIZING IMMIGRANTS

ROBERT E. BARTHOLOMEW
AND
ANJA E. REUMSCHÜSSEL

WITHDRAWN

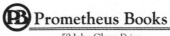 Prometheus Books

59 John Glenn Drive
Amherst, New York 14228

Published 2018 by Prometheus Books

Cover design by Liz Mills
Cover image © Everett Historical/Shutterstock
Cover design © Prometheus Books

Inquiries should be addressed to
Prometheus Books
59 John Glenn Drive
Amherst, New York 14228
VOICE: 716–691–0133 • FAX: 716–691–0137
WWW.PROMETHEUSBOOKS.COM

22 21 20 19 18   5 4 3 2 1

Library of Congress Cataloging-in-Publication Data

LCCN 2018019690 (print)
ISBN 978-1-63388-448-9 (hardcover) | ISBN 978-1-63388-449-6 (ebook)

Printed in the United States of America

To the tired, the poor, and the huddled masses
who come to America seeking a better life

CONTENTS

CONTENTS

FOREWORD

"Lustful priests." "Dim-witted," "dirty, disease-carrying Mexicans" who "multiply like rabbits." The "filthy Chinese"—a "poor, miserable, dwarfish race of inferior beings." The "childlike, barbaric, and otherwise inferior" American Indian. "Japs." "Nips." The "evil, money-hungry" Jewish "conspirators" who destroy everything that Christians hold sacred. The Muslims, a people marked by "arrogance and blood-thirsty cruelty," who are "parasitic" and "live by unproductive labor, petty trading, and graft." Wherever they have gone, they have "exercised a very baleful influence." . . . The litany of abusive, defamatory slurs American observers have hurled against dreamers who enter the United States from every continent but Antarctica is mind-numbing. But the authors of *American Intolerance* do not content themselves with an exposition on the country's benighted past; they remind us that these slurs, prejudices, and exclusionary tactics have direct relevance for the contemporary era. The country has elected a president who, during his candidacy, advocated a wall at its southern border to keep out Mexicans, and laws to exclude Muslims. Bartholomew and Reumschüssel warn us about the moral panics that the irrational fear of aliens has stirred up in the American heart.

In societies around the world and very possibly throughout human history, people have become unduly distressed and concerned that, somewhere, certain categories of humanity are engaged in despicable acts. At times, under certain circumstances, this distress and concern intensifies, breaking out into more exaggerated and overt manifestations. For as long as societies have been reasonably diverse and heterogeneous, observers have noticed this interesting phenomenon, but these early observations produced no analytic traction or intellectual progeny—nor a distinctive designation to describe it—until Jock Young, in 1971, and Stanley

Cohen, in 1972, coined a name for this state of affairs, constructed an explanation of how and why such outbreaks occur, and pointed out how they are linked to the larger social structure. Their formulations generated commentary and research that has been continuous since they launched it, and such analysis remains vigorous to this day. To quote Jason Ditton, the moral panic "has been far and away the most influential sociological concept to have been generated in the second half of the twentieth century."[1] Moral panic researchers have illuminated the sudden eruption of fear of pseudo-villainous agents who have ranged from semi-somnolent Chinese opium smokers to the gleeful horror-comic-book-reading children next door.

An essential element of the moral panic is that the concern about a particular threat be *disproportional* or *exaggerated* as compared with what a clearheaded, empirical, and factual investigation would tell us. The exaggerations may pertain to the gravity of the threat—the number of victims, the seriousness of the harm, the cost of the damage to the society—or it may even involve whether such a threat exists in the first place. No one questions the right of someone to run away from a screaming, knife-wielding maniac. But the actual menace posed by many supposed threats, objectively assessed, turns out to be minor or nonexistent. Hence, the moral panics researcher is forced to be a skeptic. Is this fear based on something material? If so, what is the risk? Where is the evidence and what does it say? For the student of moral panics, data counts; facts matter. Let's do some comparisons, these theorists insist. Did the Chinese opium smokers *really* entice white children to take up the habit, seduce and enslave our wives and daughters, and corrupt and bring down Western civilization? Was it really *true* that reading comic books turned our adolescent boys into juvenile delinquents? Let's check, then let's find out why such beliefs are plausible at certain times and places. Why this issue? Why this supposed threat? Why these targets?

The most classic panics entail *mobilization*. Protests, demonstrations, posses, meetings, speeches. They are typically characterized by violence, threats, denunciations, and heated arguments, the formation of political action groups, and social movements. There are laws, bills, prohibitions, arrests, and imprisonments. Articles about the presumed threat are published in newspapers and magazines, the social media, fiction of the day, and angry letters to editors. In the modern era, anxious tales are broadcast about the outrage and threat of the putative menace in television news reports, and in film. Governments often jump on the bandwagon and generate budget allocations to address the problem. Police stand alert to spot and take action against the accused miscreants. In short, what do the members of a society *do* when they learn of the threat supposedly facing them?

What about immigrants? What makes the arrival of foreign-born folk to our shores a matter of exaggerated concern? As historian Matt Jacobson writes in *Whiteness of a Different Color*, in 1891, anti-Italian riots erupted in New Orleans as eleven Italians were lynched following the outcome of a murder trial that had been rigged by the local Mafia.[2] An editorial in the *New York Times* defended the lynching, declaring that the mob was made up of the city's "best element," wielding the incident to suggest that the behavior of the Italian immigrants was racially determined, and questioning their fitness for citizenship.[3] The editorial referred to "sneaking and cowardly Sicilians" who are ruled by "lawless passions" and distinguished by "cutthroat practices." Rattlesnakes, the editorial concluded, "were as good citizens as they." In the 1890s, when a journalist asked an American construction worker if Italians were white, "No, sir," he replied, "an Italian is a Dago." In a like fashion, political cartoons published in the nineteenth century depicted Irish immigrants as hot-tempered, savage, and threatening, and looking distinctly swarthy and "Negroid" in countenance. Signs appeared on establishment doors: "NO IRISH NEED APPLY!" To many long-established Yankees of impeccable WASP ancestry, the Irish were not quite white, but rather a species of being categorically and distinctly inferior to themselves and therefore deserving of no rights. And very possibly a threat to the rest of us. Drunkards. Criminals. Papists.

Inferior to the rest of us. A different species of being. A threat. For much of American history, the people who migrated from other lands generated a measure of fear, suspicion, and concern among a substantial number of vociferous native-born Americans, and, under certain conditions, these emotions erupted into virulent incidents. They aren't like us, these nativists claimed; they engage in wicked, unwholesome practices, and hold insidious beliefs. Keep them out. Are undocumented Mexican immigrants really "criminals, drug dealers, and rapists," as presidential candidate Donald Trump claimed during his campaign? As any fact-checker will tell you, Mexican immigrants are less likely to commit crimes than native-born Americans; thus, Trump's statement turns out to be not only exaggerated but untrue—in fact, a lie. Do *some* illegal Mexican immigrants commit crime? Of course. Do some Muslims commit terrorist acts? We already know that "some" do. Members of all groups, in some measure, do as well.

As Bartholomew and Reumschüssel masterfully argue, in this, a land *populated* by immigrants and their descendants, immigrants have been demonized for almost two centuries. They are the "Other," America's "folk devils," a "suitable enemy"—in short, *deviants*. The case studies the authors investigate focus on the *deviantization* of historically successive immigrant categories. *American Intolerance* skillfully links the dehumanization that racism accomplishes with the stigmatization process of turning categories of humanity into deviants, not because of what they've *done*, but because of who they *are*. Here, we are in the territory of Erving Goffman's "tribal stigma of race, nation, and religion," those shameful categorical blemishes that "can be transmitted through lineages and equally contaminate all members of a family."[4] The philosopher David Livingston Smith covers this ground in his insightful volume, *Less Than Human: Why We Demean, Enslave, and Exterminate Others*. To that roster of "othering" actions we might also want to know why some of us *exclude* others from this country of ours. Yes, it's true that we dehumanize others, but there's a twist: We also fear that these others are all too human, and so we need mechanisms to reassure us that they are not *quite* so human.

And that's where Bartholomew and Reumschüssel guide us through America's long history of its "exaggerated fear" of immigrants. Catholic aliens are unworthy of citizenship because, zombie-like, they take orders from Rome. Because, within those closed-off church convent compounds, nuns and priests engage in unholy acts of depravity and perversion. Because they murder babies conceived in these unholy acts. The tribal stigma—that taint, the *human stain*—born by particular categories of humanity—Mexicans, Chinese, American Indians, Germans, Japanese, Jews, Muslims—those aliens whom nativists endeavored to exclude, seemed manifestly self-evident. Red-blooded, native-born citizens of the United States of America considered them unassimilable because they were incapable of becoming authentic Americans; if allowed to enter our country, they would menace our sacred way of life. Sneaky, dangerous, barbaric, brutish, un-Christian. Keep 'em out.

Exaggerated fear? Moral panic? During the historical apex of the scapegoating, the nativists did not think so—the categories they attempted to exclude were a foregone conclusion. Imagine the society we would live in today had these sentiments not gotten riled up, these bans not put in place. Perhaps even then, we wouldn't have become a cosmopolitan paradise, but at least Donald J. Trump would not have been elected president of the United States. *American Intolerance* admirably lays the groundwork for explaining why such a paradise was not to be.

Erich Goode
Sociology Professor Emeritus, Stony Brook University

Erich Goode is the author of several influential books in the field of sociology, including *Moral Panics: The Social Construction of Deviance* (2010), *Drugs in American Society* (2014), and *The Handbook on Deviance* (2015).

FROM OUT OF THE SHADOWS

Moral Panics and the Search for Scapegoats

Those who do not remember the past are condemned to repeat it.
—George Santayana, *The Life of Reason*, 1954

In folklore, the bogeyman is the embodiment of evil, a sinister creature lurking in the shadows that is used to scare children into behaving. It has no set form, allowing it to reflect our innermost fears. The bogeyman serves as a cautionary tale. A parent might tell their child, "Don't walk home alone after dark or the bogeyman will get you!" Most children grow out of their fear and eventually see it for what it is: a figment of their imagination. The bogeyman is a metaphor for the dark side of human nature and the potential evil that could be lurking around the next corner. Remarkably, from time to time, groups of adults come to believe in the existence of bogeymen—not as monsters from their childhood, but as real-life evildoers who pose an imminent threat to society. They are what anthropologists refer to as "the Other": people who are so alien in appearance and custom that they are seen as irrational, immoral, perverse, and—all too often—evil. These bogeymen are the product of fear, ignorance, and prejudice, and they appear in the form of social panics that arise from deep-seated tensions that accumulate during times of national crisis such as the specter of war, civil unrest, and economic turmoil.

In this book, we examine several waves of panic in American history involving the exaggerated fear of immigrants. Outbreaks reflect popular stereotypes of groups targeted solely for their ethnicity or religious beliefs. During periods of great fear, there is a tendency to release pent-up tensions by creating scapegoats. Psychologists refer to this as the "kick-the-dog syndrome" or displaced aggression. When someone has a bad day at work, he may come home and yell at his wife, who in turn may scold her son for the smallest infraction. Having no one to take out his anger on—the son kicks the dog. A similar process occurs in society. During times of crisis, people search for scapegoats.[1] Ironically, the most vulnerable are the easiest targets: immigrants, asylum-seekers, and minorities. This process of blaming others for society's problems reduces anxiety and offers a simplistic explanation for complex issues of the day.

Despite its reputation as the world's leading light for justice and equality, the United States has often failed to uphold these ideals. At the base of the Statue of Liberty rests a bronze tablet with the words: "From her beacon-hand glows worldwide welcome . . . 'Give me your tired, your poor, your huddled masses yearning to breathe free. The wretched refuse of your teeming shore. Send these, the homeless, tempest-tost to me. I lift my lamp beside the golden door!'" Written by Jewish poet Emma Lazarus, these words have come to symbolize America's history of welcoming immigrants from every corner of the globe, and embracing them regardless of skin color, ethnic heritage, or religious beliefs. Yet this often-touted pillar of American democracy with its emphasis on acceptance, tolerance, and diversity has been true only *some* of the time. It is more myth than reality. For at certain times in our history, the golden doors have been slammed shut, and the welcome mat removed. These periods of intolerance and fearmongering are fueled by sensational media reports and alarmist claims by politicians, police, lobbyists, and vigilante groups, who are worried over the new threat. Momentum soon snowballs into an unstoppable force that gives rise to harassment, persecution, and scapegoating.

During the nineteenth century, Americans endured the Great Catholic Scare, fostered a fear of Mexicans, imposed a ban on Chinese migrants, and engaged in the systematic persecution of Native Americans. At the time, "Indians" were not citizens and were considered foreigners in their own land. A second wave of scares arose during the twentieth century, amidst the fog of war: the German-American hysteria of World War I, the internment of Japanese Americans after the bombing of Pearl Harbor, and the Jewish refugee spy panic of World War II. In each instance, people of a particular ethnicity or religious affiliation were under suspicion for aiding and abetting the enemy, usually on the flimsiest of evidence and little more than rumor and hearsay. One prominent example were Jewish refugees who desperately sought sanctuary on American soil after fleeing Nazi brutality, only to be refused entry over fears that they were agents for Hitler. As a result, countless men, women, and children perished in the Holocaust. These events parallel the American government's present-day reluctance to accept Islamic refugees, over fears that they are terrorists. The overwhelming majority of the world's Muslims are peaceful, law-abiding citizens. In any given year, Americans are more likely to die from falling out of bed or slipping in their bathtub than at the hands of a terrorist.[2]

Throughout history, every society has experienced scares involving sinister forces. Whether the threats are real or imaginary, fear stokes the flames of hysteria far beyond the actual danger posed to the public. Sociologists refer to these episodes as *social panics*. Over the past fifty years, there have been many examples. They range from sensational claims over the dangers of the spread of AIDS and video-game violence, to serial killers, overuse of mobile phones and the internet by teenagers, and Satanic cults.[3] While no one denies that serial killers exist, or that teens are not preoccupied with social media, in each instance, the threat is dramatically overblown.

During the 1980s and early 1990s, there were a spate of claims about a network of Satanic cults abusing children and sacrificing infants during secret rituals.[4] Many people were falsely accused. During the early 2000s, a similar panic emerged over the threat posed by online sexual predators, which prompted US Attorney General Alberto Gonzalez to name as his top priority in 2005 the apprehension of an estimated 50,000 online offenders. A flurry of news reports highlighted the problem. In May 2006, *ABC News* reported that one in five children had been approached by an online predator. This claim was traced to a study that defined "sexual solicitation" so broadly as to include teen-on-teen flirting. This explains why *not one* of the "solicitations" led to a sexual encounter or assault.[5] As for the claim of 50,000 web predators, it turns out that it was from the TV show *Dateline NBC*. When pressed for their source, host Chris Hansen admitted that there was none; he had attributed the figure "to law enforcement, as an estimate."[6]

In chapter 1, we examine Roman Catholics. From 1830 to 1860, a fear of all things Catholic swept America. While followers were a feature of the social landscape since colonial times, anti-Catholic sentiments rose dramatically in the 1830s with the upswell of nativism, which held that established or native-born citizens were superior to new or recent arrivals. Nativists opposed all immigration, but especially the immigration of Catholics, who were rumored to owe their allegiance to the Pope instead of the president of the United States. Followers were widely believed to be part of a conspiracy to bring down the government and install a Catholic leader.[7] In the three decades before the Civil War, anti-Catholic propaganda was rife in the popular press.[8] During the scare, riots broke out in several cities. One of the worst clashes took place in 1844 when the streets of Philadelphia ran red with blood as thirteen people died and Catholic homes and churches burned to the ground. Within this cauldron of suspicion and fear, misinformation and wild tales flourished. Rumors centered on claims that convents were hotbeds of depraved sexual activity and moral perversion, including accounts of orgies and the ritual killing of babies born to deflowered nuns.[9]

Chapter 2 investigates the unequal treatment of Americans of Mexican ancestry since the 1840s, when the US "annexed" parts of Mexico and the inhabitants became citizens. Mexican Americans were portrayed as an inferior race that was dirty, lazy, and inherently prone to thievery and gang recruitment. Signs proclaiming "No Dogs, No Negroes, No Mexicans" were proudly displayed in the windows of many bars and restaurants across the American Southwest from the late nineteenth century to the early 1950s. Between 1848 and 1928, nearly six hundred people of Mexican heritage were lynched.[10] During the Great Depression, upward of a million Mexicans were forced onto trains and sent back to Mexico over the misguided belief that they were taking "American" jobs. Many were lawful American citizens or residents who had every right to stay. When in 2015, then presidential candidate Donald Trump warned of Mexican immigrants being rapists and drug dealers, he evoked stereotypes that older Mexican Americans would vividly recall.[11]

President Trump's efforts to ban travelers and refugees from several Muslim-majority countries for fear of them being terrorists parallels the events of 1882 when Congress blocked Chinese immigration for ten years. In chapter 3, we examine this period, which was in response to fears that Chinese migrants were taking jobs from "real" Americans, and diluting the "racial purity" of the "white" population. Instead of reducing tensions with the Chinese community, the law's passage triggered a surge in reports of harassment and violence along the West Coast. There were even several murders of Chinese workers after they refused to leave their gold claims or defied attempts to run them out of town. By 1892, the ban was extended and was not repealed until 1943.

Chapter 4 looks at attempts to eradicate "savage" customs of Native Americans by declaring them criminal offenses punishable by fines and hard labor.[12] At the time, "Indians" were considered foreigners; they were not granted citizenship until 1924. As Europeans immigrated to the New World, the clash of civilizations resulted in violent skirmishes with the early colonists. Even after the government made peace with the various tribes, the fear of Native culture remained so great that in 1883 war was declared on Native "superstitions." The Code of Indian Offenses outlawed such practices as plural marriages, traditional dances, communal feasts, and the use of medicine men. The code was a form of ethnocide—an attempt to wipe out an entire set of cultures and insert in their place "superior" Western values. The code was not amended until 1933.[13]

During World War I, the fear of German spies and saboteurs gripped the nation. At its height in 1917, President Woodrow Wilson warned Congress that German subversives loyal to the fatherland "filled our unsuspecting communities with spies and conspirators."[14] Chapter 5 documents this tumultuous time as German Americans were harassed or beaten on suspicion of having sympathies with the kaiser. Several were murdered by vigilante mobs. Many communities took the extreme measure of banning the teaching of German in schools and the playing of German music, while Germanic-sounding businesses, streets, and cities were given English-sounding names. Some families sought to avoid suspicion and harassment by adopting anglicized surnames: Schmidt became Smith, and Müller was changed to Miller.

Chapter 6 examines the plight of Japanese Americans during World War II, when the Justice Department ordered the internment of citizens of Japanese heritage, fearing that they were sympathetic to the emperor and might act as spies and saboteurs. These bleak, remote "relocation centers" were essentially prison camps set up soon after the attack on Pearl Harbor. Upward of 120,000 ethnic Japanese were forced to leave their friends and neighbors and live in isolation. Walt Disney was even enlisted by the War Department to produce racist propaganda films and cartoons depicting buck-toothed Japanese soldiers as demonic, animalistic, and subhuman.[15] The scare did not happen overnight, but had its roots in the long-standing fear of Japanese in California beginning in the 1890s, and the widespread belief that they were part of an inferior Mongolian race. America was also at war with Italy and Germany, yet these nationalities and ethnic groups were not subjected to mass internment.

The disturbing account of the US government's treatment of German Jews fleeing the Nazis during the Second World War is the subject of chapter 7. Despite widespread reports of persecution, America closed its doors to most Jewish refugees amid fears that they were Nazi spies or that their values would corrupt the moral fabric of society. Shaped by wartime paranoia and bigotry, it was not until 1944 that the government reversed its policy after the Treasury Department issued a scathing report on anti-Semitism in the State Department. Sadly, for many Jews, it was too late. Parallels are drawn with recent attempts by the Trump administration to bar Islamic refugees. Of the approximately 1.7 billion Muslims who constitute 23 percent of the global population, the Central Intelligence Agency estimates that only a tiny fraction are terrorists.[16] The risk of any one person becoming a casualty of a terror attack is minuscule. Since the late 1960s, the number of Americans killed in such attacks is about the same as those struck by lightning.[17] One recent study of terrorist acts on US soil over the last forty years found that the odds of dying at the hands of a refugee in such an attack are one in 3.64 billion.[18] You are more likely to be killed by a vending machine toppling over or being crushed by a falling TV.[19] Our treatment of Jewish refugees from Germany in World War II continues to haunt America's legacy as an inclusive and tolerant people.

Chapter 8 explores the present-day hysteria over the threat from Islamic terrorists intent on mass murder, slipping into the country by posing as refugees and immigrants. The statistics tell a different story. While the threat is real, it is primarily from within. Most American terrorists are homegrown. It is estimated that the government spends $75 billion annually to combat domestic terrorism.[20] This expenditure is far out of proportion to the external threat from migrants. A recent study of domestic terrorism in the United States spanning four decades found that out of 3.2 million refugees, not one death was caused by a Muslim. The odds of an illegal immigrant killing someone in a domestic terrorist attack are over 10 billion to one.[21] Attempts to halt the intake of refugees and immigrants from several Muslim-majority countries because they allegedly pose a security threat is based on fear. It is an exercise in chasing ghosts. The Trump administration's attempts to use a religious test to determine who can or cannot enter the country sets a dangerous precedent.

In chapter 9, we look at the lessons from our history of fear and intolerance of foreigners, how to identify social panics, and the enormous toll that these scares take on society. Foremost are those who have been unable to flee war-torn countries such as Syria after being refused entry into the United States on the grounds that they themselves were terrorists. The failure to take in Syrian refugees in their hour of need parallels the treatment of German Jews fleeing Hitler during the Second World War. The evidence is clear: refugees—Syrian or otherwise—pose little risk from terrorism. The pursuit of phantom enemies and the exaggerated strength of real ones place a strain on the country's human and financial resources and threaten to stain America's global reputation as a tolerant and welcoming society.[22]

THE SCIENTIFIC STUDY OF SOCIAL PANICS

The term *moral panic* was popularized by sociologist Stanley Cohen, who gained international prominence for his 1972 book, *Folk Devils and Moral Panics*, about two English youth groups—the Mods and the Rockers. In May 1964, the British press published sensational accounts about the supposed threat from these two rival gangs as they engaged in violent clashes along the country's south coast, prompting outrage and alarm. Over a thousand youths took part in the unrest, jeering, throwing stones, and destroying deckchairs that were used to make bonfires. Cohen found that journalists, politicians, and the police had overreacted to a series of relatively minor incidents. The media stoked fears by using inaccurate terms like "riot," "orgy of destruction," and "gangs."[23] The groups were not even gangs, but unrelated youths who were loosely lumped together. While some panics are forgotten and pass into folklore, others have lasting repercussions and can result in new laws and permanent government policies.[24]

Social panics are part of the human condition. They function to unify communities against a common threat and help people to feel better by blaming their problems on others. Common historical scapegoats include religious and ethnic minorities, foreigners, Jews, heretics, women, indigenous peoples, and the poor. In short, anyone who is different from those in power. In recent times, Islamic refugees have been targets. The greatest social panic of the twentieth century was the fear of Jews in Nazi Germany between 1933 and 1945. Likened to rats and parasites, Jews were portrayed as amoral, obsessed with money, and conspiring to destroy the German culture and economy. Jews became scapegoats for all that was wrong in German society. It is the ultimate example of what can happen if a panic is allowed to grow unchecked.

Migrants often bear the brunt of stereotyping and scapegoating, due to their appearance and customs. Society often casts a suspicious eye on those who are different from what is considered to be the norm for a particular time and place. We are all potential deviants, which is just a label given to someone who breaks the norms of society. During the Salem witch trials of 1692, most of those suspected of practicing witchcraft were women who stood out for having been overly assertive or eccentric for the time. The first three women to be accused had dubious reputations.[25] Sarah Osborne had a volatile temper and stopped attending church. She raised eyebrows when, shortly after the death of her husband, she married her servant, before which time they had apparently been engaging in premarital sex. Osborne and her new husband drew further ire of the community for trying to disinherit her sons, which was widely viewed as a family betrayal. Sarah Good was destitute and forced to live off the charity of others for her survival. She was known for her aggressive begging and was described as sharp-tongued, with a grumbling disposition; she was someone who smoked a pipe, rarely bathed, and was suspected of having loose sexual morals. In short, these women were ideal candidates for being accused of practicing witchcraft.

The first suspected witch, a Barbados slave named Tituba, stood out for her dark skin and unfamiliar customs. She had a penchant for storytelling and a vivid imagination. At one point, upon being accused of witchcraft, she described Satan as "a thing all over hairy, all the face hairy, and a long nose."[26] Bridget Bishop, the first to be hanged, was described as fun-loving and fond of wearing flamboyant attire—unpopular traits in conservative Puritan New England. One resident accused her of having threatened to corrupt the morals of young folk as she "did entertain people in her house at unseasonable hours in the night to keep drinking and playing at shuffleboard."[27] She was previously convicted in court for fighting with her husband. On other occasions, she was hauled before a judge for using foul language and was accused of stealing.[28] As someone on the margins of society, she was vulnerable to accusations of witchcraft.

Cohen's research has been the basis for many studies on an array of social panics. A notable example was the outrage over plans to build an Islamic cultural center and mosque near the site where the World Trade Center once stood prior to its destruction by al-Qaeda on September 11, 2001. Attempts to block construction of the so-called Ground Zero Mosque included claims that it was in poor taste and insulting to those who died in the attacks. Social commentators even claimed that it was a "sacred site." This assertion held little weight, since the area was the home to several strip clubs.[29] Despite the uproar, the center did eventually open its doors to the public in 2011.[30]

EVIL EVERYWHERE—HALLOWEEN SADISM

Social panics can persist for decades if the claim is relentlessly promoted in the media and by law enforcement, as with the Halloween candy-tampering scare. For decades, stories have circulated about perverse sadists poisoning candies and inserting needles and razor blades into apples and candy bars. Sociologist Joel Best has reviewed press reports of these incidents dating back to 1958, including the medical literature, and found just five incidents. Not one held up to scrutiny.[31] The fear of Halloween sadism is a classic example of a social panic.

In 1970, five-year-old Kevin Totson of Detroit reportedly died after eating heroin-laced Halloween candy. An investigation revealed that the candy was drug-free. He had tragically stumbled upon a cache of heroin at a relative's house. A second case involved Texas boy Timothy O'Bryan, who died suddenly after eating a cyanide-tainted Pixie Stix—a sugary powder sold in colorful straws. Police eventually charged his father with poisoning his son and making it look like the work of a Halloween psychopath so that he could collect several life insurance policies. The 1978 death of two-year-old Patrick Wiederhold of Flint, Michigan, also raised fears of a crazed killer on the loose, when he died after eating Halloween candy. Tests revealed his death was due to natural causes. The fourth incident in 1990 involved seven-year-old Ariel Katz of Santa Monica, California, a little girl who collapsed and died while trick-or-treating. A coroner later ruled that the cause of death was an enlarged heart. A fifth report, from Vancouver, Canada, in 2001, attributed the death of a four-year-old girl to poisoned Halloween candy and prompted police to warn parents to dispose of their treats. An autopsy revealed that she had died of streptococcus infection.[32]

Several independent studies confirm Best's conclusions. One examined efforts by newspapers to trace all local stories of Halloween sadism in America during 1973. It concluded that "virtually all" were hoaxes.[33] Another study for the year 1982 identified 270 claims. After analyzing the suspected treats, the Food and Drug Administration found no evidence of tampering in over 95 percent of the cases. The remaining 5 percent were dubious, such as an innocent nick on an apple or the inadvertent tear of a candy wrapper that was reported as attempted tampering. These findings led an FDA official to describe the wave of reports as an episode of "mass hysteria."[34] Since the early 1970s, Best has located just three cases of people ingesting foreign bodies attributed to Halloween perpetrators; each was suspicious.[35] The annual Halloween candy scare has occasionally merged with other panics, such as Islamophobia. Soon after the 9/11 terror attacks, rumors began circulating in e-mails urging caution when trick-or-treating, after it was claimed that two suspicious "Arab-looking" men had entered a wholesale store in Hackensack, New Jersey, and bought $15,000 to $20,000 worth of candy. An FBI investigation would later determine that only one man was involved, and the amount purchased was $7,000. He was a wholesaler who had bought the candy to resell it. Such large transactions are common.[36]

HISTORICAL PERSPECTIVE ON A MODERN CRISIS

Recent concerns over Islamic terrorists infiltrating the country in the guise of immigrants taking advantage of American generosity are not new. The fear of foreigners threatening our security, creating social unrest, taking jobs, and corrupting the moral fabric of society has a long and storied history that is vital to understanding the present-day immigration crisis. During the late nineteenth century, Congress began passing a series of laws to keep out the world's downtrodden, fearing that they would contaminate the Anglo-Saxon stock on whom it was believed the nation was founded. American anthropologist Madison Grant warned that unless immigration was curtailed, the country would soon be awash with "the weak, the broken and the mentally crippled of all races" who threatened to fill "jails, insane asylums, and almshouses" with "human flotsam."[37] Within this climate of fear, intolerance, and racism, Congress tightened immigration laws, turning away everyone from paupers and polygamists to the handicapped. Anyone appearing odd or unusual was at risk of deportation, including those deemed physically unattractive. Early federal immigration laws were loosely written, and if an inspector did not like you, he could often find a reason to have you deported.

SORTING THE DEFECTIVE MASSES

The inspection system was particularly harsh toward the poor and disabled. The Immigration Act of 1891 expanded the power of the federal government to deport immigrants who were paupers, that is, people so poverty-stricken as to need state charity to survive. The act included a clause about persons *likely* to become paupers, giving immigration officers a wide latitude to keep out undesirables. Being poor in America at this time was a sign of defective character and inferior breeding; those with physical defects were thought to be deficient mentally and morally. Labor leader Eugene Debs summed up popular sentiment by describing immigrant paupers as "vagrants, vagabonds, tramps, idlers by choice, and generally criminals by profession."[38] In 1903, the law was expanded to include public begging. It is ironic that this further tightening of immigration law that was intended to keep out the destitute occurred during the same year that Emma Lazarus's poem "The New Colossus," was placed at the Statue of Liberty, touting America as a refuge for the world's "homeless" and "poor."

Determining who was acceptable was often a reflection of the inspector's prejudices. This was a concern given the prevalence of racist attitudes, especially toward Asians, Jews, Slavs, and Africans. For instance, an inspector who was anti-Semitic could create an excuse to deport a Jew by citing medical reasons. In 1909, the Hebrew Sheltering and Immigrant Aid Society of New York City raised concerns that Jews were being singled out for deportation under the diagnosis of "lack of physical development."[39] Near the turn of the century, there was a vigorous scientific debate as to whether Jews suffered disproportionately from an assortment of physical and mental defects. Immigration officers at Ellis Island were familiar with the medical discussion depicting Jews as biologically inferior: undersized, weak-muscled, poorly developed, and mentally unstable.[40] As one Ellis Island surgeon wrote in *Popular Science Monthly*, Jews were "a highly inbred" race with high rates of insanity and mental disorders. He supports this stance by citing statistics for 1907 on the number of new arrivals diagnosed as mentally defective: although Jews composed only 14 percent of the island's immigrant hopefuls, nearly one-third of them were diagnosed as defective mentally.[41] Far from proof of the surgeon's claim, these figures were a reflection of the racially biased decisions of immigration officers and doctors.

Many inspectors made no secret of their biases. One remarked that "no one can stand at Ellis Island and see the physical and mental wrecks who are stopped there . . . without being a firm believer in [immigration] restriction."[42] Another inspector equated migrants to cars: "It is no more difficult to detect poorly built, defective or broken down human beings than to recognize a cheap or defective automobile." One immigrant was rejected based on his appearance and the size of his genitals: On June 30, 1922, Israel Raskin was refused entry because he was "physically defective and likely to become a public charge." His medical certificate stated that he had a "lack of sexual development which may affect his ability to earn a living." The US Surgeon General later justified his and similar exclusions for posing bad economic risks, as it would be "difficult for these unfortu-nates to get or retain jobs, their facial and bodily appearance, at least in adult life, furnishing a patent advertisement of their condition."[43]

Aside from outright discrimination toward certain ethnic groups, those who drew attention to themselves were subject to higher rates of secondary inspection. Once under closer scrutiny, examiners were more likely to discover other health issues, raising the risk of exclusion.[44] The process was heavily visual and subjective. Immigrants were made to file through inspection stations like cattle; anyone who stood out by walking with a limp or appearing frail or unusual was separated, and a letter was chalked on the back of their clothes: H for suspected heart problems, L for lameness, and so on.[45] Those appearing inattentive or confused were marked with an X for possible mental illness.[46] This situation was a recipe for misunderstandings and mistakes. Immigrants arriving from long over-seas voyages often endured crowded, unhygienic conditions. It would not be surprising for those fresh off the ship to appear haggard and lethargic from the sheer strain of the journey. First-class passengers typically had their own rooms and ate in separate dining halls, while the poor were crammed into the lower decks, where it was hot and noisy. Sometimes hundreds of passengers had to share a single bathroom. One investigation revealed the barely tolerable conditions: "The ventilation is almost always inadequate, and the air soon becomes foul. The unattended vomit of the seasick, the odors of not too clean bodies, the reek of food and the awful stench of the nearby toilet rooms . . ."[47] Differences in language, customs, and literacy levels could easily result in singling someone out for further inspection.

In 1905, Armenian Turk Donabet Mousekian was selected for deportation after being diagnosed with "feminism," a code word for poorly developed sex organs. At his hearing, there was no mention of his "condition," and he was asked only a few questions about his background. The transcript read as follows:

> Mr. Rotz: In view of the Doctor's Certificate I move to exclude him as
>   likely to become a public charge.
> Mr. Ryan: Second motion.
> Mr. Smiley: Excluded.

His appeal was upheld by the Ellis Island immigration commissioner, partly because of his physical appearance: "Appellant is devoid of every external evidence of desirability. He is weak . . . repulsive in appearance, the doctor's certificate . . . furnishing sufficient indication of his physical defects."[48] Seven years later, when Nicolaos Xilomenos was rejected for "lack of sexual development," the commissioner upheld the decision, observing that while appearing "strong and robust," he likely suffered from "perversions or mental instability."[49]

When in March 1902, thirty-five-year-old Domenico Vozzo arrived from Italy, he passed through immigration without difficulty. Three years later, upon returning after a short visit to his home country, he was detained at the port of Boston as a risk to become a public charge. Vozzo was fit and strong, with a successful work history in America. His inspection certificate stated that while appearing "perfectly healthy" below the neck, he had a "curiously shaped head, and his skin looks rather white, almost bleached, and his ears are quite thin." The Boston immigration commissioner reviewed the case and decided for deportation. He then sent a note to the Immigration Secretary: "I enclose his picture which I think will convince you that he is not a desirable acquisition."[50] Once again, a migrant's appearance was used as the basis for rejection.

America's treatment of the poor and disabled at the turn of the century parallels present-day anxieties. Fears of the impoverished and "defectives" overwhelming social-service agencies resembles present-day concerns that Mexicans and other "free-loading" foreigners will turn America into a welfare state. Where today we fear Islamic terrorists, a century ago the threat was from Jews, Asians, and Africans, who were seen as compromising national security by diluting the Northern European racial stock on which the country was supposedly founded. Recent attempts to ban people in certain Muslim-majority countries are reminiscent of the Asiatic Barred Zone of 1917, which excluded immigrants from India, Siam, Burma, the Malay States, Afghanistan, Arabia, parts of Russia, and most of Polynesia. The ban remained in effect until 1952.[51]

THE PANIC OVER REDS AND GAYS

While America is often touted as "the land of the free," this did not extend to expressing even passive support for Communism or promoting alternative lifestyles among consenting adults. One of the more unusual social panics in American history involved the convergence of two fears: Communism and homosexuality. For Americans living in the 1950s, gays were considered sexual deviants with Communist tendencies. While the

Immigration Act of 1917 did not mention the word *homosexual*, it barred the "mentally defective," under which gays were categorized. At the time, "homophiles" were considered sex perverts akin to pedophiles. Many lied about their orientation, but if a criminal-records check revealed a conviction for homosexuality, they were rejected under federal law from entering the country. Gay immigrants who were not citizens lived under constant fear of being outed and deported. Republican Senator Keith Wherry of Nebraska was one of many politicians who viewed closeted homosexuals as a threat to national security, believing that they were susceptible to blackmail by Communists who could enlist them to act as spies and subversives. He worried that Soviet leader Joseph Stalin had obtained a list of closeted homosexuals and would use it to recruit spies in the civil service.[52] The fear of homosexuals compromising the nation's security has been dubbed the "Lavender Scare."[53]

The man who started the Communist witch-hunt in early February 1950, Wisconsin Senator Joseph McCarthy, acknowledged the gay "threat," making references in his speeches to "queers" and Communists. He asserted that both were suffering from mental defects and maladjustment.[54] When asked to produce evidence of "Red" infiltration, on February 20, McCarthy stood on the Senate floor for six hours, giving details on eighty-one known cases of Communist spies in the government, including a "nest" of "homos."[55] Eight days later, a congressional hearing was told that as many as ninety-one homosexuals had been dismissed from the State Department over concerns that their sexuality compromised the nation's security. Most were allowed to resign quietly.[56] The anti-gay campaign quickly intensified. The *New York Times* proclaimed, "Perverts Called National Peril," while the *Washington Times-Herald* declared "War on Perverts."[57]

By 1953, President Dwight Eisenhower issued Executive Order 10450, giving the federal government the power to dismiss any civil service employee for the "sexual perversion" of homosexuality. At least five thousand workers lost their jobs for being "perverts" who posed security risks.[58]

Once homosexuals were deemed to be a threat to the nation's welfare, the FBI went to great lengths to infiltrate the subterranean world of homosexuals, even enlisting postal workers to monitor recipients of male physique magazines, who were then placed under surveillance. Postal inspectors were sometimes asked to subscribe to pen pal clubs and initiate suggestive correspondence with suspected homosexuals. If the response was positive, their mail was traced in hopes of identifying other gays.[59]

Amid growing hysteria over Communists infiltrating the country, in 1952 Congress passed legislation excluding people solely for their ideological beliefs. The new law gave the government power to deport immigrants or citizens born outside the country, if they were known or suspected of being Reds. The criteria for deporting a suspected Communist was conveniently vague. As politicians feared attempts to infiltrate or overthrow the government, the search was on to identify and purge Communists wherever they may be. Those receiving the most suspicion were schoolteachers, union leaders, and anyone associated with Hollywood, which was synonymous with left-wing leanings and homosexuality. The treatment of Claudia Jones is typical of the extreme reaction to all things Communist. At age eight, she immigrated to the United States with her family after living in the British West Indies. In 1953, after thirty-two years in her adopted country, she was deported for the crime of organizing Communist activities. At her trial, she openly admitted to supporting Communist ideas, which she asserted posed no threat to the United States, and contrary to popular belief, stated that she had no interest in overthrowing or destroying the American government. She told the judge: "Quite candidly, Your Honor . . . I proudly plead guilty . . . which by your own prior rulings constitutes no crime—that of holding Communist ideas."[60]

The search for Reds and "homophiles" were modern-day versions of the Salem witch-hunts in a different cultural guise. While these social panics occurred over two and a half centuries apart, the backdrops are hauntingly similar: outside evildoers were believed to be in their midst, conspiring to destroy the cherished values of democracy and family. Just as suspected witches were asked, "What evil spirit have you familiarity with?" members of the House Un-American Activities Committee impatiently queried, "Have you ever been a member of the Communist Party?" Government investigators also inquired of civil servants, "Is it true that you're a homosexual?"[61] During both eras, suspects were pressured by their interrogators to reveal the names of co-conspirators. In Salem, a special court was convened in which basic rules of evidence were ignored, there were no defense attorneys, and the accused were presumed guilty until they could prove their innocence. During the 1950s, congressional hearings turned into public spectacles in which McCarthy bullied witnesses, asking them leading questions, and treating them as if they were guilty without a trial in a court of law. This failure to follow proper procedure and short-circuiting of the American legal system led Minnesota Senator Hubert Humphrey to complain that the behavior of McCarthy was "totalitarian" and "undemocratic" and made a mockery of Western law.[62] Accusations of homosexuality by government investigators often included high-pressure tactics behind closed doors. One lesbian was told: "We have your friend in the next room. She's already told us that you're gay. You give us the names of others, and we'll go easier on you."[63]

Before subsiding, the Communist Scare reached ludicrous levels. At one point, the owners of the Cincinnati Reds baseball team briefly changed the name to the Redlegs to show their patriotism and avoid sending the wrong message to the nation's youth. Some citizens even tried to censor the publication of *Robin Hood* for being a Communist parable, since the hero robbed from the rich and gave to the poor.[64] To underscore the exaggerated response to the threat, historian Angus McLaren observes that despite all of the fuss and whoopla over the security threat from gays, there is not a single documented instance of an American homosexual being blackmailed by a Communist agent.[65]

In 1965, Congress amended the immigration law to include the term "sexual deviation," making it explicit that homosexuals were unwelcome.

It even sought the opinion of the Public Health Department, which assured them that a sexual deviant included "homosexuals and sex perverts."[66] In 1973, the American Psychiatric Association changed its designation of homosexuality from "sociopathic personality disturbance" to a sexual variation akin to left-handedness. It is not surprising that immigration laws would reflect popular and scientific views on homosexuality. However, what is remarkable is that once the majority of psychiatrists no longer considered homosexuality an abnormality, it took seventeen more years for Congress to change the laws and allow gay immigrants into the country in 1990.[67] It would take five more years before the federal government banned the use of sexual orientation to deny employment.[68]

NEGROPHOBIA

One of the longest-running social panics in US history involves the exaggerated fear of African Americans, especially males. Ever since the country's founding, they have been portrayed as violent, with primitive, animalistic sexual urges, prompting fears of rape and interracial breeding. Medical authorities considered blacks to be mentally inferior, inherently lazy, and morally deficient; it was widely thought that their extended interaction with white youth would lead the latter astray, justifying the later need for segregation. Popular belief masqueraded as scientific fact as one nineteenth-century physician observed that Africans were "defective" and lacking in "cerebral matter," rendering them "unable to take care of themselves."[69]

Immediately after Abraham Lincoln freed the slaves on January 1, 1863, his executive order was met with widespread trepidation among Southern whites as a threat to their safety and values, and a strain on government resources and charities. Reaction to their newfound freedom was swift. By the 1870s, signs reading "Colored" and "Whites Only" appeared across the South, mostly in eating and drinking establishments.

In 1896, the US Supreme Court upheld the bans. For the next fifty-eight years, segregation was the law of the land and soon expanded to include buses and trains, parks, libraries, restrooms, theaters, and cinemas. For some, there was no escape even in sickness and death, as hospitals and cemeteries were segregated. The view of African Americans as inferior to those of European heritage did not begin to change until the 1920s and 1930s, with the work of anthropologists such as Franz Boas, who viewed culture and environment to be the main influences on behavior. Even today, despite modern science dispelling the myth of race, America has been besieged by a series of moral panics suggesting that blacks are inherently criminal and violent.[70]

Over the years, blacks have been the subject of numerous scares among whites. One poignant contemporary example occurred during the late 1980s and early 1990s when the media reported on a worrisome new crime perpetuated mostly by impoverished African American women: "crack babies." Mothers addicted to crack cocaine were reportedly giving birth to babies with permanent brain damage. Not only were the claims unsupported by the scientific evidence, experts now agree that crack is less harmful to unborn babies than alcohol is, and it is comparable to the effects of smoking tobacco.[71] A twenty-year study of two hundred "crack babies" found "no differences in the health and life outcomes between babies exposed to crack and those who weren't."[72] More recent scares involving African Americans have included the exaggerated fear of blacks, including Hispanics and Afro-Caribbeans, randomly assaulting whites[73] and gang-raping white women.[74]

A poignant example of the lack of regard for black lives and how they have been unfairly targeted and exploited even after their emancipation, took place in Brooke County, Georgia, when nineteen-year-old Sydney Johnson was arrested for the crime of "rolling dice." He was fined and jailed because he could not afford what was then the considerable sum of thirty dollars. Johnson was freed by a white plantation owner, Hampton Smith, who had an abusive reputation and such difficulty keeping workers that he made a habit of bailing out African American prisoners in return for their services in what was tantamount to indentured slavery. After enduring beatings and being forced to work while sick, Johnson shot Smith dead. A mob of local whites scoured the countryside. Over the next several days, they took their revenge by lynching thirteen blacks, several of whom had no involvement in the murder. Johnson was eventually tracked down and would be the last to die. Mary Turner, the wife of one of the victims, was eight months pregnant at the time and vehemently protested her husband's innocence, threatening to obtain statements from witnesses and have the perpetrators arrested. Turner was captured by the mob. The *Atlanta-Journal Constitution* reported what happened next, from an eyewitness, Philip Dray: "There, before a crowd that included women and children, Mary was stripped, hung upside down by the ankles, soaked with gasoline, and roasted to death. In the midst of this torment, a white man opened her swollen belly with a hunting knife and her infant fell to the ground, gave a cry, and was stomped to death."[75] Even this was not sufficient to satisfy the mob's rage. Historian Christopher Meyers writes that her body was then riddled with so many bullets that "she was barely recognizable as a human being."[76] This shameful episode in American history took place in May 1918. Despite the number of murders committed, their callous and brutal nature and hundreds of witnesses, no one was ever charged in the killings.

A SOCIAL PANIC CHECKLIST

There are five tell-tale signs of a social scare: (1) concern, (2) hostility, (3) consensus, (4) disproportion, and (5) volatility. First, there must be sufficient *concern* that the perceived threat poses a serious risk to traditional values and must be measurable. Statistics and opinion polls are often used to sound the alarm, but they are not always accurate. Statistics are notoriously easy to manipulate. A 2015 TV ad for Hillary Clinton's presidential campaign stated matter-of-factly that the American "epidemic of gun violence" was so out of control that each day about 90 people were killed by guns. While technically true, this figure makes gun violence appear worse than it is. When the ad aired, the latest statistics from the Centers for Disease Control had recorded 32,888 deaths from guns, yet the more accurate figure is 11,208. The Clinton campaign added the 505 accidental gun deaths and 21,175 firearm-related suicides in order to swell the total. In reality, gun violence was responsible for 5.1 deaths for every 100,000 Americans—roughly 32 per day. The Clinton camp inflated the figures for dramatic effect. The number of Americans who die from accidental falls or poisonings is an even greater problem, claiming over 30,000 lives during the same year, yet these events receive far less attention.[77] Moral panics do not occur out of thin air: there must be a "grain of truth" to start with, that becomes distorted and exaggerated.

The second component of a social panic is *hostility* toward the person or group that is seen as a threat. This often involves sit-ins and marches to draw attention to the perceived menace or lobbying legislators to pass laws to contain it. Social media campaigns may be organized and flyers distributed on street corners or handbills posted to raise awareness. Sometimes law enforcement unwittingly create anger by acting on baseless claims. In August 1983, a worker at the McMartin Preschool in Manhattan Beach, California, was suspected of child abuse. Judy Johnson told police that she believed that Ray Buckey had molested her young son after noticing the boy's bottom was red after returning from the school one day. The local police chief soon sent a warning letter to parents. "This Department is conducting a criminal investigation involving child molestation . . . [by] Ray Buckey." It continued: "Please question your child to see if he or she has been a victim. Our investigation indicates that possible criminal acts include: oral sex, fondling of genitals, buttock or chest area, and sodomy, possibly committed under the pretense of 'taking the child's temperature.'" The letter stated that Buckey may have taken nude photos of the children, and it asked if anyone had observed Ray "leave a classroom alone with a child during any nap period, or if they had ever observed Ray Buckey tie up a child."[78] Outraged parents began questioning their impressionable children. Over 360 came forward to report that they too had been molested by Buckey or his co-workers. All of those accused were acquitted after it was revealed that the children's interviews were laden with leading questions. One investigator wrote: "There was not one spontaneous 'disclosure' on any of these tapes. . . . On all of the videotapes shown, the children repeatedly denied witnessing any act of sexual abuse of children. The interviewer . . . continued to coax and pressure the child for accusations."[79] What was then the most expensive civil trial in American history had essentially been triggered by an overprotective mother, an overzealous police chief, and diaper rash. In classic social-panic fashion, the defendants were tried in the media, with stories and commentaries portraying them as guilty even before their case was heard in court. One headline in *Time* proclaimed: "Brutalized," while *People* magazine described the school as "California's Nightmare Nursery."[80]

For moral panics to develop there must be a third element: *consensus* within a significant segment of a population that the threat is both real and serious. There is no set number or percentage of people who must be involved to reach a tipping point. Some researchers cite opinion polls or the sudden rise in the number of protests or news reports on a particular threat. In a 2011 Harris poll of Halloween risks, parents with children placed the fear of tampered or poisoned treats at 24 percent. This was a global survey, suggesting that the myth of Halloween sadism had spread beyond the United States.[81] During the nineteenth-century anti-Catholic hysteria, a vast literature of books, newspapers, and magazines appeared that seemed to confirm the danger posed by Catholic immigrants and to vilify followers as depraved cultists. Similarly, a 2015 poll on Syrian refugees entering the United States found that 45 percent of Americans deemed them to be a major threat to the security of the country.[82] In reality, you are far more likely to die from chronic constipation (one in 2.2 million) or in a flash flood while visiting the Grand Canyon (one in 14.2 million) than in a terrorist attack by a refugee in America.[83]

Another indicator of a panic is the threat being out of proportion to reality. Statistics are instrumental in generating the perception of danger as claim makers generate alarm by citing inflated figures about the number of crimes, deaths, injuries, addicts, terrorists, and money amounts. These figures are used as evidence to confirm that there is some degree of objective harm that can be quantified and used to construct charts and graphs to highlight the danger.[84] At the height of the Red Scare of the early 1950s, anti-Communist crusaders claimed that Soviet spies had infiltrated all levels of government and were lurking in thousands of communities across the country. Similarly, during March 2000, a panic erupted in Slovenia after three teens were caught killing and torturing cats. Fueled by sensational media reports, it was soon claimed that cat killing and torture were major issues in Slovenian society. Sociologist Gregor Bulc observes that suddenly, the TV news and press were flooded with "images of dead cats and cute kittens" and claims that such events were common. In reality, he found that serial pet killings were "exceedingly rare or even nonexistent."[85]

The final characteristic of a moral panic is *volatility*. They are unpredictable and may subside, only to re-emerge stronger than ever. A panic over the threat from German spies infiltrating the American heartland reached fever pitch during World War I. Yet near the war's end, reports of harassment and discrimination had leveled off dramatically, only to reignite during Hitler's ascension to power in 1930s. In rare instances, social panics can persist for centuries, such as the persecution of "witches" in Europe between 1400 and 1650. Conservative estimates place the death toll from witch-hunts at half a million.[86] And in 1285, 180 Jews were burned alive in Munich, after rumors circulated that they had sacrificed a Christian child as part of a religious ritual. Panics involving anti-Semitism have flared up on a regular basis since the Middle Ages, and were often triggered by tales of Jews poisoning wells or spreading the Bubonic Plague. At Guyenne, France, in 1321, upward of 5,000 Jews were burned alive for allegedly poisoning the water supply.[87]

A classic example of a recurring panic is the White Slavery Scare. Between 1880 and 1917, stories circulated in Europe and North America that gangs controlled by Jews abducted "white" girls and women, plied them with drugs, and forced them into the sex trade.[88] In May 1969, a similar scare—equally unfounded—spread across France, when it was reported that women were being drugged inside the fitting rooms of Jewish-run clothing stores and smuggled out of the country to work as prostitutes in North Africa.[89] The present-day scare over an "epidemic" of child abductions can be traced back to 1750, when a kidnapping panic swept through the streets of Paris, prompting extraordinary scenes. Suspected abductors ran for their lives as angry mobs chased them through the streets and back alleys. The episode began with the spread of rumors that King Louis XV was suffering from leprosy and was having children kidnapped to cure his condition by bathing in their blood.[90]

THE POWER TO SHAPE HISTORY

At different times in our history, immigrants have been singled out as scapegoats for a multitude of social problems plaguing the country. During these periods of intolerance and fear, there is a temptation to suspend laws, ignore civil rights, and deport new arrivals back to where they came from. In doing so, we risk redefining a religion as a cult, devoutness as fanaticism, and diversity as perversity. Foreigners with strange customs are susceptible to demonization as "the Other," while unfamiliar traditions may become perceived as irrational superstitions. Our differences are a testament to human imagination and creativity. Studying these panics allows us to appreciate the rich tapestry of human diversity while underscoring the importance of standing up for basic rights when those differences are under threat.

The United States has accepted tens of millions of immigrants during its relatively short existence, but there is a dark legacy that is often overlooked. At certain times, the American dream has been denied to those who were pregnant, poverty-stricken, skinny, short, handicapped, physically unattractive, dark-skinned, or polygamist. Often these categories were mere excuses for thinly veiled racism and bigotry. At other times, people were rejected solely because they were gay, Communist, anarchist, Native American, Mexican, Chinese, Japanese, German, Jewish, or Muslim. The list is far from exhaustive.

We must avoid simplistic labels and sweeping generalizations about entire groups based solely on superficial qualities such as ethnicity, religion, ideology, sexual preference, and skin color. Using such labels places people in boxes and reinforces popular stereotypes: "Blacks are violent"; "Mexicans are rapists and drug dealers"; "Muslims are terrorists." If we give in to such temptations, we risk dehumanizing those who are different from the mainstream and creating a world of "them" versus "us." This book is a timely reminder of the historical context for the present-day American immigration debate involving Mexicans, Muslims, and others. These are defining issues of our time. Armed with insights from similar social panics in our history, it is time that America lives up to the promise etched into the base of the Statue of Liberty and fulfills its destiny as a tolerant and just society. This book will help Americans look inward to overcome their fear of the foreign and reach the inevitable realization that the bogeymen we have for so long come to fear are nothing more than shadows of our own creation.

CHAPTER 1

"THEY'RE PLOTTING TO OVERTHROW THE COUNTRY!"

THE GREAT CATHOLIC SCARE

*No passion so effectively robs the mind of all its powers of
acting and reasoning as fear.*
—Edmund Burke, *A Philosophical Inquiry into the
Origin of Our Ideas of the Sublime and Beautiful,* 1756

During the 1830s, an extraordinary agitation swept across the American landscape as suspicions arose that Catholic immigrants from Germany and Ireland were part of a vast conspiracy to take over the country. Many Protestants considered the plot to be plausible. To understand why, it is important to examine the historical context. In 1535, Henry VIII, angry with the pope for not granting his divorce, broke with Rome, officially declaring himself head of the Church of England. For the better part of the next three centuries, Catholic worship was outlawed under penalty of death. While this bitter rift had begun to heal by the 1830s, American's Protestant majority still looked upon Catholics with suspicion. Many saw it as a sinister institution demanding absolute loyalty from its followers, who were willing to blindly obey the orders of its leaders who were puppets of the pope.

This turbulent period parallels present-day fears that Muslim sleeper cells have infiltrated the West and are secretly planning attacks, including claims that hundreds of ISIS terrorists are scattered across Europe, awaiting a signal from their leaders to strike.[1] There have been similar reports that America was under threat from a network of jihadists with tentacles in every state, with one headline proclaiming: "Massive Number of ISIS Sleeper Cells Spanning United States Uncovered—Training Camps and All."[2] As with any good social panic, there were grains of truth. ISIS had tried to recruit agents to carry out attacks at home, but rumors of their minions infiltrating the American heartland in such large numbers were ludicrous.

Undoubtedly, many Catholics despised Protestant America and would have liked to have seen a Catholic president. But to think that tens of thousands of immigrants had organized themselves into an extensive network of subversives who were secretly planning to topple the government was equally preposterous. There were also claims that voter fraud was rampant among Irish Catholic immigrants, who were either voting illegally as noncitizens or casting multiple ballots in the same election to steal the outcome for their candidates.[3] In the aftermath of the 2016 presidential election, Donald Trump made similar allegations, charging that millions of ballots were cast by "illegals," which cost him the popular vote. He told congressional leaders that he would have won a clear majority "if 3 million to 5 million immigrants living in the country illegally hadn't voted."[4] His claims were as baseless as those that had been made against the Irish immigrants. A study of all known cases of voter fraud in America between 2000 and 2014 has identified just thirty-one credible incidents out of over 1 billion ballots cast.[5]

The Catholic Scare would grip the hearts and minds of citizens for the next three decades, waning only with the outbreak of the Civil War in 1861. During the crisis, Catholics were the subject of vile rumors, harassment, discrimination, protests, and vigilante attacks. Anti-Catholic riots rocked several cities, resulting in widespread destruction to property and dozens of deaths. The most incredible claims centered on convents and accounts of priests taking out their sexual fantasies and perversions on youthful innocence. Stories of nuns serving essentially as sex slaves captivated the public imagination and were a common theme in the sizable literature that sprang up at this time. Rumors spread that many nuns had been coerced or brainwashed. Convents were said to contain dungeons where acts of torture took place and the newborns of forbidden liaisons were sacrificed in macabre rituals, their bodies disposed of in vats of acid.[6]

Within this atmosphere of fear and hysteria, stories began circulating of Catholic plots to overthrow the government. These sentiments are epitomized in the writings of Samuel Morse, inventor of the telegraph and developer of Morse Code. The son of a Protestant preacher and a virulent anti-Catholic, he saw conspiracies everywhere. In 1835, he published a popular book outlining a papal plot aimed at the downfall of the American government and eventual world domination. For Morse, the flood tide of Catholic immigrants was part of a carefully orchestrated scheme. In *Foreign Conspiracy Against the Liberties of the United States*, Morse wrote of the urgent need to counter the threat: "The enemy . . . has spread himself through all the land. The ramifications of this foreign plot are everywhere visible to all who will open their eyes."[7] He believed that European powers, acting on orders from the pope, were sending money and agents into the country as a prelude to a Catholic insurrection. He also made the alarming claim that "hundreds of Jesuits and priests . . . have a complete military organization through the United States."[8] A key strategy in the papal plot supposedly involved perverting the morals of Protestant girls who were being taught by nuns in convent schools. As evidenced by the surge in Catholic hate literature during this period, a significant segment of the population either accepted the claims at face value or held them to have some truth.

Several political movements sprang up to combat the perceived threat. These parties and their affiliated societies had patriotic names like the Order of the Star Spangled Banner. Supporters lobbied Congress to halt or restrict all immigration and to ban foreign-born citizens from holding government jobs or political office. Some wanted only to stop the flow of Catholic immigrants and demanded an investigation into claims of convent abuses. Laws prohibiting Catholics from holding public office were passed in states such as New Jersey and New Hampshire, and they were not rescinded until the 1870s.[9] The parallels with today's Islamic Scare are unmistakable, with calls to ban only Muslim immigrants and admit only Christians in their place. This paranoia is epitomized by Fox News TV commentator Sean Hannity, who charged that unless Muslim immigration is halted, some neighborhoods would be turned into Islamic Caliphates: non-Muslim no-go zones ruled by Sharia law. He also made the outlandish assertion that Great Britain had no less than eighty-eight working Sharia courts.[10]

Catholic hostilities flared in 1834, when a mob in Charlestown, Massachusetts, enraged by rumors of abuse involving a local nun, burned a convent to the ground. Five years later, residents in Baltimore were left shaken by three days of riots protesting the alleged mistreatment of nuns at the local Carmelite convent after fantastic claims circulated in the press. In 1844, dozens of people died on the streets of Philadelphia as Catholic homes and churches were set alight. Violence peaked in the summer of 1854 when riots left ten dead in St. Louis after rumors that Irish and German immigrants were about to cast illegal ballots in city elections. Stones, bricks, and the smell of gunpowder filled the air as the combatants fought pitched battles. The following August, at least twenty died in bloody skirmishes in Louisville when a band of Protestants backed by city police tried to stop a group of determined Irish and German citizens from voting. The events became known as Bloody Monday.[11]

ROOTS OF THE SCARE

Hostile attitudes toward Catholics had been brewing long before British settlement in the New World. In the sixteenth century, a rift appeared in the Catholic Church after Martin Luther embarked on a historic mission of reform, unhappy that the Bible was written in Latin and had to be interpreted by Catholic priests on behalf of their followers. He believed that a commoner could have a relationship with God without having to go through priests. Luther wanted the holy book translated into different languages so everyone could interpret it for him- or herself. His supporters became known as Protestants, for "protesting" the control of the church by the pope. When King Henry VIII broke with Rome in 1535, Catholic-Protestant tensions rose and soon found their way to the New World. Over the next several years, Henry dissolved all convents and monasteries in England, Wales, and Ireland. The ban was not fully lifted until 1829. As a result, many early British settlers to America had vague notions of convents as sinister places.[12]

The Puritans sailed to the Massachusetts Bay Colony, hoping to gain "purification" from Catholic influences at home by rejecting their use of rituals and prescript prayer and opting instead for plain services and spontaneous worship.[13] Prior to leaving for the New World, many Puritans were convinced that Catholic subversives were bent on overthrowing the Crown.[14] This helps to explain why, in 1700, the colony enacted a law making it illegal for a Catholic priest to reside there. The punishment was death.[15] A popular children's game of the early Protestant colonists was Break the Pope's Neck. It involved spinning a plate on its edge and letting it go to see which way it fell. The act of letting it go was known as breaking his neck.[16] Seven of the thirteen original states banned Catholics from holding public office. Hostilities rose to even greater heights during the late 1700s, when the New England colonists began to mark November 5th as Pope's Day with parades culminating in burning effigies of the Holy Father.[17]

These deep divisions provide a context for the rise in anti-Catholic paranoia that was to follow. During the 1820s, a surge in Irish and German immigrants of Catholic persuasion caused growing alarm among Protestants. In the first four decades of the nineteenth century, over a million Roman Catholics poured into the country.[18] Feelings of nativism rose with the belief that the interests of native-born citizens and established inhabitants were more American than those of newcomers who were often more skilled in a variety of trades and provided a cheap labor pool. Another factor stoking tensions was a lack of familiarity with convents by English Protestants. By the mid-1830s, just a few hundred nuns were scattered across the country. An air of mystery surrounded convents because they were secretive institutions closed to outsiders.

For many Protestants, the vows of Catholic celibacy were a perversion of nature and a rejection of the traditional family. For mothers, nuns threatened to replace their role as caregiver, shouldering the responsibility for the education and religious training of their children.[19] Anti-Catholic literature was filled with dire warnings to would-be students of convent schools. In *The Testimony of an Escaped Novice from the Sisterhood of St. Joseph*, the editors suggest that any girl educated in a nunnery would find it difficult to find a husband: "For a young girl educated in a convent to be a good wife and a good mother is a thing most rare . . . because, not educated in the family, she knows nothing of domestic life."[20] They conclude that "few are the husbands who have not speedy cause to repent of marrying a young girl just out of the convent." In his introduction to *Female Convents: Secrets of Nunneries Disclosed* (1834), Thomas Roscoe writes: "Every girl who has been educated in an American nunnery has departed from it . . . with every refined feminine sensibility destroyed."[21]

Within this backdrop of long-standing tensions between Catholics and Protestants, and fanciful conspiracies about papal plots, a flurry of sensational books appeared about runaway nuns.[22] Captivity novels depicting escaped nuns had been circulating for centuries across Europe, providing a ready-made template for New World writers. Some of the stories were so similar that their authors were accused of plagiarism.[23] By 1834, several popular European "No-Popery books" had begun to appear in America. In these books, Catholicism was depicted as an immoral system rife with lustful priests breaking their vows of celibacy by violating young womanhood. Historian Ray Billington writes: "These books spread tales of secret passageways connecting nunneries with the homes of the clergy, of babies' bodies found beneath abandoned convents, and of confessors who abused both their trust and the young ladies whom they confessed."[24] These writers created the impression that convents were hotbeds of vice and lust. Prior to the destruction of the Charlestown convent, notices had appeared in the area proclaiming: "When Napoleon opened the Nunnerys of Europe, he found cords of infant skulls!!"[25] These depictions generated anger that evildoers were in their midst. Worse yet, they were teaching Protestant children in convent schools.

HOSTILITIES EXPLODE

Catholic hostilities came to a head in the summer of 1834 outside Boston. On August 11, the Mount Benedict boarding school for girls in Charlestown was burned to the ground by a mob whipped into a frenzy by rumors that the building had been the scene of ongoing abuses against the young nuns inside. Most of the students were the daughters of wealthy Protestants. The school had an excellent reputation, drawing pupils from around the country. The Ursulines were hardly the evil cult they were made out to be by the locals. They were an Italian order dating back centuries, known for nursing the sick and educating girls. The Charlestown riot broke out amid fears that convent schools were central to the plot to make Catholicism the main religion by introducing it into Protestant homes through impressionable female students who were "easily swayed by the seductive charm of sisters, and of Roman Catholic rituals."[26]

Concerns over the goings-on at Mount Benedict had been brewing since 1831, when a local woman, Rebecca Reed, spread shocking tales about her brief time there. Reed's accounts of mistreatment and escape spread by word of mouth across the region, gaining traction after a nun had reportedly escaped captivity. This was the tipping point for the nunnery riot after Sister Mary John suffered a nervous breakdown on July 28, 1834, wandering away from the convent grounds and raising fears for her well-being.[27] She soon returned to the nunnery accompanied by the bishop of Boston, Benedict Fenwick, and her brother, amid rumors that she had done so under coercion and was being held captive in a basement dungeon.

These rumors and hearsay took on a semblance of fact when on August 8, the Boston *Mercantile Journal* published a story about a nun who had "escaped" from Mount Benedict and was never heard from again—suggesting she may have been murdered. Within two days, the story of the missing nun was reprinted in newspapers throughout Boston, while handbills were posted calling for the destruction of the convent. Reports of the captive nun would have outraged readers and resonated with Boston Protestants. Even more alarming, the woman had been born into an upstanding Protestant family, only to have renounced her religion and converted to Catholicism. Historian Maureen McCarthy writes on the alarm such a story would have created: "Local people heard a story of a young woman—probably Protestant—seduced into becoming a nun, prohibited from leaving the convent, and now inaccessible, maybe even murdered."[28] While the newspaper account was heart-wrenching, it was riddled with errors and innuendo. For instance, the nun was not exactly a "young woman," but in her thirties, and she had worked at the school for twelve years, serving as a teacher.[29]

On Saturday, August 9, a local official named Edward Cutter visited the nunnery and met with Sister Mary John, who reassured him that she was well and had not been coerced into returning. The next day, the Reverend Lyman Beecher delivered three impassioned sermons at separate Protestant churches in Boston, warning of the dangers of Catholicism, and urging audience members to take decisive action.[30] In the years prior to Beecher's addresses, Boston-area ministers and the religious press had attacked the convent, claiming that the students and nuns were being conditioned to owe their allegiance to the pope. This led to warnings "that the leading citizens of Massachusetts would eventually all be Romanists."[31]

On the 11th, Mr. Cutter led five selectmen on an inspection of the convent with Sister Mary John as their guide, convincing them that the claims of captive nuns were tall tales and the product of overactive imaginations. The men promised to publish their findings in an official statement in the newspapers the next day. Tragically, by morning the school and convent would be a pile of smoldering ambers. The Mother Superior defiantly stood up to the crowd and told them to address their questions of abuse to local officials. They ransacked the compound and set it alight. Sister Mary John (whose real name was Elizabeth Harrison) had told the selectmen that if a mob threatened the convent before their report appeared, she would address them. Unfortunately, fate intervened. The Mother Superior later testified that she intended to have Sister Mary John appear at a window to calm the mob, but, overcome with emotion, Harrison collapsed.[32] Mother Superior could produce Harrison, but in her fragile state, it might have had the opposite effect and confirmed their suspicions of abuse. On the other hand, if she had refused access, it would have appeared that the nuns had something to hide.

The final assault on the compound was a surreal scene. A crowd of men and boys began waving clubs and makeshift weapons, and shouting anti-Catholic slogans, before they set the compound alight. Fortunately, no one was killed or injured in the peculiar events that ensued. Historian Daniel Cohen examined the trial records and observes that as the convent burned, the mob took a bizarre, festive turn and a carnival-like atmosphere ensued. "During the course of the night, participants donned schoolgirls' dresses or religious garb looted from the convent, swigged wine . . . staged a mock procession around the gutted building, and held a sham auction of looted books. As they watched the . . . property go up in flames, tired but exultant rioters and friendly spectators alike sang songs, smoked cigars, lounged casually on the grass, and even snacked on cheese and crackers."[33] Two separate trials of the perpetrators were held. It is a testament to the anti-Catholic hysteria of the period that twelve of the thirteen people charged in the attack were acquitted. The one person who was found guilty was always going to get off: a teenage boy. The young man was convicted of conducting a mock auction of the bishop's books, tossing them into the bonfire as bids were called out. He was certainly no ringleader. As expected, he was pardoned by the governor seven months later after a public outcry; even Mother Superior and the bishop petitioned for his freedom.[34]

The tragic circumstances surrounding the destruction of Mount Benedict did little to slow the spread of Catholic hate literature. One survey identified no less than thirteen magazines and twenty-five newspapers with editorial stands or articles against Catholics, and hundreds of books.[35] While claims of captivity and abuse at Mount Benedict were untrue, rumors of similar evils committed within nunnery walls continued to draw attention to the issue. One New York–based anti-Catholic paper even suggested that the riot had been instigated *by Catholics* to gain sympathy.[36] Post-riot fears of nunnery abuses were driven by the appearance of two sensational and wildly popular books, supposedly written by escaped nuns. The first was Rebecca Reed's *Six Months in a Convent* in 1835,[37] followed by Maria Monk's *Awful Disclosures of the Hotel Dieu Nunnery of Montreal* the next year. These works enjoyed wide readership, and their authors became household names. The books set off a fierce anti-Catholic backlash. It would later be uncovered that both books were works of fiction, and their so-called authors had considerable help from ardent anti-Catholics in writing their accounts.

Rebecca Reed entered Mount Benedict in 1831 with hopes of becoming a nun after giving away all her worldly possessions, including a pair of earrings, a handkerchief pin, and at least one goldfish. She left four months later after having been found unsuitable.[38] An investigation into the riot found that rumors of sexual misconduct and physical abuse spread by Reed were circulating around Boston just prior to the unrest and contributed to the tumultuous events.[39] The riot conveniently served as free publicity for Reed's book, which appeared in mid-March 1835. Her story had an enormous following. The book was one of the bestselling publications of the nineteenth century, selling 200,000 copies in its first month alone.[40] Its appearance had a huge impact on the Catholic Scare since it was the first truly American escaped-nun book in what would quickly become a popular genre. It also provided a blueprint for the avalanche of future escaped-nun books to follow.[41] Overlooked by its many supporters was the suspicious timing, coinciding with the second trial of her brother-in-law for his part in the Mount Benedict riot, and with the debate over whether or not to compensate the convent for its losses.[42] Reed's allegations were refuted by the Mother Superior, who pointed out the many inconsistences in her story.[43] Far from being seduced into Catholicism, she noted that it was *she* who had pursued *them*, begging to be let into the convent, only to be rejected. The Mother Superior asserted that Reed told her that due to her decision to turn Catholic, family members "beat her till she was bruised in every part of her body." She said that Reed had even threatened suicide if she was not admitted. Finally, in September 1831, Mother Superior allowed her to join as a charity case, sympathetic to a young woman who had been evicted from her home and rejected by friends and family for having converted.[44] There is also evidence that local Catholics had encouraged Reed to convert and gave her religious books. The case of Rebecca Reed stirred strong emotions on both sides of the Protestant-Catholic divide.[45]

THE MONK AFFAIR

The popularity of Reed's book was rivaled only by Maria Monk's *Awful Disclosures of the Hotel Dieu Nunnery of Montreal* in 1836. A runaway bestseller, it led to more waves of anti-Catholic hysteria. Monk claimed to have escaped from the convent after falling pregnant to a priest and fearing her newborn baby would be murdered.[46] The Hotel Dieu was a hospital serving the poor, which was attached to a convent. She claimed that priests from an adjacent seminary would sneak through a network of secret tunnels to engage in sexual escapades with the nuns. Reed's book was tame in comparison. Reed described physical and mental punishment through rigorous penance but made no claims of sexual impropriety. In contrast, Monk's "autobiography" was filled with sensational allegations of seduction, rape, ritualized baby-killing, and torture at the hands of depraved priests. So sexually charged was the content that some commentators feared that reading it might permanently corrupt female morals. It became one of the bestselling books of the nineteenth century! Instead of repulsing readers, it titillated the sexually repressed populous.[47] The contemporary adage that "sex sells" was as true then as it is today, and by 1860, *Awful Disclosures* had sold 300,000 copies.[48] By twenty-first-century standards, the writing was modest and left much to the imagination, although there is little doubt that most readers would have understood what was being conveyed. For example, Maria told of meeting a thirteen-year-old girl who described "the conduct of a priest" while taking confession, that "was of so criminal and shameful a nature, I could hardly believe it."[49] In another instance, she wrote: "Father Dufrèsne called me out, saying he wished to speak with me. I feared what was his intention; but I dared not disobey. In a private apartment, he treated me in a brutal manner; and from two other priests, I afterward received similar usage that evening. Father Dufrèsne afterward appeared again; and I was compelled to remain in company with him until morning."[50]

The impact of *Awful Disclosures* was enormous. For those who did not read the book, it was excerpted in countless newspapers and magazines across the country. Monk was portrayed as either an innocent victim who was the subject of abuse and exploitation by the nunnery, or a villain—a lady of the night with a vivid imagination. Pro-Catholic handbills characterizing her as a liar and a prostitute were posted around New York City. Monk reached such notoriety that several mock trials were held in public, and shops sold her pictures. One could choose between a solo shot and one with her holding the baby she had allegedly conceived at the nunnery. In November 1936, a Boston newspaper declared that she was "As familiar as that of any political personage whose name is before the public."[51] Ghost written by a group of Protestant ministers, Monk's book contained descriptions of the depraved goings-on at the convent. Her story was attractive to Protestants, highlighting their benevolence and kindness in counseling a young woman in distress after abuse at the hands of degenerate Catholics. She asserted that the babies of priests' unions were baptized, smothered with ruthless efficiency, and buried in the cellar.[52] Monk claimed that up to twenty babies were murdered during her time at the convent. "When he [the priest] had baptized the children, they were taken, one after the other, by one of the old nuns, in the presence of us all. She pressed her hand upon the mouth and nose of the first so tight that it could not breathe, and in a few minutes, when the hand was removed, it was dead. She then took the other, and treated it in the same way. No sound was heard, and both the children were corpses. . . . The little bodies were then taken into the cellar, thrown into the pit. . . ."[53]

During the night, she said that priests would enter through secret passageways leading into the convent and rendezvous in special rooms where they would have intercourse. While some nuns were willing participants, those who refused soon turned up missing. Monk claims to have witnessed the ritual murder of a young nun who declined to participate in murdering babies. She was bound, gagged, placed between two mattresses, and smothered: "One of the priests, named Bonin, sprung like a fury first upon it, and stamped upon it, with all his force. He was speedily followed by the nuns, until there were as many upon the bed as could find room, and all did what they could, not only to smother, but to bruise her. Some stood up and jumped upon the poor girl with their feet, some with their knees, and others in different ways seemed to seek how they might best beat the breath out of her body, and mangle it, without coming in direct contact with it, or seeing the effects of their violence."[54] Her lifeless body was then dragged into the cellar and unceremoniously dumped into a hole, covered with lime, and sprinkled with a mysterious liquid, presumably acid. Monk told how nuns were trained to treat priests with unquestioned obedience and how she was forbidden from speaking without permission, a claim intended to raise Protestant fears of the threat posed by convent schools. Cohen observes that the thought of nuns in secretive convents "subject to the sexual proclivities of unmarried, childless priests, and working with these same clerics to bring new women into the Catholic fold, raised fears that Protestant women . . . would spread alien beliefs to impressionable children and bring about the Catholic takeover of the United States."[55]

In reality, Monk had not been a nun; she was a mentally deranged prostitute who was cared for by a Catholic asylum for prostitutes in Montreal. Discharged in 1834 after becoming pregnant, she soon formed a liaison with an anti-Catholic reverend named William Hoyt, who exploited her imaginative tales of abuse at the hands of the sisters.[56] Monk died penniless in 1849 at a house for the poor in New York after having been sent there following her arrest for pickpocketing while plying her trade.[57]

In October 1835, Monk's mother signed an affidavit declaring that her daughter was mentally unstable and was being used as a pawn to make unfounded accusations against Catholic priests and nuns in Montreal. It stated that "at the age of about seven years, she broke a slate pencil in her head; that since that time, her mental faculties were deranged, and by times much more than at other times . . . she could make the most ridiculous, but most plausible stories; and that as to the history that she had been in a nunnery, it was a fabrication, for she was never in a nunnery."[58] The accident left her easily manipulated and prone to fantasy.

If these disclosures were not enough to deter even the most ardent believer, when the building was opened to inspection, not a shred of confirming evidence was found. The Protestant editor of the *New York Commercial Advertiser*, Colonel William Stone, had initially supported Monk and wanted to check out her story firsthand. He traveled to Montreal to examine the building where the abuses had allegedly taken place. He found that Monk's detailed descriptions of the convent did not match the claims in her book, including the gate that she had supposedly escaped through, which did not exist.[59] Protestant supporters of Monk quickly countered with a booklet of their own, refuting Stone's claims and calling him a liar. The anonymous authors made the unlikely claim that Stone's motive for "covering up" the truth of *Awful Disclosures* was financial, as most of his Canadian subscribers were Catholic and would be inclined to cancel their subscriptions if they knew the truth.[60] But given the testimony of her own mother, Monk's reputation was severely tarnished.

In typical moral-panic fashion, claims as to the scale of the threat were exaggerated, sometimes to the point of being absurd. At one point, Monk reports that about twenty infants had died over her two years at the nunnery, but later claimed to have found a book of which twenty-five pages had listings of the names of either novices or murdered infants during her stay; with fifteen entries per page. Colonel Stone did the math, which did not add up. "Now, we will allow twenty pages for the records of admissions of novices, and five for the births of the murdered children. Fifteen entries on a page, twenty pages, will give us the number of THREE HUNDRED admissions in two years.—Now there are but thirty-six nuns in all, and seldom more than four or five novices, or postulants."[61] Given that there are five pages devoted to birth records, Stone conservatively calculated that there would have been seventy-five births over the same period. He notes that out of the pool of thirty-six nuns, over half were not of menstruating age, and therefore could not have given birth. "Taking Maria's statements, therefore as correct data, and each of these fifteen nuns—striking the average—must give birth to two and a half children every year!!"[62] Later in 1836, she published a sequel, *Further Disclosures of Maria Monk*.[63] Public support and sympathy waned in 1838, after she gave birth to a second child out of wedlock.

Awful Disclosures wet the public appetite for similar works. Many of these novels described how nuns, having managed to escape the clutches of vile priests, upon returning home, fell in love, raised a family, and lived happily ever after.[64] Others were less fortunate, such as the sad tale of young Anna Howard, the central figure in *The American Nun* (1836).

The book was a cautionary tale about the dangers posed by the nunnery, to young, susceptible minds. Anna had naively decided against marrying her boyfriend to whom she had been engaged. Instead, she sought a life of adventure and liberation, only to be disenchanted with the nunnery. After realizing her folly and escaping, by the time she returned home, her mother had died and a friend had married her boyfriend. As if this was not heart-wrenching enough, the couple had produced a little girl named Anna. Overcome with emotional conflict and guilt, she soon died, mentally tortured and barren.[65]

The theme of escaped nun stories is an indictment on both the Catholic Church and the naivety and rashness of impulsive young women of the time, whose judgment and vulnerability were also on trial. Historian Susan Griffin points out that according to these works of fiction about escaped nuns, in order to atone for her sins, the initiate was typically forced to endure an array of physical and mental torments, from "being forced to lick the shape of a cross on the ground" to "solitary confinement, starvation, and even murder. All communication with the outside world is cut off: letters are destroyed, visitors denied, false communications issued in the protagonist's name. Her privacy is systematically violated: her captors invade her room, eavesdrop on her conversations, spy on her actions." Convents are portrayed as prisons that served as brothels for priests, and provided "a training ground for spies and teachers of Catholic propaganda" whose goal was nothing less than the control of the United States government.[66] Nuns are portrayed as either nymphomaniacs or the pitiful victims of physical, emotional, and sexual abuse. Griffin continues: "Those who refuse the priests' attentions are punished and, like the infants born as a result of priests' and nuns' illicit relations, eventually murdered. In the passages and rooms beneath the convent, dreadful penances are exacted, recalcitrant nuns imprisoned, and bodies disposed of. In several versions of the escaped nun's tale, the protagonist becomes the auditor or reader of other nuns' sad stories of entrapment and torture."[67]

Many writers tried to capitalize on the success of the books sold under

Reed's and Monk's names. *Six Months a Nun* soon spawned similar titles such as *Six Hours in a Convent* and *Six Months in a House of Correction*. Titles and subtitles often made reference to Monk or Charlestown, such as *Maria Monk's Daughter*, *The Chronicles of Mount Benedict*, and *The Convent's Doom: A Tale of Charleston in 1834*. Some titles were longwinded, apparently to be able to include the tie-in to either author. Notable examples were: *The Nun of St. Ursula; or, the Burning of the Convent; a Romance of Mt. Benedict* and *Hannah Corcoran: An Authentic Narrative of Her Conversion from Romanism, Her Abduction from Charlestown, and the Treatment She Received during Her Absence.* [68]

While confessional novels from supposedly escaped nuns ruled the day, priests soon got into the act. During the Catholic Scare, several men stepped forward claiming to have been ex-priests and wrote about the shenanigans that went on behind closed doors. A popular author of several books on the Catholic menace was Father William Hogan, who described how priests wore down their victims during confession by offering a sympathetic ear to their most intimate secrets at close physical proximity until succumbing to their sexual desires.[69] The Irish-born Hogan had been kicked out of the church in 1924 after a bitter dispute in which he was charged with attempted rape.[70] His main grievance was with the church's act of confessing sins to a priest. Hogan viewed confession as dangerous since it could be used to uncover Protestant secrets. Prone to making sweeping generalizations with little or no supporting evidence, Hogan claimed that "almost all the immoralities" by Catholics stemmed from the confessional.[71] He believed that confession allowed priests the opportunity to plant impure thoughts into the minds of their confessors, and to engage in sexual encounters with the young and vulnerable. One reason for his popularity may have been that his talks were laced with sex and scandal, titillating his conservative audience. Hogan claimed that some nuns who fell pregnant from their confessors had the babies baptized before they were strangled or aborted.[72] The confessionals by ex-priests helped to validate the many escaped-nun stories. Catholic historian Patrick Carey observes that by the 1830s, confessionals were being portrayed by anti-Catholic campaigners as hotbeds of perversion and sexual exploitation and a threat to the stability of the American family. Several former priests used the surge in anti-Catholic sentiments to tour the country, lecture on the evils of the confessional, and sell their books.[73]

ANTI-CATHOLIC RIOTING

Occasionally, anti-Catholic hostilities spilled over into full-scale riots that paled in comparison to the events at Charlestown. During the later 1830s, rumors and misinformation about the perversions committed behind convent walls swirled as a result of the surge in anti-Catholic propaganda and the rapidly accumulating literature on captive-nun tales. It did not matter that most of the accounts appeared as fiction, or that those authors claiming to have written autobiographical works were lacking evidence. The pattern in Charlestown was soon repeated in Baltimore in 1839, when thousands of outraged citizens marched on the Carmelite convent, rioted for three days, and threatened to destroy the building, under the misguided belief that it was holding captive nuns. The convent was a magnet for Catholic hostility, led by a group of reformed Protestants who had vehemently opposed its construction in 1831. Rumors of captive nuns had been circulating in the city since 1835, when the Protestant-controlled *Baltimore Literary and Religious Magazine* whipped up a public outcry by publishing claims of abuses behind the nunnery's walls. In one instance, it reported that a man repairing a house near the convent told of hearing a noise like someone lashing a whip, and in a window he could see "*a man dressed in black, flogging a female with what he took to be a cowskin.*" In a separate incident, no less than six citizens were reported to have heard screams from the fourth floor. Their signed statement, read in part: "The sound was that of a female voice, indicating great distress; we stopt and heard a second scream; and then a third, in quick succession, accompanied with the cry of *HELP! HELP! OH LORD! HELP!*" After waiting near the window for several minutes, the group moved on.[74] Given the deluge of anti-Catholic propaganda that was circulating at the time, authorities rightfully looked at the claims with great skepticism. In fact, police ignored this report, as it was made by members of a Protestant congregation returning from a meeting.[75] It was within this backdrop of suspicion that on Sunday, August 18, a nun was spotted wandering about East Baltimore, seeking shelter and making vague complaints of ill treatment. Tensions were further enflamed when the *Baltimore Post* erroneously reported that a group of physicians at nearby Washington College had examined the young woman, Sister Isabella Neale, and found her to be mentally sound. The report prompted greater concern over the nun's welfare and claims of abuse at the nunnery. The crowd was temporarily appeased when a group of physicians declared that Sister Neale was indeed mentally ill. Despite this, tensions were high and a militia remained at the nunnery for three weeks in order to prevent further mob actions amid threats to burn down the convent. The tense atmosphere only subsided after the nuns allowed authorities to inspect the convent and question the women inside. Each said they were there of their own free will. [76]

The worst anti-Catholic riots broke out at Philadelphia in 1844; these riots stemmed from arguments over which version of the Bible to use in public schools. Each day, students would listen to biblical readings from the King James edition favored by Protestants. Catholics preferred the so-called Douai Bible—a translation from a group of scholars at a seminary in Douai, modern-day France. Even though the messages were nearly the same, Catholic immigrants were upset that a "Protestant Bible" was being used to teach their children in a public school. So when in 1842 the city's Roman Catholic bishop asked the Philadelphia Board of Controllers to include other versions of the Bible in schools and that Catholic students be excused from sitting through Protestant religious classes, they agreed. This was seen as a fair compromise to appease the ever-growing Catholic population, whose ranks had swelled from 35,000 in 1835 to 170,000 by 1850.[77]

The issue over which Bible to teach in public schools erupted into riots amid rumors that Catholics were planning to remove all versions of the sacred book from public schools. Rioting broke out over several days in May and July, after it was erroneously reported that a Catholic school director named Hugh Clark wanted *all* Bible reading in public schools to cease, which infuriated Protestants and prompted a swift backlash. The first series of riots in May occurred in the Irish-dominated suburb of Kensington, where fourteen people died and two churches were destroyed. Rioting again flared up in July, when five thousand militiamen were called in to restore order, but not before at least a dozen more people were killed.[78]

On August 6, 1855, rioting broke out in Louisville, Kentucky. The targets were mostly Catholic immigrants; rioters left a path of destruction in their wake, and at least twenty dead. The so-called Bloody Monday riots occurred amid growing tensions with the flood of immigrants from Germany after the failed revolutions of 1848 and 1849, and from Ireland during the Irish Potato Famine. By 1850, one-third of the white population of Louisville was composed of recent migrants.[79] Prior to the violence, the anti-foreigner, anti-Catholic Know Nothing Party had a powerful influence on the city and enjoyed the support of its mayor, John Barbee. Another sympathizer was George Prentice, editor of the *Louisville Journal*, which was a pro-slavery newspaper through which he tried to influence public opinion against the newcomers. Amid an increasing atmosphere of intolerance and bigotry, just before the riot, he had written an inflammatory article in the *Journal* intended to whip up hostilities: "Rally to put down an organization of . . . priests and other papists, who aim by secret oaths and horrid midnight plottings, to sap the foundations of all our political edifices."[80] The riots were triggered when Know Nothings who were in control of the polling stations tried to stop naturalized immigrants from voting. Full-fledged citizens of the United States under the law, they had every right to vote, but the Know Nothings were determined to stop them from exercising that right.[81] As tensions grew between the two factions, gunshots rang out from both sides and houses were torched as mobs of Know Nothing supporters were soon roaming the streets, terrorizing German and Irish citizens.[82] The anti-Catholic fervor only subsided by the early 1860s as public attention was diverted to the more-pressing issue of the Civil War.

Protestant leaders and sympathetic politicians had exploited the hysteria to advance their agenda through legislation intended to bar Catholics from government jobs and halt the flow of Catholic immigrants. The exaggerated threat from Catholics has many parallels with more recent concerns involving Muslim immigrants and refugees. During the nineteenth century, many right-wing politicians engaged in fearmongering by using the Catholic Scare to drum up support for their agenda of stemming the flow of foreigners who were said to pose a threat to the country. Similar scare tactics have been used more recently by politicians who claim that many American towns and cities are rife with "sleeper cells" secretly plotting our downfall. Some fear that these newcomers owe their allegiance to foreign clerics, terrorist organizations, or countries with fanatical ideologies. The terrorist threat from these immigrants has been dramatically overstated and used to advance the isolationist agenda supported by politicians such as Donald Trump.

The most remarkable aspect of the Catholic Scare is how it parallels exaggerated fears over Muslim refugees who are fleeing war and persecution. The risks of being murdered by a refugee in a terrorist attack in the United States are an astronomical 3,500,000,000 to 1 (3.5 billion to one).[83] This Islamic Scare is driven by fear, not facts; illusion instead of reality. In a similar fashion, despite countless allegations of abuse and perversions at the hands of Catholic priests, not a single claim was ever confirmed. While there is some evidence that Rebecca Reed may have witnessed the mistreatment of a fellow nun dying of tuberculosis, even if that is true, it is a far cry from the many claims of systematic rape and murder of nuns, ritualized infanticide, and the existence of dungeons and torture chambers.[84] If these crimes were committed, and on such a vast scale as were claimed, why were the perpetrators never brought to justice? In some contemporary cases, such as the claims of "escaped nun" Helen Jackson in the late nineteenth century, a cash reward was offered by Catholics to anyone who could substantiate her assertions. The money was never paid.[85] There is not one instance where someone collected a reward for a confirmed case of nunnery abuse. The Catholic Scare is a testament to the human propensity to create, believe, and spread salacious stories driven by long-standing stereotypes, rumors, and fear. It exemplifies the power of belief, which is all too real in its consequences. It is a story that is as relevant today as it was 150 years ago.

CHAPTER 2

"NO DOGS, NO NEGROES, NO MEXICANS"

THE SOUTHERN BORDER MENACE

When Mexico sends its people, they're not sending their best. . . . They're sending people that have lots of problems, and they're bringing those problems with [sic] us. They're bringing drugs. They're bringing crime. They're rapists. And some, I assume, are good people.
   —Donald J. Trump, campaign speech, June 16, 2015

The signs in front of businesses enforced the prevailing attitude: No Dogs, No Negroes, No Mexicans.
       —Francisco Natera, *Coyame: A History of the American Settler*, 2012

When in 2015 presidential candidate Donald Trump warned of Mexican immigrants being a threat to American society as rapists, drug dealers, and gang members, he evoked painful memories of ill treatment that were still vivid for many older citizens of Mexican ancestry. Animosity was once so great that until 1890, a person of Mexican heritage had the same chance of being lynched as an African American did.[1] Old, young, rich, poor, male, female—no one was spared from the brutality of the era. On a warm summer's evening in June 1911, a Mexican American citizen named Antonio Gómez was minding his own business, whittling a shingle of wood outside a saloon in Thorndale, Texas. After being repeat-edly harassed by several men for dropping his shavings on the sidewalk, he was beaten, sworn at, and called a "skunk." Humiliated and enraged, he fought back, lunging at one of his tormentors with his knife and stabbing him in the chest. Gómez was quickly tracked down by a group of vigilantes, attached to a chain, and dragged behind a horse through the center of town as upward of two hundred residents looked on with approval. He was then lynched from a ladder. Antonio Gómez was just fourteen years old. The four men charged with his murder were all found not guilty.[2] During this period, Mexicans were loathed as an inferior race who were a threat to American's economic growth and social progress.

Throughout our history, hostilities have often come to the fore over the misguided belief that citizens of Mexican ancestry were taking "American" jobs. To stop the corruption of the Northern European racial lineage, laws were passed to prevent them from marrying "whites." Harassment and violence were mainstays of everyday life in the early years of America's colonial presence in the Southwest.[3] Starting in the mid-nineteenth century and persisting to the present day, Mexican Americans have been the subject of several waves of panic, which waxed and waned with popular sentiment and political expediency. In 1929, Americans of Mexican descent were classified as white. With the onset of the Great Depression and the rising tide of jobless, in the 1930 census the govern-ment tried to limit immigration by categorizing them as nonwhite. A decade later, when there was a shortage of factory labor and soldiers to cope with the demands of the Second World War, they were conveniently reclassified as white again.

Until the early 1950s, Mexican Americans living in the Southwest were treated like second-class citizens. Signs proclaiming "No Dogs, No Negroes, No Mexicans" were proudly on display in the windows of many bars and restaurants across the region. A widespread fear and aversion to Americans of Mexican ancestry has permeated society in these con-quered lands ever since the annexation of northern Mexico in the 1840s, when the inhabitants could become citizens. As Anglo Americans began pouring into the region to work as ranchers, farmers, and miners, conflicts arose because the local residents were not accepted as equals. By mid-1850, anti-Mexican violence had spread to California and across the entire Southwest, as the result of competition for jobs, racist attitudes, and the growing belief in manifest destiny. White American settlers believed that it was their destiny to expand to the West Coast, spreading their superior European civilization and Christian values, while enlightening the "primitive" peoples of the region. Hispanics and Native Americans were in the latter category. Manifest destiny became a convenient rationale to justify the annexing of the territories of the Southwest and the subjugation of their people.

From the time Texas became an independent country in 1836, until its full annexation a decade later, its citizens of Mexican heritage were widely viewed by their Anglo conquerors as members of a lower race. They were seen as a strange mixture of "Negroid," "Mongoloid," and "American" racial types who were dirty, lazy, untrustworthy, and prone to thievery and gang activity. These traits were seen as the predictable outcome of poor breeding between the African, Spanish, and Native American races. Rufus Sage lived through this period. He describes Mexican Americans as "mongrels" with despicable morals, people who were incapable of self-government, and who needed to be "kept in their place by force, if necessary."[4] He wrote that, "As servants, they are excellent . . . but are worse than useless if left to themselves." Historian Reginald Horsman observed that a major rationale for America having invaded northern Mexico was that "Mexicans, like Indians, were unable to make proper use of the land. The Mexicans had failed because they were a mixed, inferior race with considerable Indian and some black blood. The world would benefit if a superior race shaped the future of the Southwest."[5] Many Americans steadfastly opposed annexing parts of Mexico—not on moral grounds, but over the fear of race mixing and contamination by inferior people.[6] During the 1840s, newspaper editors and politicians debated the benefits of annexation. Many urged President James Polk to avoid taking tracts of land with large numbers of Mexicans.[7] Polk wanted to claim all of Mexico but compromised on the amount of land that was eventually seized, over the dilemma of Mexicans becoming citizens. Polk annexed only Mexico's sparsely populated northern regions, obtaining the most land with the fewest Mexicans—about 100,000.[8]

THE BLACK LEGEND

While Spain was part of Europe, many of America's early settlers looked down upon the Spanish as an inferior race that was prone to cruelty and sadism on the basis of the atrocities they committed in their colonial conquest of Central America and Mexico. Spanish historians would later refer to this negative perception and hostility as the Black Legend. The Spanish conquest of these regions had a devastating impact on the native peoples. The spread of diseases such as smallpox, for which there was no natural immunity, killed large swaths of indigenous inhabitants. Enslavement and the use of natives for hard labor led to more deaths, while priests outlawed religious and cultural traditions that had developed over millennia, supplanting them with Christianity. Ironically, Americans of Northern European ancestry had short memories, as they had taken part in similar acts of cruelty and barbarity to Native Americans, denigrating their culture, displacing their people, and deliberately spreading smallpox to exterminate entire tribes. Despite these inconvenient facts of history, by the mid-1800s, a number of Anglo American writers began exaggerating the exploits of the Spanish and demonizing them as an evil race. According to historian David Weber, "Englishmen and Anglo Americans who wrote about the Spanish past in North America uniformly condemned Spanish rule. . . . Anglo Americans had inherited the view that Spaniards were unusually cruel . . . treacherous, fanatical, superstitious, cowardly, corrupt, decadent, indolent, and authoritarian."[9] This demonization of the Spanish helped to justify American's expansion into the Southwest and further stigmatized the inhabitants as the product of inferior cultures and breeding.[10] Lothrop Stoddard's popular books on racial types reinforced these views; he warned of the perils of race-mixing along the Southwest border, which he concluded would lead to the inevitable contamination of the "pure" Nordic stock. He believed that poverty and political instability in Mexico and the Caribbean were the result of their having been "largely hybrid mixtures of whites, Indians, and negroes."[11] Stoddard's view of the mixed-breed Mexican peasant was far from complementary, describing them as "a poverty-stricken, ignorant, primitive creature, with strong muscles and just enough brains to obey orders and produce profits under competent direction."[12]

Stoddard believed that Mexican ancestry made people prime targets for manipulation by unscrupulous leaders, especially Communists. As such, they posed a threat to the nation as potential followers of revolutionary movements and rebellions. He saw Mexican peasants as "about the most 'alien,' unassimilable creature that could be imagined."[13] He continued, "His temperament and outlook on life are absolutely opposed to those of the typical American. Low in intelligence and almost devoid of individual initiative, the Mexican Indian is likewise splendid revolutionary material, because he is *a born communist*." Another popular nineteenth-century stereotype was that of the Mexican bandit, which reinforced the belief in that Mexicans were natural followers. Historian James Evans writes: "The Mexican bandit, like the typical Mexican, would rather steal than work, but he differed from the masses in that he possessed the ambition and physical stamina necessary for bandit activities."[14] Given their diminished mental capacity as an inferior race, Anglo Americans of the period held that the bandit leader could easily acquire "a following of admirers and thieves and cutthroats who became members of his band and participated in his raids." The modern-day equivalent is the Mexican as a natural gang member, ready to carry out the orders of his leaders without question. In the years following the Immigration Act of 1924, which significantly restricted the number of incoming immigrants from all parts of the world, the porous southern border was viewed as America's Achilles' heel. As a result of this demographic shift, and with no scientific backing, many of the leading proponents of immigration restriction suddenly viewed Mexicans as among the worst offenders for racial contamination. In 1927, Stoddard wrote that in all likelihood, the non-Nordic races from outside northern Europe "can eventually be absorbed into the nation's blood without such alteration of America's racial make-up as would endanger the stability and continuity of our national life. But what is thus true of European immigrants, most of whom belong to some branch of the white racial group, most emphatically does not apply to non-white immigrants, like the Chinese, Japanese, or Mexicans."[15] Stoddard worried about a possible immigration invasion from the hordes of inferior races in Central and South America.[16]

AN INFERIOR PEOPLE

The widespread notion that Mexican Americans are of lower intelligence than "whites," has continued in recent times. They are commonly portrayed on American TV as unsophisticated, subservient, dimwitted and born followers.[17] This bias was evident in 1982, when controversy erupted in California after a set of test scores were invalidated due solely to their high results, and the ethnic background of those taking them. When the Princeton Educational Testing Service reviewed scores for the state, they found that the highest pass rates for the advanced calculus exam were from Garfield High School in Los Angeles. The school had a poor track record of exam success and a high proportion of Mexican American students. Fourteen of the eighteen who passed were suspected of cheating and were made to re-sit a different exam. While two of the students refused because they did not need the credits to pass, the remaining twelve took the new test. They all passed. School officials angrily asserted that the students would never have been singled out if it had not been for their Spanish surnames or had they not come from low-income neighborhoods. The episode was turned into the 1988 film *Stand and Deliver*.[18] In 2016, the US Postal Service issued a stamp honoring their teacher, Jaime Escalante. After serving seventeen years at the school, Escalante left in 1991. Calculus scores immediately plummeted. The events at Garfield High highlight the importance of school environment and nurturing by exceptional teachers in getting good grades. Genetics had nothing to do with it.[19] As one journalist wrote, the key to his success was how he "cajoles, inspires and truly teaches them the difficult subject of calculus, and in so doing creates in them an enduring feeling of self-worth."[20]

In recent decades, several researchers have claimed that race itself can predict intelligence. In 1987, a pioneer in the field of intelligence testing, Lloyd Dunn, made the stunning claim that differences in measured intelligence between Latinos and whites were partly due to heredity. He wrote that "while many people are willing to blame the low scores of Puerto Ricans and Mexican-Americans on their poor environmental conditions, *few are prepared to face the probability that inherited genetic material is a contributing factor.* Yet, in making a scholarly, comprehensive examination of this issue, this factor must be included."[21] Dunn said that it would be naïve and irresponsible to claim that a ten- to twelve-point difference in IQ scores was solely caused by social and cultural factors.[22] However, an array of influences can account for the differences in test scores, including teacher attitudes and expectations, and disparities in resources and funding between schools.[23] Other researchers note that in culturally diverse, bilingual children, scores will reflect their degree of familiarity with Standard American English and the level of cultural assimilation.[24]

Dunn's conclusions fall into the realm of pseudoscience and quackery since he fails to accept the consensus within the scientific community that race is a biological myth. Race is also a social reality. Thus, if a student believes she is part of an inferior race, her belief may act as a self-fulfilling prophecy. She may lack self-confidence, stop trying, or give up altogether.

Many factors influence standardized test scores, not the least of which is culture. Law scholar Steven Bender observes that Latino families emphasize the importance of respecting authority and the collective good, while downplaying individual assertiveness. This outlook can influence student achievement. He writes: "In the classroom, this submissive tendency may be regarded by teachers as apathy to be contrasted with the aggressive, 'engaged' participation of Anglo students. Because teachers tend to reward the most active class participants with positive feedback, superior grades, and recommendations, this culture of the American classroom contributes to the negative channeling of Latina/o students away from college and academic pursuits."[25] Dunn's biased interpretation of the data hides his deeper political agenda. His findings that most Mexican American children lack sufficient scholastic aptitude or linguistic competency to master two languages led him to conclude that English should be the *sole* language of instruction in American schools.[26]

Given what we now know about the powerful role of social environment and self-belief in achievement, it is no wonder that Mexican American students have a poor history of achievement on exams and standardized tests. During the first half of the twentieth century, those of Mexican heritage living in the American Southwest were the subject of government campaigns to Americanize them in the hope that these children would begin to assimilate into society and start to lose their "peasant culture," which was seen as an impediment to modernization. Sociologist Carina Bandhauer writes that this new policy created a war on Hispanic culture and customs. As a result, "Mexican American children were taught that they were dirty, [were] unacceptable, spoke a forbidden language," and that their community, family, and culture were obstacles to successful schooling.[27] In teaching students about their inferior culture, it would have undoubtedly damaged their self-confidence and dampened any ambitions they may have had, other than aspirations of being house cleaners and low-level laborers.

EUGENICS—THE SCIENCE OF RACE

By the early 1910s, the eugenics movement had become part of mainstream science, and was being used to control "inferior" races, including Mexicans, to ensure that they did not spread disease and vermin. Medical researchers and public-health officials used statistics to justify claims that certain races were disease carriers and were over-represented in mental asylums. Such figures conveniently failed to count private mental institutions, which were more likely to be occupied by well-off whites.[28] By 1917, quarantines were established along the Southwest border with Texas in an effort to "protect" Americans from lower-class, disease-carrying Mexicans. Wealthier Mexicans and Europeans traveling by first-class rail were not subject to any restrictions. It was thought that those who had accumulated wealth were the products of better breeding and were more clever and sophisticated than their inbred compatriots. Meanwhile, Mexicans in the second-class cars were treated like animals and subjected to the indignity and humiliation of delousing. They were forced to strip naked, inspected for lice, doused in kerosene, and sprayed with an assortment of chemicals—including Zyklon B, a cyanide-based pesticide that would later be used by the Nazis in the mass murder of Jews. Those with lice were forced to shave their body hair with clippers and bathe in a mixture of vinegar and kerosene. In January 1917, the Bathhouse Riots broke out at a disinfection station on the Santa Fe Bridge linking El Paso, Texas, with Juárez, Mexico. Led by two hundred exasperated women, the unrest lasted several days after rumors that rail inspectors had taken nude photos of Mexican women and were selling them in the shops of El Paso.[29] The notion of Mexicans as a dirty, disease-carrying race were pure stereotype and were not borne out by the statistics. For instance, during a four-month period in early 1917, there were three fatalities from typhus along the US–Mexican border. This number is miniscule when considering that during this same period, inspectors examined over three-quarters of a million people.[30]

During the first half of the twentieth century, American eugenicists tried to weed out inferior gene pools by placing "defective" members of certain races in institutions for either mental or behavioral problems. Some facilities in California had up to a quarter of their population as Mexican Americans.[31] These behaviors were viewed as medical conditions that needed to be addressed by separating the afflicted from the rest of society in institutions for delinquents. Many were forced to undergo sterilizations in the misguided notion that doing so would prevent them from having defective or inferior children. Hispanic women who had children out of wedlock were branded as suffering from a hyperactive sex drive and were classified as delinquents. Mexican American males who committed petty crimes or were truant from school were also placed in institutions for the delinquent.[32] Between 1909 and 1979, the state of California oversaw about twenty thousand sterilizations, many without consent or under duress or coercion. Most occurred during the first half of the century.[33] Some facilities refused to release the patients until they agreed to the procedure, essentially rendering them prisoners of the state. Many only learned of their sterilizations after the event. Historian Natalie Lira studied the California eugenics archives and found that a disproportionate number of Mexican Americans were sterilized. Fortunately, the procedure rapidly declined in usage by the early 1950s.[34]

There was great enthusiasm when the first eugenics law was passed in Indiana in 1907. Scientists and social reformers were excited about the prospect of applying this new "science" to solve long-standing social problems. In California, eugenicists defined the genetically "unfit" as those who had disabilities and were of low income and education. The notion of social Darwinism was popular at this time, so a person's level of wealth and education were seen as a reflection of his or her inherited intelligence. Conversely, middle- and upper-class "whites" were encouraged to procreate and strengthen the Nordic racial stock for the benefit of the country. The state of California viewed Mexicans and Indians as the foremost racial problems facing the state.[35] There was a major concern over what was believed to be their prolific breeding ability and the potential strain on welfare services. Charles Goethe, the cofounder of a San Francisco–based eugenics club, warned that the surge in Mexican peasants crossing the border posed a menace to society because they "multiply like rabbits."[36] This attitude appears in a 1920 California school report, which claimed that Mexican living standards "do not accord with ours, but it is more likely that intellectual differences account for most of their unsocial conduct."[37] The report asserts that Hispanic students were inherently deficient in intellectual ability. "Mexican children do not learn readily at school, and few of them ever pass above the third grade. Recent studies have indicated that this failure to learn is not because of language difficulties, but is more likely due to low intelligence." The author went on to claim that "the average intelligence of Mexican children in Southern California is not greater than three-fourths that of American children." As a result, the report concluded that "nearly one-half of the Mexican children in our schools are feeble-minded."

In one instance, state officials targeted a "half Spanish, half Indian" woman who had given birth to eleven children from two different fathers. Despite normal IQ scores, she was classified as a "high moron" and sent to a home for the mentally defective and eventually marked for sterilization, against her parents' wishes. Her misfortune was to have been of Mexican origin, to desire a large family, and to be poor.[38] The IQ ranking placed "idiots" as those with a score of twenty-five or lower; "imbeciles" as those with a score of twenty-five to fifty; and "morons"—those with a score of fifty to seventy-nine—who were seen as especially dangerous because they could pass as normal and spread their genes, thus diluting the purity of the population.[39] In most instances, "morons" appear to have been "normal" members of the Mexican American community who fared poorly on the IQ test. In 1975, several Mexican American women filed suit in court against non-consensual or coerced sterilizations. At the trial, it became evident that long-held stereotypes of Mexican Americans were alive and well in California. A medical student testified that she had heard one of the sterilizing physicians remark that "poor minority women in L. A. County were having too many babies; that it was a strain on society; and that it was good that they be sterilized."[40] She further testified that he stated it was his intention to see "how low we can cut the birth rate of the Negro and Mexican populations in Los Angeles County."

SECOND-CLASS CITIZENS

More recently, Donald Trump has threatened to round up and send non-resident Mexicans back over the border. His remarks have generated anxiety for Americans of Mexican heritage, stirring up memories of the Repatriation from 1929 to 1936. During the Great Depression, the administration of Herbert Hoover launched a campaign of mass deportations to purge the country of Mexican American citizens, legal residents, and illegal aliens, who were blamed for taking jobs from "real" Americans. This episode occurred amid a wave of anti-immigration hysteria. Upward of two million were sent back to Mexico, 60 percent of whom were American citizens.[41] Those of Mexican heritage were the logical targets, as they were the most recent major group of immigrants.[42] In many cases, government officials knocked on the doors of families and tried to persuade them to leave—going so far as to give them free tickets back "home" to be with their "own kind." Many county governments cut welfare payments to Mexican families in an effort to discourage them. While the program was called the Mexican Repatriation, a more apt description would be the Great Deportation. The word *repatriation* evokes connotations of voluntary participation. In this instance, they were pressured, and sometimes forced, to cross the border, usually on trains or buses. County agents would knock on doors and say, "You would be better off in Mexico, and here are your train tickets. You should be ready to go in two weeks."[43] One appalling example involved Ignacio Pena of Idaho. Historian Francisco Balderrama recounts that as his family was about to eat breakfast, sheriff's deputies entered the house. "They took everybody in custody, and they were told that they could only leave with the clothes that were on their back. They could not bring any of their personal belongings, and they were placed in a jail. His father was working out in the fields, and he was also placed in a jail."[44] After a week, they were shipped by train across the border to Mexico. "They never were able to recover their personal belongings, even though they were told that those belongings . . . would be shipped to them. And among those belongings was a documentation of his father having worked in the United States for over 25 years. Among those belongings was his and his sisters' and his brothers' birth certificates, having been born in the United States."

Mexican American citizens faced continuing discrimination throughout the first half of the nineteenth century, with efforts to block them from exercising their basic democratic rights to vote in state and national elections. In 1870, the Fifteenth Amendment to the US Constitution gave every citizen the right to vote regardless of race, color, or creed. The practical reality was very different. White lawmakers in many states found ways to keep new immigrants and unwelcome minorities from making their voices heard at the ballot box. This was especially true in the Southwest, where many communities had a majority of Mexican American residents. State leaders realized that if they voted as a block, they could exercise considerable political clout. Many state legislatures circumvented federal law by requiring residents to pay a poll tax or pass a literacy test to be eligible to vote. In 1894, California required voters to be literate in English, thus eliminating many residents who were uneducated or fluent in Spanish as their first language. They also required a fee to be eligible to vote. Hispanics were among the state's poorest residents and could not afford to pay. Texas followed suit in 1902, requiring a poll tax of between $1.50 and $1.75—a hefty sum at the time, especially for the poor. Some states stipulated that poll taxes be collected annually. These laws endured for several decades until they were challenged by the courts and deemed illegal. It was not until 1964 that the Twenty-Fourth Amendment abolished poll taxes in national elections. Two years later, the US Supreme Court abolished them in state elections.[45] Some people believe that new voter identification laws in several key states during the 2016 presidential election may have contributed to the loss of Hillary Clinton. Trump narrowly won the state of Wisconsin by 22,728 votes. Conspicuously, the state had its lowest voter turnout in two decades, about 41,000 fewer than in the previous presidential election. Milwaukee County Clerk Joe Czarnezki is convinced that the voter ID laws handed the election to Trump. "I believe it was voter suppression laws from the state government that crushed turnout," he said, noting that those most affected were poor minorities who did not own a motor vehicle or a driver's license.[46]

The rights of Hispanic Americans were continually trotted upon during the first half of the nineteenth century. The heartbreaking case of New York orphans epitomizes their social position. In 1904, forty Anglo American orphans were sent to live with Hispanic families in Arizona Territory, outraging local whites who held fierce protests over allowing Nordic children to be raised by "half-breeds." Vigilante groups seized the children and placed them with white families. It is a testament to the deeply held racist sentiments of the time that the Arizona Supreme Court sided with the white parents, who were essentially kidnappers and child abductors. The court referred to the vigilantes as "committees." The New York orphanage was legally powerless to get the children back, and the children spent the rest of their lives with their new, white families.[47]

In 2018, the Trump administration exhibited a similar callousness in its treatment of refugees and asylum seekers from Latin America who were trying to enter the country at the Mexican border. The administration's policy of separating infants and children from their families as part of a deliberate strategy to discourage them from seeking safe haven in the United States was widely condemned, both domestically and internationally. As part of the zero-tolerance policy, persons who were not processed at one of the officially designated ports of entry were labeled as having attempted to enter the country illegally. However, many people were turned away at the ports of entry, or, after waiting days or weeks without being processed, they eventually crossed elsewhere in frustration. Many did not have the means to reach a port of entry, and they crossed the border somewhere else without obtaining a visa, only to be branded as criminals. In many of these cases, upon entering the United States, the asylum seekers immediately sought out Border Patrol agents to request safe haven, only to find themselves under arrest and separated from their children.[48]

Present-day fears over the perceived threat posed by Mexicans, and the reluctance to fully accept Mexican Americans as equal citizens, continue to pose a challenge for our reputation as a tolerant and welcoming country. In June 2016, Donald Trump evoked race when he claimed that the judge presiding over a lawsuit against Trump University should recuse himself from the case because his parents were of Mexican ancestry. To insinuate that US District Judge Gonzalo Curiel could not rule fairly because of his Mexican heritage, since Trump proposed to build a wall between the two countries, has alarming racial overtones. While the United States promotes itself as a melting pot of ethnic and religious diversity, it has a checkered history when it comes to putting these ideals into practice. People of Mexican ancestry are but one of a long list of culturally diverse groups and nationalities that have been vilified as leeches on the American welfare system and a threat to our national security. Immigrants are some of the most vulnerable people on Earth, and make easy scapegoats for complex problems of the day. The efforts by President Trump to build a wall along our Southwest border, physically separating Mexico and the United States, is the most visible attempt to further underscore our differences, instead of focusing on our common humanity.

CHAPTER 3

"THE MONGOLIAN HORDES MUST GO!"

THE CHINESE MIGRATION BAN

[Chinese] are uncivilized, unclean, and filthy beyond all conception, without any of the higher domestic or social relations; lustful and sensual in their dispositions. . . . The first words of English they learn are terms of obscenity or profanity. . . . Clannish in nature, they will not associate except with their own people, and the Chinese quarter of the city is a by-word for filth and sin. Pagan in religion, they know not the virtues of honesty, integrity or good-faith.

—Horace Greeley, "Chinese Immigration
to California," *New York Tribune*, September 29, 1854

Amid fears that the country was being overrun by hordes of immigrants from the Far East who would corrupt the American way of life, in May 1882 Congress took the extraordinary step of banning Chinese laborers. It was the first significant legislation in American history in which a group of migrants were excluded from settling on US soil based solely on their race and class. The anti-Chinese hostilities would not end until the early twentieth century, when all migrants from China were banned. Passage took place at a time when scientists thought that the world was divided into racial groups. The existence of superior and inferior peoples was a cornerstone of the curriculum in high school and university biology classes across Europe and North America. The Chinese were believed to be a branch of the Asiatic "Mongol Race," a step above the "Negro," but well below whites. In 1866, the editor of the prestigious *Anthropological Review* described them as an inferior "infantile" race, as evidenced by their "backward" art, literature, and government. "They are beardless children, whose life is a task, and whose chief virtue consists in unquestioning obedience," he wrote.[1] A few years later, in 1871, attitudes had changed little, as Ohio Congressman William Mungen stood on the floor of the House of Representatives and complained about the wave of Chinese immigrants who were taking jobs from more worthy Americans, referring to them as "a poor, miserable, dwarfish race of inferior beings."[2]

Many newspapers and scholarly journals of the period published apelike images of the Chinese, implying that they were lower on the evolutionary scale. There were many comparisons to insect swarms, especially bees, ants, and locusts. They were portrayed as mindless followers who looked alike and acted with a common purpose.[3] This imagery frightened white Americans. Perhaps more than any other factor, the belief in different racial types is what fueled the anti-Chinese hysteria, although economic factors certainly played a role. The initial ban was for ten years, but it was renewed and eventually expanded to include *all* Chinese by 1902. The policy would not be abolished until the Second World War, when politicians finally relented after the United States and China found themselves as allies in the fight against Japan.

The backdrop of the scare was the sudden influx of Chinese immigrants arriving on the West Coast during the second half of the nineteenth century, as they fled civil war, economic turmoil, and political unrest in their native land. Many took jobs in the California gold mines, where tensions soon boiled over. The views of San Francisco attorney John Boalt were typical of the period. He wrote that white and Mongolian races were incompatible, observing that their physical peculiarities were so repulsive as to "prevent any intimate association or miscegenation [sexual intercourse] of the races."[4] California politicians shrewdly capitalized on the anti-Chinese mood to gain votes.[5] They did not fear a backlash from Chinese voters, because foreign-born Asians were ineligible for citizenship and could not cast ballots.[6]

INVASION!

The initial surge of Chinese migrants was in response to the California gold rush of 1848, and later to build the western branch of the transcontinental railroad. Others took jobs in the agricultural and fishing sectors. For company bosses, they were a welcome supply of cheap labor who had a reputation for hard work. Most were willing to do any job, including those that their white counterparts were reluctant to fill. During the 1850s, an Anglo American earned about three dollars a day in the gold fields. Their Chinese counterparts were paid as low as $1.25 for the same work, and most were paid at least a dollar below that of a white laborer.[7] In 1850, a mere 660 Chinese were living in California, most hoping to make their fortune mining gold.[8] Within two years, 25,000 more would pour into California. By 1880, more than 105,000 Chinese had made the voyage across the Pacific in search of a better life in America—most in California. Only one in five was an American citizen.[9] In 1868, Congress passed the Fourteenth Amendment to the Constitution to ensure equality for the recently freed black slaves. It stated that all persons born or naturalized in the United States were American citizens, including blacks. This allowed Chinese immigrants the chance to obtain citizenship, which was for the courts to decide, on an individual basis. That changed in 1878 when a California court ruled that members of the Mongolian race were of neither Anglo nor African descent. While Chinese born in the United States could still become citizens, those born outside the country were now prohibited from applying.[10]

Anti-Chinese hostilities grew steadily in the 1870s. Once the transcontinental railroad was completed in 1869, thousands of Chinese workers flooded the West Coast job market at a time of economic hard-ship. Attempts to address concerns over the growing number of Asians entering the labor force prompted Congress to act in 1875, banning the immigration of convicts or prostitutes from any country. It was a thinly veiled attempt to reduce the number of unskilled Chinese laborers from entering, and to stop the flow of Chinese women to lower their birth rate. At the time, Chinese women were portrayed as sexually promiscuous and natural prostitutes who posed a threat to the morals of America's youth. The law did little to slow the arrival of Chinese immigrants.[11] As fears grew over cheap Chinese labor taking jobs from white citizens and corrupting American values, calls to address the issue grew louder. William Lock-lear observes that the Chinese migrant was viewed as "a slave of another color," willing to undercut white labor. To him, they were a cunning and godless race with no respect for American morals. "He lived in 'herds' amid squalor, gambled, smoked opium and forced Chinese women into prostitution, thus endangering the health and morality of the commu-nity."[12] Anti-Chinese sentiments reached such levels that many Anglo Americans vowed never to live in a house previously occupied by "filthy" Chinese, and complaining that whenever they moved into a neighbor-hood, property values dropped.[13] The Chinese were demonized by poli-ticians and journalists alike, culminating in the Exclusion Act of 1882. The act was a form of scapegoating for the wage decline of the 1870s, but the reality was very different. The presence of Chinese workers had little impact on the overall economy. In the 1880 census, those of Chinese descent comprised a mere 0.002 percent of the nation's population—just over 100,000 out of 50 million. While the law was worded in economic terms, it had racist overtones.[14]

The 1882 ban exempted the Chinese upper class: diplomats, mer-chants, students, teachers, and travelers, but it prevented *all immigrants* from China from becoming naturalized citizens.[15] These well-to-do new-comers were believed to have had better breeding by virtue of their wealth. It was assumed that those who were financially better off were naturally smarter than poorer Chinese, as their intelligence had allowed them to accumulate wealth. In 1888, the law was expanded to bar the return of Chinese immigrants who had temporarily left the country, stranding about 25,000 of their compatriots overseas. By 1893, amid the continuing clamor from white voters to address the so-called Yellow Invasion, lawmakers expanded the definition of *laborer* to include merchants, miners, laundry owners, and those in the fishing industry. By 1902, the issue was emphatically resolved when *all Chinese immigration was prohibited.*[16]

It was no small irony that the better life so many Chinese had come searching for was itself a fiction, an embellished image that was packaged and sold by shipping companies to promote their self-interests: making as much money as possible by filling their vessels to capacity for the voyage to America. As they docked in port cities like Canton and Hong Kong, broadsheets were handed out to lure locals into taking the voyage. One company urged residents to seek their fortune in the California goldfields. Their handbill read: "Americans are very rich people. They want the Chinaman to come and will make him welcome. There will be big pay, large houses, and food and clothing of the finest description.... Such as wishes to have wages and labor guaranteed can obtain the security by application at this office."[17] Dreaming of gold and wealth, many sold their homes and fishing boats, or borrowed money from relatives to make the long journey. They were soon to be disillusioned by what they found.

THE DRIVE TO PURGE THE HORDE

To the surprise of many, the 1882 Immigration Act not only failed to placate supporters and calm anti-Chinese sentiments but also had the opposite effect—igniting and emboldening opponents. As hostilities grew, many residents living in western states formed anti-Chinese organizations for the purpose of lobbying for even stricter laws to combat the perceived threat to their jobs and the American way of life. Some encouraged boycotts of Chinese goods and businesses, harassed Chinese citizens, and, in several instances, ran Chinese residents out of town. In 1884, Congress made it more difficult for merchants and travelers to obtain an exemption by expanding the definition of *merchant* to include peddlers and fishermen.[18] By 1892, all existing Chinese exclusion laws were renewed for another decade. The racist nature of the act was evident in its language. The law stipulated that any Chinese laborers residing in the country had to register with the government and obtain a special certificate allowing them to stay. Anyone found without a certificate was subject to a year in prison followed by deportation. However, people could be saved from this fate if a "credible *white* witness" was to testify on their behalf that they were indeed US residents who had a good excuse for failing to register. In 1893, the law was amended to include "one credible witness *other than Chinese*" to prove residency.[19] By the turn of the century, white animosity toward the Chinese was stronger than ever. In 1901, San Francisco Mayor James Phelan viewed the campaign against Chinese immigrants as a titanic struggle for the future of white humanity. He proclaimed that California government officials were "wardens of the Golden Gate; we must stand here forever in the pathway of the Orient. . . . It is for us to sound the alarm. I regard the Chinese question as a race question . . . and above and over all, a question involving the preservation of our civilization."[20]

While the most intense hostilities were concentrated in California, other western states were also forced to address the issue. In Montana during January 1886, a group of women who washed laundry for a living placed a notice in a Helena newspaper complaining that "Mongolian hordes" were putting them out of business. Predictably, the editor came out in support of the women and against the "almond-eyed citizens."[21] The Montana papers were filled with anti-Chinese sentiments at this time, depicting them as unscrupulous, perverse, unclean, uncivilized, and ungodly. Throughout the state, they were commonly referred to in the press as John Chinaman and Chink Chink Chinaman.[22]

FROM MODEL CITIZENS TO INFERIOR MENACE

Historian Stuart Miller found overwhelmingly negative images of Chinese in American books, newspapers, and magazines in the century leading up to the 1882 Exclusion Act. He observes that during the first half of the century, most of what trickled down to the American masses were reports from diplomats, missionaries, and merchants who had visited China, recounting stories of Chinese idolatry, cruelty, infanticide, and sexual perversity.[23] However, California newspapers had an overwhelmingly positive description of these strange newcomers. The image would quickly change. These early press accounts held them to be well-dressed, refined, and civilized. For instance, the prominent *Daily Alta California* had nothing but praise. A typical comment appeared in the paper on May 12, 1851: "Scarcely a ship arrives here that does not bring an increase to this worthy integer of our population.... Perhaps the citizens of no nation except the Germans, are more quiet and valuable." Another issue described them as possessing a lofty moral and industrious character: "They make good, honest and industrious citizens, and no one of them has ever yet been before the authorities for larceny or any other criminal charge."[24] By 1852, California Governor John McDougal not only praised them as "one of the most worthy classes of our newly adopted citizens," he pushed for land grants to attract greater numbers of Chinese migrants to America.[25] The tide would quickly turn. Later that same year, with the swearing in of Governor John Bigler, anti-Chinese sentiments had well and truly taken hold. Bigler supported a bill that would halt further immigration of unskilled Chinese laborers.[26] By 1862, Governor Leland Stanford took up the cause with vigor, referring to local Chinese as "dregs"—worthless people. His position was the height of hypocrisy. At the same time, thousands of low-wage Chinese workers were being imported to construct the Central Pacific Railroad. Stanford was the railroad's president. From 1865 to 1869, over ten thousand Chinese were hired to construct the railway, at two-thirds the wages of whites. They were shamelessly exploited in other ways, such as having to provide their own shelter and food. The use of Chinese workers saved the company an estimated $5 million—an enormous sum at the time.[27] The exploitation of migrant workers to cut costs remains prevalent across America today, as does the taking advantage of migrants who are deemed to have illegally entered the country and fear deportation if they complain. For example, during the demolition of a building to make way for the construction of Trump Tower in Manhattan, Donald Trump was aware that many of the construction workers were illegal Poles, whom he threatened with deportation when they complained over a pay dispute.[28]

These early press accounts fail to mention that trouble was brewing in the gold mines where Chinese workers were resented for their thrift and willingness to accept low pay. Tensions had been building for several years, even if they did not often make the newspapers.[29] With few blacks and Native Americans involved with mining, and with the exodus of Mexicans and South Americans due to taxes, Chinese miners became the obvious targets of abuse given their numbers, different physical appearance, and seemingly strange customs. Difference was quickly equated with inferiority. The predominantly white miners also considered the Chinese to be part of a colored race.[30] By May 1852, one California newspaper made a reference to them as "cloven-footed inhabitants of the infernal regions" and called for their removal from the mines. In September, a state mining convention voted to call on Congress to protect the industry from Chinese immigrants. They complained about the state policy "by which whole hordes of degraded, dark colored and worthless laborers, of mongrel race and barbarous education, are allowed, and even invited, to come hither merely to rob the rightful owner" of their mining treasures.[31]

By 1853, the *Alta California* had changed ownership and with it had taken an anti-Chinese stance. In November, the same paper that just two years earlier had characterized Chinese migrants as model citizens was now portraying them as a criminal race. Historian James Evans writes that "a petty crime committed by or blamed on a single Chinaman was publicized as though it evidenced that all Chinese were criminals endangering the state. The Chinese sector of San Francisco was now pictured as a squalid area of filth and vice rather than a place where thrifty immigrants lived quietly."[32] Evans continues: "These diminutive little folk who had previously been an amusing but admirable novelty from a distant land and had been the epitome of virtue, thrift, and picturesqueness in San Francisco were now regarded as pig-tailed barbarians. . . . Their ability to live cheaply was no longer evidence of the virtue of thrift; it was proof that they could survive at a degraded level unfit for white men."[33] San Francisco was the epicenter of the anti-Chinese movement since large numbers of new arrivals disembarked and made their home there. Alarmists in the state spread baseless claims that the Chinese were responsible for spreading every disease under the sun, from cholera to small pox and leprosy.[34] During this period, in the eyes of many Anglo Americans, the Chinese could do little right. They were deemed to have been a public-health threat, a view espoused by no less an authority than the *Police Gazette*. Its March 21, 1868, edition described Chinatown as a repulsive cesspool: "That this eye-sore, this great fountain head of disease and death, this corruptor of our youth, this destroyer of morals, this blight upon property, this strain upon the escutcheon of the city itself, this putrid, rotten, 'damned spot,' should be allowed to lay and fester, spreading its death smell, like the deadly upas tree, all around . . . [is] a profound mystery."[35] Ironically, many of the rundown buildings in Chinatown were being rented out by prominent white citizens.

Depictions of the Chinese in California would soon reach new levels of vitriol, even among those entrusted to be neutral and maintain law and order. In the April 4, 1868, issue of the *California Police Gazette*, the editor described the Chinese as "the rat-eating, mooneyed, lying, thieving Mongolians, who have no affinity with us either in race, religion or customs." Such attitudes highlight the racist feelings held by not only many California police officers but also the criminal justice system, as Chinese were at a disadvantage in court. They could not testify against whites after an

1854 ruling in the California Supreme Court that gave them the same legal status as American Indians. In 1869, the same court ruled that Chinese could not even testify in court against the "lowly Negro."[36]

On August 8, 1853, the *Alta California*—a paper now known for its anti-Chinese stance, published a story about the treatment of a Chinese man, which even it described as disgraceful. It underscores the injustice of the period, and the intensity of anti-Chinese feelings: "An American yesterday attacked a Chinaman in Dupont street, beating him shamefully. The Chinamen in the neighborhood were afraid to interfere, and the Americans, of whom there was a large crowd, stood by and saw the poor Chinaman abused. . . . [Soon] a policeman came up, saw by his bloody face that he had been in a fight and arrested him. Unlucky John slept in the Hotel de Ville last night; the fellow that beat him was lucky enough to get off without being arrested." Even the editor of the *Alta California* had to admit the unfairness of a legal system that barred Chinese from giving testimony against non-Chinese. On March 26, 1854, he noted his opposition to the law, even though he considered them a lower race: "justice to ourselves, as well as to them, demands that they should be permitted to testify like persons of other colors. Their evidence should not carry . . . so much weight with a court or jury as that of a white man; but it does not follow that their evidence should be excluded entirely. . . . Although the majority of the negroes, Chinese, Malays, and Indians are not reliable witnesses, yet, there are exceptions."

During the latter half of the nineteenth century, Californians commonly referred to the Chinese as "heathens," not because of their non-Christian beliefs, but because it was a derogatory term.[37] The word *heathen* became synonymous with *Chinese* thanks to the 1870 publication of a poem by Bret Hart in which he made reference to "the heathen Chinee." It was certainly not complimentary and told of a Chinese man who had cheated two Western miners at cards.[38] Other common descriptions were the terms "moon-eyed" and "slant-eyed" in reference to the epicanthic fold, which causes the eyes to appear slanted. Anti-Chinese clubs popped up like mushrooms across the West Coast during the 1880s and 1890s. They held conventions, circulated petitions, and lobbied lawmakers to purge the region from the scourge of the Chinaman. Some groups encouraged boycotts, reasoning that if every resident refused to buy Chinese goods or employ Chinese, they would be forced to return home. Manufacturers were encouraged to place labels on their products affirming that they were made without Chinese labor. Many businesses tried to capitalize on the hysteria, with anti-Chinese displays. One such advertisement was used by a meat seller: "BE CAUTIOUS! A DUE RESPECT FOR A NATURAL prejudice against using MEATS Handled by Chinese and kept in their Unventilated Dens until sold for market use, has decided us to advertise the fact that we SELL NO MEATS that have been handled by CHINAMEN."[39] Politicians jumped on the anti-Chinese bandwagon. The influx of Chinese was often referred to as the Yellow Invasion, yet it was the height of hypocrisy that these same Americans who had invaded and conquered the Indians, were themselves complaining about being invaded. Given the importance of the labor vote in California, gaining support often meant being more anti-Chinese than a politician's opponent.[40] To gain a sense of how engrained and pervasive anti-Chinese hostilities were, in 1899, US Supreme Court Justice Stephen Field wrote that to preserve America's independence, the country must be on guard from Chinese immigrants, whom he described as "vast hordes of people crowding in upon us" and who constituted "a different race" who were deemed to be "dangerous to peace and security."[41]

POPULAR FICTION WARNS OF THE ASIATIC SWARM

Fear of a Yellow Invasion by Chinese migrants along the West Coast was fueled by racially charged novels. One such work was *Almond-Eyed: The Great Agitator* which was published by Atwell Whitney in 1878.[42] Set in "Yarbtown," California, where factory owner Simon Spud (a not so subtle hint that he was Irish) decides to hire a large number of Chinese laborers. After littering the town with their refuse and driving many white residents out of business, the new workers from the Orient spread small pox. Eventually, a group of white workers who had lost their jobs to the Chinese begins to riot, resulting in a massive fire. After the factory and Chinatown are rebuilt, the new factory manager vows to only hire white workers. Because the Chinese remain, racial tensions continue unabated, leaving Whitney to write of perpetual conflict.[43] "The stream of heathen men and women still comes pouring in, filling the places which should be occupied by the Caucasian race, poisoning the moral atmosphere, tainting society, undermining the free institutions of the country, degrading labor, and resisting quietly, but wisely and successfully, all efforts to remove them."[44]

In Pierton Dooner's *Last Days of the Republic* (1880), the Chinese government tries to take over the United States through unlimited migration. Eventually, a race war breaks out, and America becomes a territory of China. The Chinese characters in the novel are cunning and power hungry. Dooner portrays Chinese workers as mindless zombies willing to give their lives for their race and who are ready to carry out the wishes of their leaders at a moment's notice. Historian William Wu observes that the invasion is successful due to their hordish character, allowing for "absolute, unquestioning, immediate obedience to the government of China." Wu writes that "Dooner's image of the Chinese as a mindless mass is required in order to make plausible the slow process of infiltration and the subsequent arming and training of the Chinese in the United States."[45] Treating the Chinese as a swarm or herd reflects the belief that their actions stemmed not from free will but from their racial makeup. Hence, they could not be dealt with rationally any more than a herd of cattle or a swarm of insects could be reasoned with. They were an irrational force that had to be kept out at all costs.[46]

Other novels would further highlight the invasion threat. Robert Woltor's *A Short and Truthful History of the Taking of Oregon and California by the Chinese in the Year A.D. 1899*, resembles a history book.

Published in 1882 and written by "a survivor," it tells of the conquest of California and Oregon following a series of uprisings aided by a visiting Chinese flotilla. Woltor claims that the Chinese were deliberately massing in urban ghettoes for strategic purposes, and that they were able to act in unison as a large organism with a single-minded purpose: conquest. He depicts the Chinese as mindless puppets.[47] Woltor's novel exploits racial stereotypes of the period: "Our enemy, moreover, possess two great elements . . . which may well be the envy of warmer-blooded races, namely a stoic indifference to pain, which makes them fearless to deeds of blood, and a certain coolness in moments of excitement and danger." In contrast, Woltor portrays the Europeans as less primal and more cerebral leaders.[48] Despite these qualities, the "Asiatic swarm" is victorious in conquering the West Coast. Perhaps the most dire scenario was portrayed in Oto Mundo's *The Recovered Continent: A Tale of the Chinese Invasion* from 1898. In it the Chinese invade Southeast Asia, pour across Europe, and eventually take over the United States and conquer the world.[49] The portrayal of Chinese settlers in the literature of the early twentieth century was unflattering and racist. Even religious publications routinely referred to them as inferior and heathens.[50] During this time, Chinese women continued to be portrayed as prostitutes.[51]

THE WHITE BACKLASH TO THE YELLOW PERIL

While discontent with Chinese miners first broke out in the California goldfields in the late 1840s, it was not until the following decade that the situation reached crisis proportions. The fear of Chinese taking white jobs prompted a fierce backlash. Mobs and vigilante groups systematically drove the strange newcomers off their claims, often at gunpoint, seizing and destroying their tools, tents, and supplies. In many cities and towns across the west, especially along the coast, law and order broke down. One trouble spot was Shasta County, California, where during the winter of 1858–59, a race war erupted as anti-Chinese riots spread throughout the county. In Shasta City, a mob forced a group of Chinese men to parade through the streets as jeering townsfolk pelted them with stones. Riots sprung up in several small mountain towns, including Middletown, Oregon Gulch, and Horsetown. Sheriff Clay Stockton eventually managed to restore order and quell what became known as "the Shasta wars." Many vigilantes were rounded up and brought to trial. Each was found not guilty.[52] In 1853, upward of 3,000 Chinese were working the mines of Shasta County. By 1860, that number had dwindled to 160,[53] many of whom were working under the protection of European employers.[54] During the 1880s, two riots broke out which claimed the lives of dozens of Chinese Americans and prompted the call for federal troops to quell tensions. In September, a race riot in Rock Springs, Wyoming Territory, left 28 Chinese dead and $150,000 in damages as the local Chinatown was leveled. That same month, an attack on a remote campsite by a group of angry residents at Squak Valley in Washington State killed three Chinese hops pickers. Several days later, there was a midnight raid by a band of masked men who burst into the sleeping quarters occupied by 37 Chinese workers of the Oregon Improvement Company mine in Coal Creek, Washington. They ordered the workers outside and burned down the building. In early November, a white mob in Tacoma, backed by the police and mayor, entered the Chinese district and ordered the inhabitants to leave. They were forced onto a train bound for Portland. During February 1886, a riot broke out in Seattle during attempts to remove the city's Chinese inhabitants. Marshall Law was declared and federal troops were summoned to restore order.[55] Between 1850 and 1890, Chinese migrants in the western United States endured verbal abuse and threats, fistfights, biased news reports, segregation from whites, shootings, stabbings, the destruction of Chinese property, and premeditated murder.[56]

One of the worst acts of violence took place on March 14, 1877, when four Chinese agricultural workers were murdered in Chico, California, at the hands of white supremacists. The killings occurred amid a series of arson attacks on Chinese homes in the area, and businesses employing Chinese. While on a mission to burn down Chico's Chinatown, several arsonists shot the four migrants, doused them in kerosene, and set them alight. The perpetrators were members of the Order of Caucasians. The incident coincided with a period of global economic decline between 1873 and 1896, which some writers refer to as the Second Great Depression. The men were soon captured and put on trial for murder and arson. Four of the men received life sentences, while the others were given ten to twenty years for arson. A social commentator would later remark: "Had their victims been white men, they would have been hanged. In fact, they would have been . . . accorded that special type of hanging termed lynching."[57]

On February 14, 1879, Senator James Blaine, the nation's foremost advocate for Chinese exclusion, proclaimed that "either the Anglo-Saxon race will possess the Pacific slope or the Mongolians will possess it."[58] A week later he referred to Chinese migrants as criminals and compared their spread to that of a disease: "If as a nation we have the right to keep out infectious diseases, if we have the right to exclude the criminal classes from coming to us, we surely have the right to exclude that immigration which reeks with impurity and which cannot come to us without . . . sowing the seeds of moral and physical disease, destitution, and death." Blaine's influence cannot be overstated. At the time of his speech, he was the leading candidate for the Republican nomination for president, and although unsuccessful, he would serve as secretary of state under James Garfield. Many of Blaine's Republican colleagues enthusiastically supported his views on immigration. Representative Addison McClure of Ohio echoed Blaine's racist sentiments, quipping: "Alien in manners, servile in labor, pagan in religion, they are fundamentally un-American."[59] Wisconsin Senator George Hazelton likened them to "packs of dogs," while other politicians equated the Chinese to swarming insects and rats: creatures considered pests and devoid of moral character.

Waves of violence and intimidation would continue across the country into the new century, with friction especially prevalent in the western states, and along the West Coast where the Chinese were most concentrated. Even those who had been fortunate enough to be exempt from the exclusion legislation, such as Chinese government officials, were not immune from the intimidation and harassment. One notorious episode involved Tom Kim Yung, a military attaché based in San Francisco. On September 13, 1903, he was handcuffed by two city police officers, tied by his hair to a fence, and then severely beaten. A former bodyguard of the emperor of China, he was so distraught at having been falsely accused of starting the altercation that shortly after the incident he committed suicide. Prior to the attack, Yung was walking back to the Chinese embassy with several merchants and was just a few feet from the door when a police officer grabbed him. A *San Francisco Call* journalist describes what happened next, based on eyewitness accounts: "He was met by Policeman Kreamer ... who took hold of him rudely and made an improper remark in pigeon English. The colonel shook off the policeman's grasp with an angry gesture, whereupon Kreamer struck him a severe blow in the face," after which a second officer arrived and the beatings intensified. Several witnesses to the incident later testified that the police had started the altercation.[60]

ROADBLOCKS

Even before the 1882 Exclusion Act, California lawmakers were busy thinking up new and ever more creative ways to make life difficult for Chinese migrants in the hope that they might become discouraged and leave the country. In 1852, foreign miners who were not eligible to become citizens had to pay a monthly fee of $3—a hefty sum for the time. It was no coincidence that most foreign miners who were ineligible for citizenship were Chinese. Within three years, the fee would double. Two years later, the California Supreme Court gave Chinese the same legal status in court as "Red Indians" and determined that they could not testify against whites—a ruling that endured for the next eighteen years. In 1862, all Chinese living in California were forced to pay a police tax of $2.50 cents for the cost of looking after their health, safety, and moral conduct. The tax was a reflection of stereotypes of the Chinese as dirty and unhealthy people who were inherently inclined toward smoking opium, gambling, and prostitution. Those refusing to pay the tax had their property seized and sold at public auction.[61] By the end of the year, the State Supreme Court ruled the law to be unconstitutional. In 1863, Chinese were barred from giving testimony in civil and criminal court cases. The most outlandish law was the Cubic Air Ordinance of 1870, which targeted Chinatown, known for its congested living arrangements. The law made it illegal "to rent rooms with less than 500 cubic feet of air per person." Ironically, county jails could not even meet the requirement, so the law was voided.[62] Since the Chinese were the only people who carried clothes and vegetables on the end of poles, that same year the Sidewalk or Pole Ordinance was passed, prohibiting anyone from walking on the sidewalk using poles to carry goods.[63] Another unusual law involved hair. In 1873, the city of San Francisco passed an ordinance banning male Chinese prisoners from wearing braids—a long-standing cultural tradition. Also known as the Pigtail Ordinance, it was intended to stop Chinese from committing crimes, as losing one's braid was a sign of disgrace. Although the mayor vetoed the bill, a similar version passed in April 1876. The law was thrown out in 1879 after Ho Ah Kow sued the local sheriff and was awarded $10,000 in damages.[64] In 1880, California amended its thirty-year-old law prohibiting marriage between blacks or "half-castes" with whites, to include Mongolians. It was specifically meant to prevent marriages between Europeans and Chinese. A dozen other states soon followed as Chinese were banned from marrying whites in such places as Arizona, Georgia, Louisiana, Mississippi, Nebraska, Nevada, Virginia, and Wyoming.[65]

There were also attempts to prevent the Chinese from attending school with whites. In 1859, the San Francisco School Board closed a public school for Chinese students but were then forced to reopen it. However, between 1871 and 1885, state officials were able to shut down Chinese American schools. Legal historian Joyce Kuo writes that during this time, "the Chinese were explicitly excluded from the all-white and even the separate schools in the public school system."[66] During this period, the Chinese were denied a public education despite their tax dollars going to fund the education of the other races. Some Chinese children were homeschooled or sent to expensive private schools; others were tutored by missionaries; but not all could afford the expense. In 1884, the Chinese exclusion policy was challenged in court and deemed to have been illegal, prompting the establishment of separate Oriental Public Schools.[67] By 1896, the US Supreme Court had rendered its historic *Plessy v. Ferguson* case, allowing for public segregation of whites from nonwhites in public places ranging from schools to movie theaters, parks, swimming pools, school buses, and even libraries and hospitals. The court ruled that nonwhites could be excluded from white public schools so long as the state provided "separate but equal" facilities. This became the law of the land until 1954, when the Supreme Court deemed it illegal, resulting in mass desegregation of schools across the country. From the 1850s until well into the next century, there were numerous attempts in California to segregate Chinese students from their white counterparts in school. In 1855, the state enacted discriminatory legislation stipulating that school instruction had to be in English.[68]

The power of the times to influence one's views can be found in the US Supreme Court. In his legendary dissent in the *Plessy v. Ferguson* case, Justice John Marshall Harlan wrote that the government has a responsibility to ensure "equality before the law of all citizens of the United States, without regard to race."[69] Harlan has been hailed as a visionary for his position on equal rights for blacks. However, in his very next paragraph, he mentions the Chinese: "There is a race so different from our own that we do not permit those belonging to it to become citizens of the United States. Persons belonging to it are, with few exceptions, absolutely excluded from our country. I allude to the Chinese race. But by the statute in question, a Chinaman can ride in the same passenger coach with white citizens of the United States, while citizens of the black race [are not allowed]." While this curious passage is often ignored by his supporters, legal scholar Gabriel Chin has examined Harlan's past decisions and writings and concluded that he was a "faithful opponent of the constitutional rights of Chinese for much of his career on the court." Justice Harlan was a product of his times. Chin observes that reprints of Harlan's dissent often omit the Chinese passage.

FROM PUBLIC MENACE TO MODEL MINORITY

An extraordinary turn of events would see the axing of the Chinese Exclusion Act, and renewed friendship between America and China. This remarkable attitude shift took place over a span of a few years starting in the late 1930s and would become crystalized by a single event: the Japanese attack on the American naval base at Pearl Harbor in Hawaii. On December 8, 1941, the day after the attack, the United States and China both declared war on Japan and became instant allies. Public opinion had already begun to change with the Japanese invasion near Peiping in northern China during July 1937. The very next month, an American poll found 43 percent of the populace was sympathetic to the Chinese. By 1939, favorable ratings had risen to 74 percent.[70] By the early 1940s, a series of influential newspaper and magazine editorials appeared, underscoring the importance of China as a friend to the United States and an influential partner in the war effort.[71] This new alliance created an awkward situation given the US treatment of Chinese laborers over the previous sixty years, and the inflammatory rhetoric that was often spouted by anti-Chinese politicians and activists during this period. China was now seen as a key ally because Washington's main aim was to retake Europe. It was hoped that the Chinese could keep the Japanese at bay while the United States focused on its "Europe First Policy." Toward this end, in January 1942, the United States lent China half a billion dollars to help fight the Japanese.[72]

The imperial government tried in vain to break the new bond by reminding the Chinese of America's shameful policy on Chinese migration. After Pearl Harbor, Japan began to refer to its war as the Greater East Asian War and claimed that its purpose was the liberation of East Asia from the "Anglo-Saxon imperialists." By February 1942, the Japanese insisted that their war effort was aimed at emancipating Asian peoples, with the goal of "racial equality and harmony." In a clear reference to the Chinese Exclusion Act, the imperial leaders observed that America was exploiting Asian peoples.[73] By June, the *Asahi Shumbun* newspaper published a series of "Open Letters to Asian Peoples," proclaiming that "Asia must be one—in her aim, in her action and in her future," noting that "when Asia becomes one in truth a new order will be established throughout the world."[74] The pressure was now squarely on the shoulders of the American government to counter the campaign by the Japanese propaganda machine—a campaign that had a stinging reality. Attempts to drive a wedge between America and China were destined to fail, since each side needed the other more than ever. For their part, the Chinese went on a charm offensive, with the wife of leader Chiang Kai-shek visiting the country between November 1942 and May 1943. She worked vigorously to build support for a new US–China relationship. An eloquent speaker, she was given the rare privilege of addressing both Houses of Congress in mid-February, hailing democratic values and talking about the need to build a world "based on justice, coexistence, cooperation, and mutual respect."[75] Throughout the spring, she traveled the country, calling for more military aid and better relations. As a result, politicians and media commentators emphasized the similarities between China and America and began pressing for a repeal of the Exclusion Act.

By May 1943, a group of prominent intellectuals formed the Citizens

Committee to Repeal Chinese Exclusion and Place Immigration on a Quota Basis. Among them was the influential founder of *Life*, *Time*, and *Fortune* magazines, Henry Luce, and writer Pearl S. Buck. An acclaimed novelist known for her stance on human rights, Buck grew up in China as the daughter of missionaries. She played a role in swaying public opinion, pointing out that the Japanese were winning the propaganda war against the United States by exploiting America's treatment of the Chinese. She called for cooperation between people of all races, colors, and nationalities if the war was to be won.[76] Adding further momentum to the movement, thousands of Chinese Americans were serving their country in the armed forces, underscoring their sacrifice in the war effort and earning them the nickname of the "model minority." As American political scientist Harold Isaacs would observe, the perception of Chinese Americans had shifted from the "Age of Contempt" to the "Age of Admiration."[77] The deluge of sentiments for ending racial discrimination against the Chinese finally bore fruit on December 17, 1943, when Franklin Roosevelt signed into law the Chinese Exclusion Repeal Act. Events had come full circle. Our longtime enemy, the Yellow Menace, was now our best friend. But while there was a thaw in US–Chinese relations, a new villain had just as quickly filled the void, as Americans found another scapegoat for their problems: Japanese Americans.

CHAPTER 4

"CHILDLIKE, BARBARIC, AND OTHERWISE INFERIOR"

THE FEAR OF NATIVE AMERICANS— FOREIGNERS IN THEIR OWN LAND

Indian-ness was conflated with foreignness, which placed Native Americans outside the nation—as foreigners in their own land.

—Robert Elias, *The Empire Strikes Out: How Baseball Sold US Foreign Policy and Promoted the American Way Abroad*, 2010

What would happen if the United States government made it illegal to practice religious beliefs, outlawed celebrations on the Fourth of July, and banned gift giving at Christmas? How would you feel if it were a crime for adults to tell their children about the Easter Bunny and the Tooth Fairy, and if those practicing such traditions were publicly chastised and labeled as ignorant for spreading superstitions? What if those convicted of these offenses were fined, thrown in prison, or forced to endure hard labor? Incredibly, just such an event occurred in 1883 when the American government issued the Code of Indian Offenses. The code was a watershed moment during which, virtually overnight, an array of customs and ceremonies that had been practiced for millennia were suddenly deemed to be crimes. While some resisted the new laws by worshipping in secret or fought the rules in court, most attempts at resistance were futile. The result was a decimation of Native American culture. It is a testament to the deeply ingrained prejudices of the era that the code was not abolished until 1933, fifty years after its inception.

By the 1880s, Native Americans were essentially displaced immigrants, strangers in their own land, who were moved onto reservations and would not be granted citizenship until 1924. The new policy, the Code of Indian Offenses, was designed to wipe out centuries of sacred tradition that many Christians believed were contaminating "white" values. The justification for such actions was "The White Man's Burden," a term used by Rudyard Kipling in 1899 in his poem of the same name, which was used to describe the presumed moral responsibility of white Europeans to oversee the everyday affairs of nonwhites because the latter were seen incapable of governing themselves. Indian activist Walter Echo-Hawk writes that during this period, Native American cultures were viewed "as childlike, barbaric, or otherwise inferior and in need of European guidance for their own good."[1] Europeans justified these colonial conquests as noble acts of charity, but in reality the opposite was true—"the white man became the burden of the black, brown, yellow, and red men and women."

Books on Native American history are filled with the words *acculturation*, *assimilation*, and *civilization*. They are but euphemisms for the systematic attempt to destroy Native American culture through government policies. These same books contain words such as *displacement* and *geographical transition*—which are different ways of saying forced removal. Terms like *reservation* and *refugee* are but code words for segregation and internment. The need to address the "backward" ways of Native Americans, which was fueled by Anti–Native American sentiments, had long been viewed by whites as a problem during the nineteenth century, with individual states and territories passing laws to control the perceived menace. These hostile views were evident at the highest echelons of political office. During his annual address to Congress in December 1833, President Andrew Jackson spoke of Native Americans in the most disparaging, subhuman terms: "They have neither the intelligence, the industry, the moral habits, nor the desire of improve-ment. . . . Established in the midst of another and a superior race, and without appreciating the causes of their inferiority . . . they must necessarily yield to the force of circumstances and ere long disappear."[2]

WHAT'S IN A NAME?

Native Americans have been marginalized by the use of the word "red" to describe their skin color, which serves only to emphasize their per-ceived difference. Historian Nancy Shoemaker observes that eighteenth-century descriptions of American natives "tended to follow the pattern set by the earliest European explorers of the Southeast, the Spanish, who described them as 'brown of skin.'"[3] Native American law analyst Bethany Berger notes that they were not commonly referred to as "red" until the 1700s, with the most common description being "tawny"—orangish-brown or yellowish-brown. The earliest use of the term "red skins" came about because of their common use of red paint on their faces.[4] While the father of botany, Carlolus Linnaeus, referred to American natives as *Americanus rubescus* ("reddish"), his actual description was "tanned."[5] Just how he had come up with the color red is still unclear. He may have read accounts of red-painted natives.[6] The eventual adoption of the term "red" to describe them also has political roots. While some tribes described themselves as "red," the meaning goes deeper. Berger writes that during diplomatic negotiations, tribes in the southeastern US typically described themselves as "the red people," while the colonists were referred to as "the white people." She continues: "For these tribes, red signified matters of war, while white signified domestic affairs. Tribal politics was divided between red chiefs who governed war and state, and white chiefs who governed internal matters. By calling themselves the 'red people,' these tribal negotiators were both establishing themselves as part of a comple-mentary governmental system and downplaying English skill at war." As a result, red became synonymous with Native Americans, even though their skin color was not.

SOPHISTICATED SAVAGES

The European newcomers typically viewed the natives as primitive, lawless, simplistic, and childlike people requiring the guidance and protection of the white settlers with their superior culture and laws. Fear of their heathen customs and strange ways drove the settlers, especially missionaries, to one conclusion: Native Americans needed the help of whites to become civilized by embracing Christianity and become productive members of the new society that Europeans had established in the New World. That could only happen through assimilation. In reality, Native American culture was as advanced as any in Europe. Before the arrival of the first known white settlers in 1492, their nations were structured under tribal laws. Governing bodies resolved conflicts, regulated land use, and exerted jurisdiction over criminal matters by norms and values that had existed long before the white man's arrival to their shores.

Before European contact, the Americas were a diverse place where millions of natives from an array of tribes and independent nations roamed. Yes, there was barbarity: war, slavery, and injustices committed by one tribe to another. However, similar acts of barbarism were common in Europe, which had long been plagued by war, atrocities, and intolerance of religious diversity, as well as political and ethnic injustice. There are many examples of just how sophisticated the justice systems of the "savages" were. Among the Yuroks in what is now northwestern California, *crossers* advocated for crime victims. Typically two nonrelatives from different communities would support an aggrieved Yurok who felt he or she had a legitimate complaint. The accused could equally employ the services of nonrelatives from a community that was not his or her own. Crossers mediated between the victim and the accused, weighing the evidence and reaching a verdict or setting a payment to compensate for damages according to a scale that was known to all members of the tribe. Each crosser was usually paid in shell currency called a *moccasin*.[7] In the Great Plains, the Cheyenne employed restorative justice with a focus on preventing further harm to any party involved, reestablishing harmony to the community, and renewing damaged relationships. In contrast, the dominate retribution system in Western cultures was punishment. When one Cheyenne killed another, the murder was considered a stain on both the tribe and the murderer, with the perpetrator banished for between one and five years. As a result, only sixteen murders among the Cheyenne were recorded from 1835 to 1879, while in the coexisting frontier towns, homicides were a common sight, with offenders hanged in public. In these frontier towns, those found guilty of other crimes such as indebtedness, manslaughter, rape, arson, and assault were kept isolated in prisons under harsh and often unsanitary conditions. Little rehabilitation took place in these settings, and if a person had been falsely accused and was not a criminal before he went in, he likely would have been by the time of his release. In contrast, the Cheyenne justice system prized demonstrations of repentance and regret, the sorrow of the perpetrator being an indicator of his or her willingness to resume life by Cheyenne values.[8] While we are not advocating one system over the other, we acknowledge that the Native American judicial schemes were not nearly as crude and simplistic as they are often portrayed in novels and Westerns.

The European legal system originated in the Middle Ages when the church tried to limit self-government by pagans and heathens, using force to justify its actions on religious grounds. Before Martin Luther pursued the Reformation of the Catholic Church and the Protestant movement grew stronger in Central Europe, the Catholic Church dominated European society. Dissenting religious beliefs were brutally suppressed and persecuted. While there can be no doubt that some forms of tribal justice were cruel and savage by any standard, they could not have been any worse than the legacy of European Christianity. For instance, during the notorious witch persecutions that took place across continental Europe between 1400 and 1650, historian Rossell Robbins estimates that upward of two hundred thousand died, while sociologist Erich Goode places the death toll closer to half a million.[9] During this period, men, women, and children were brutally tortured, shot, drowned, poisoned, starved, hacked to death, or burned alive at the stake for the imaginary crime of witchcraft. Even the most barbaric system of Native American justice would not have surpassed this butchery that was sanctioned by the European legal system. The circumstances under which one could find oneself accused of practicing witchcraft were so vague as to be absurd. Jules Baissac writes that neither piety nor virtue offered immunity from suspicion: "A careless gesture, look or word, whether one was rich or poor, great or lowly . . . could pass for malignant spells if that gesture, look or word happened to coincide with one of the thousand and one accidents of human life: none could feel safe. . . ."[10] Qualities such as "beauty, talent, artistic skills were grounds for suspicion; a fortune rapidly acquired could be the devil's work. Everything and anything in everyday life could furnish a pretext for an accusation of sorcery; nothing, absolutely nothing, guaranteed anyone's immunity." Given the above, it is ironic that Europeans failed to appreciate the complex social control mechanisms in many tribal societies.

A CLASH OF CIVILIZATIONS: BUILDUP TO THE ACT OF 1883

When European colonizers arrived in the New World and expanded onto Native American lands, the natives were confronted with people who were not used to cultural diversity and who sought to force European laws, customs, and beliefs onto the inhabitants. Europeans perceived the world through racial categories and saw Native Americans with their nature-centered beliefs and rituals as culturally and intellectually inferior. This worldview made it easier for whites to claim their lands and undermine their judicial systems.[11] The first encounters between Europeans and

Native Americans occurred during the 1600s along the Atlantic seaboard. The initial interactions were positive. Europeans brought clothes, metal pots, and weapons, and they traded with the natives, who in turn, provided the strangers with food and local knowledge of how to live off the land. But despite having signed treaties with many tribes, relations soured, and Native Americans were soon treated like second-class citizens.[12]

After the founding of the United States, tribal nations continued to be recognized as sovereign and independent. In 1787, the Northwest Ordinance proclaimed that the United States had the best intentions in dealing with the natives. Two years earlier, the newly formed republic had signed the first written agreement describing the power and limits to power of both the US government and a Native American government. In the Treaty of Wyandot, it was agreed that natives who committed crimes on US soil would be punished by US law, while crimes committed by settlers on native lands would fall under tribal law.[13] The treaty gave the impression that these tribes were equals with the settlers. This would soon change. A few years later, the government started diluting the regulations in the treaty when it signed the General Crimes Act in March 1817, stating that federal crimes committed on native lands fall under US law.

During the 1820s, the state of Georgia passed laws declaring that operations of the Cherokee government were illegal, including their court system. The Cherokee took the matter to the Supreme Court. In *Cherokee Nation v. Georgia* (1831), the court declared that the Cherokees were not a foreign nation as defined in the Constitution, but rather *a dependent nation*, and therefore it could not file suit in a federal court.[14] Under this pretext, a few years later, the Cherokee were rounded up by federal troops and forced to move westward.[15] More and more native nations were deemed wards of the government. After the Indian Removal Act of 1830, many tribes were forced onto reservations, which was essentially a form of apartheid.[16] Public anxiety over the threat posed by religious minorities increased in the decades after the Civil War, as more and more citizens demanded that the government intervene and address the issue.[17] Protestant Christians in particular demanded that the state take action on heathen rituals in the form of Christian sects, metaphysical movements, and Native Americans,[18] as such group members were viewed as "religious criminals."[19] While Christian organizations and state authorities worked together to end slavery, other practices were targeted as moral depravity, including polygamy, which was practiced among many native tribes and Mormons.[20]

RESERVATIONS AS A MEANS OF CONTROL

During the Second World War, the Nazis rounded up Jews and herded them into ghettos where they could be supervised and more easily controlled. Placing Native Americans onto reservations served a similar purpose. By the 1870s, most Native Americans were confined to reservations, where they could be more easily converted to the white man's religion and customs. Once there, tribes were an easy target for missionaries and state officials who served as guardians to guide them to become "civilized Christians."[21] Natives were told that their ways of life, religion, and customs were sinful. During this time, the state was viewed by most white citizens as the protector of public morality. It was only logical that the government felt responsible for the so-called civilization of natives by its own agents and Christian missionaries. Many Native American children were sent away to schools far from their families. There, secluded from their culture, they were forced to adopt Christianity, accept Anglo-Saxon names, forget their native languages, and accept Euro-American laws and customs.[22]

FROM THE COURT OF PUBLIC OPINION TO COURTS OF LAW

In 1883, the Bureau of Indian Affairs established the Courts of Indian Offenses on most reservations, with the purpose of forcing Native Americans to abandon their "primitive" practices and assimilate into wider society.[23] The courts had the power to enforce a criminal and civil code as well as the Indian Religious Crimes Code; the latter allowed agents to imprison and withhold rations from any Native American who practiced traditional religious customs that were deemed to be undermining the state's civilization project.[24] Suddenly, marrying more than one wife was illegal, as was participating in customary religious ceremonies, or serving as a medicine man. These crimes were punishable by jail time or reduced rations.[25] After being corralled onto reservations and having their buffalos hunted to near extinction, many natives were dependent on the government for food rations. Whoever chose to follow the traditional ways risked starvation.[26]

Legal historian Robert Clinton equates these reservations to concentration camps.[27] He observes that by the time the code was invoked during the early 1880s, Native American society was quickly transformed into a welfare state dependent on the government for its very existence. He gives the plight of the nomadic Plains tribes as an example: "Their traditional hunting lifestyles had been effectively destroyed by such confinement, as well as the deliberate federally sponsored eradication of the buffalo [bison] on which they depended. This forced change in tribal economies resulted in the nation's first welfare state, in which the tribal members became completely dependent on federal rations."[28] The penalty set out in the code for practicing the old ways was often the denial of rations, something that would be considered a basic human right today. Clinton writes that "the federal government's message to tribal Indians in the late nineteenth century was crystal clear—abandon your traditional culture and comply with the Code of Indian Offenses or starve." In this regard, the Code was more than a series of laws governing reservations; it was a policy of government-sponsored ethnocide with the goal of exterminating a series of ancient cultures.

There was another factor that equally drove the wish to establish a Western system of law on the reservations: Interior Secretary Henry Teller. He despised many Native American religious and cultural practices, which the new code characterized as "evil," because it was feared that native customs threatened civilized society. Teller's goal was to end "old heathenish dances" that were "intended and calculated to stimulate warlike passions."[29] Hence, the code stated: "The 'sun-dance,' the 'scalp-dance,' the 'war-dance,' and all other so-called feasts assimilating thereto, shall be considered 'Indian offenses.'"[30] The enforcement of these rules prompted heartbreaking and demoralizing scenes on reservations. Lucy, the daughter of Black Elk, a well-known spiritual leader, recalls how her father was called to cure a sick boy. In the tent where the little boy lay, Black Elk took off his shirt and made a sacred offering of tobacco while pounding his drum and called upon the spirits to heal the boy. Then a priest who had already baptized the boy and given him last rites disrupted the ancient ritual. Father Lindebner gathered up Black Elk's offerings and tossed them into a stove. He grabbed the drum and rattle and threw them out of the tent, then took her father by the neck and said: "Satan, get out!" The once-proud and respected Black Elk sat outside the tent "as though he lost all his powers."[31] Following this incident, Black Elk turned to Christianity and gave up his traditional medicine practice.[32] While sad and pathetic, this story pales in comparison to others, in which ethnocide was replaced by genocide, such as the massacre at Wounded Knee in 1890. Three hundred Lakota men, women, and children, were slaughtered at Wounded Knee, demonstrating how those who were following their own customs and religion met a bloody end.[33]

CRIMINALIZING CUSTOM: THE GHOST DANCE

In the same year as the Wounded Knee tragedy, white police were involved in the murder of the Lakota Holy Man Sitting Bull, whom they suspected of supporting the revitalization of a new ritual known as the "Ghost Dance."[34] Native American rituals posed a serious threat to the power of the state and were a hindrance to the dependence of the natives on the US government. These rituals were also feared for being "primitive" and whipping up religious excitement. No ritual was deemed more frightening than the Ghost Dance. It arose during the late 1800s in the Great Plains, at a time when many natives were being converted to the oppressor's god.[35] Within this backdrop of cultural devastation, the Ghost Dance flourished between 1889 and 1891 and promised the dawning of a new era for Native Americans. The dance was a religious movement that reenacted a series of visions by Wovoka, a medicine man from a tribe in Nevada, who, while experiencing visions induced by small pox, prophesized a golden age. During this new period of rebirth, the natives would regain control of their ancestral lands and live in harmony with non-natives. It was believed that performing the dance was necessary to fulfill the prophecy. Participants had to sing certain songs while performing the ritual and wearing "ghost shirts."[36] The dance had to be performed over five consecutive nights and repeated at six-week intervals. Many settlers were frightened by this strange new religion, which featured dancers who trembled violently or fell into trances and told of having been taken to the Happy Hunting Ground, where they met ancestors.[37] The Bureau of Indian Affairs became alarmed by the rapid spread of the Ghost Dance and called in the cavalry to regain control.[38] The movement collapsed after settlers thought that the natives were using the dance to prepare for a war with whites. Feeling it necessary to strike first, on December 29, 1890, the Seventh Cavalry surrounded a band of Ghost Dancers at Wounded Knee Creek in South Dakota and ordered them to surrender their weapons. A scuffle ensued between a native and a soldier. A shot rang out. By the time the shooting stopped, three hundred Indians—half of whom were women and children—and some sixty soldiers lay dead or wounded.[39]

The biggest enemy of the missionaries were the *wakan* men, important spiritual leaders.[40] Missionary Gideon Pond wrote that "until they are put down by the mighty operations of the Divine Spirit, through the word of Christ, they . . . will effectually baffle any effort to elevate and civilize the Dacotas."[41] Episcopal missionary Henry Swift reported: "It is the constant effort of the church to break up Indian customs, encourage industry, educate, purify the marriage relation in conjunction with and as a part of its [C]hristianizing work. In the sphere of our influences dancing and conjuring have ceased."[42] By the early 1900s, the US government and the missionaries had achieved an important goal on their way to assimilating the Native Americans: about two-thirds of all reservations were by then subject to the Courts of Indian Offenses.

A LAST ATTEMPT TO SAVE NATIVE CUSTOMS

Unable to protect their culture and customs in battle, Native Americans tried to combat the prohibition of tribal ceremonies in court on the grounds of religious freedom and compared their religious practices to those in Christianity. In 1917, when Commissioner of Indian Affairs Cato Sells planned to shorten the three-day "Medicine Dance" to one day, the Blackfeet compared their ceremony to the Christian Holy Week of Easter.[43] The tribal representative Wolf Tail compared painting the skin of babies to baptism. The Ojibwe on the Red Lake Reservation in what is now northwestern Minnesota demanded that the government allow them to practice prayer and healing, just like Christians who were allowed to worship God through singing and music.[44] Native Americans were not granted US citizenship until June 1924, so how could they expect to be treated equally to Christians in US courts? Their natural reaction was to look for other ways to bypass the rules.[45] One strategy to evade the prohibition on religious dances was to claim that they merely had a social purpose or were performed for onlookers interested in "old Indian ways."[46] Many tribes cleverly linked the dances to American holidays to increase the likelihood of having them approved by the Bureau of Indian Affairs. The Lakotas, Blackfeet, Kiowas, and Shoshone, for instance, practiced ceremonial dances on the Fourth of July. The government's fear that these dances might threaten European morals decreased as soon as they seemed secular.[47] Red Cloud, a Lakota chief on the Pine

Ridge Reservation, continued practicing the Sun Dance together with other Lakotas. Whenever an agent broke up the ceremony on one reservation, the Lakotas moved on to another agency.[48]

In some situations, the white man's quest to civilize the natives took an unexpected turn, enabling them to continue their traditions under the guise of federal jurisdiction, as tribal elders were made judges. They often found ways to mute the white man's code of punishment. During the nineteenth century, among the Crow people, Bear Claw was a tribal judge. That often meant disciplining young warriors who sneaked out of camp to go hunting or engage in sexual escapades. Perpetrators were usually flogged by a native who was in the service of the state, and ordered to hand over their weapons. All the people brought in front of him on the charge of adultery were younger than twenty-five. While it was the judge's duty, under federal law, to sentence these young men for a deed that was defined as criminal by Western culture, Bear Claw was able to follow a semblance of tribal custom. With each verdict, tribal judges such as Bear Claw strengthened their own status and the relationship to the youths of their tribe.[49] One example is the case of Robert Red Deer, who had been accused of "cohabiting" with twenty-two-year-old Amy Bear. Red Deer was sentenced to ninety days in a Native American agency guard house—a small prison operated on the reservation by the natives under the direction of the federal government. Bear Claw released him after just sixty-eight days. Even more remarkable is that this was Red Deer's fourth conviction for the same offense: cohabiting with Amy Bear. None of his previous convictions had sustained a penalty of more than a month in the guard house. For her part, Amy Bear was not charged. Bear Claw might have empathized with Red Deer's actions, as records reveal that he had been previously married five times! Native American scholar Frederick Hoxie writes that "Red Deer and [Amy] Bear emerged from a world where, as one old man told anthropologist Robert Lowie, 'women are like a herd of buffalo, and a husband who cleaves to one wife is like a hunter who has killed the last of the fugitive animals and stays by the carcass because he lacks spirit to pursue others.'"[50] Hoxie observes that public drunkenness convictions were "equally mild." He continues, "One tribal member found that on his fourth conviction for inebriation, the fine had been reduced from ten dollars to five dollars. What seems to have been at least as important as the punishment was the reinforcement of the relationship of elder to youth. Authority and prestige were the judge's reward for his service, and these could be renewed at each session of the court regardless of the presence of 'repeat offenders' or the persistence of 'immoral' conduct."[51] Despite different forms of resistance, Native American culture continued to be suppressed for decades. The code was not amended until 1933, under President Franklin Roosevelt, when all bans on dances and other customs were eliminated.

The criminalization of native customs was a form of ethnocide, prompted by a belief in European superiority, that is responsible for the devastation of Native American culture. Natives were seen as needing help and guidance from the missionaries and, later, the government, to become acceptable citizens of the newly formed United States. But Native Americans adjusted to their new reality and found ways to bypass the white man's laws or used them to their own favor. Native American history is an example of adjustment, resistance, and survival, since some traditions and customs are still practiced today, despite efforts to destroy them. In reflecting on the systematic attempt to wipe out tribal customs and spiritual beliefs, we would do well to heed the words of religious scholar Jeremiah Gutman, who observes that when foreign practices appear strange or unpopular, "A religion becomes a cult; proselytization becomes brainwashing; persuasion becomes propaganda; missionaries become subversive agents; retreats, monasteries, and convents become prisons; holy ritual becomes bizarre conduct; religious observance becomes aberrant behavior; devotion and meditation become psychopathic trances."[52] After the arriving Europeans failed to wipe out American tribes through violence and war, the Code of Indian Offenses succeeded by exterminating a significant portion of their age-old customs and beliefs.

CHAPTER 5

"DON'T TRUST THE HUNS!"

THE ANTI-GERMAN HYSTERIA
OF WORLD WAR I

"One hundred percent" Americans did not use any language other than English, did not read foreign-language newspapers or attend foreign-language church services, were not members of any clubs adhering to German customs . . . and did not criticize the government.
—Katja Wüstenbecker, *Immigrant Entrepreneurship: German-American Business Biographies, 1720 to the Present*, 2014

During World War I, the fear and suspicion of all things German swept across North America like a blight. Anti-German sentiments rose quickly with Canada's entry into the war during August 1914, in support of the British Empire. Widespread intolerance and harassment soon spread to the United States, where German Americans and immigrants were made to feel unwelcome and their loyalties questioned. During this period, German immigration slowed to a trickle. In 1911, over 32,000 Germans poured into the country. Most were welcomed with open arms as upstanding members of their communities. By 1919, the figure was just fifty-two individuals, and each was looked upon with wariness.[1] Prejudice and mistrust ran deep. Some branches of the American Red Cross, long known for neutrality and independence, excluded volunteers with German surnames, amid rumors that infiltrators were grinding up glass and placing it in bandages used to treat wounded soldiers.[2] The *New York Times* reported claims that bandages were being soaked in poison.[3] None of the allegations were ever proven. By 1918, the scare had reached such proportions that in New Haven, Connecticut, city cleaners were kept busy clearing the roadways of rocks, bottles, and eggs after a car drove through the streets dragging an effigy of the kaiser.[4] That same year, the syndicators of the popular comic strip *The Katzenjammer Kids*, about the misadventures of two German brothers, changed the name to *The Shenanigan Kids*. In the new strip, Hans and Fritz became the Dutch siblings Mike and Alec. The cartoon reverted back to the original characters in 1920, as hostilities began to subside.[5] Such was life in America during the Great German Scare.

From New York to California, paranoia and conspiracies were the order of the day as people saw plots where none existed and turned in their German neighbors, fearing they were enemy agents. One rumor held that German musicians were passing secret messages in their arrangements. According to another, German submarine captains were surfacing in remote locations along the coast and coming ashore to attend the theatre to spread influenza germs.[6] Perhaps the most far-fetched claims involved pigeons. When a new species was shot in Michigan, there was speculation that it was German and was being used to send coded messages between spies.[7] The discovery of an exhausted carrier pigeon on a farm near Brisbane, North Dakota, also caused alarm. On its legs were two bands with a series of numbers and letters. After examining the bird, a bank teller took it to authorities believing it was a "German agent" and the bands were coded messages.[8] It was also rumored that the Germans were melting the corpses of soldiers taken from the battlefield to make soap, candles, and explosives. This story was later revealed to have been an Allied fabrication.[9]

Tales of dubious German atrocities and inhumanity highlighted the ruthless nature of the enemy in order to whip up public hysteria by demonizing Germans as an evil, warlike race. This created problems for scholars who had previously written that the early American pioneers were descendants of ancient Germanic tribes. History was hastily rewritten to include the theory that most of the original inhabitants of Germany had been killed off by Asiatic barbarians.[10] The government Committee on Public Information played a major role in stifling voices of dissent and rallying public opinion behind the war effort. A nationwide poster campaign portrayed Germans as thugs and beasts. One depicted an attractive woman being carried off by a demented apelike figure wearing a German helmet—the caption reading: "Destroy this Mad Brute—Enlist!" Another showed a German soldier impaling a baby with his bayonet.[11] During the war, the American Defense Society was influential in portraying Germans as an evil, vicious race. Led by its honorary president, Theodore Roosevelt, one of its publications described Germany as "the most treacherous, brutal and loathsome nation on earth. . . . The sound of the German language . . . reminds us of the murder of a million helpless old men, women, and children; [and the] driving of about 100,000 young French, Belgian, and Polish women into compulsory prostitution."[12]

In Canada, there were fears of a surprise attack from German Americans loyal to the kaiser, who were supposedly training on the northern border of Western New York to stage raids or a full-scale invasion. The worst offender in spreading these tales was Sir Courtney Bennett, a British diplomat stationed in New York City. Bennett had a propensity for making sensational statements. In early 1915, he made the dramatic claim that as many as eighty thousand German loyalists were secretly drilling near Buffalo and Niagara Falls, New York, for an invasion. Other rumors held that a five-thousand-man German militia was operating in Chicago, and a force of eight thousand had formed in Boston. Canadian Police Commissioner Percy Sherwood was worried enough to send agents across the border to infiltrate areas where there were large concentrations of German Americans. After visiting bars and clubs in the hope of uncovering subversives, they could find no evidence of a plot to attack Canada or any attempt to recruit volunteers for an invasion.[13] Anti-German feelings reached such levels that one historian would later observe that "there was hardly a major fire, explosion, or industrial accident which was not attributed to enemy sabotage," and further investigation "invariably led elsewhere."[14] While there were mysterious fires, explosions, and equipment failures during the war in both Canada and the United States, it is difficult to know which were sabotage. The small number of confirmed incidents were more of a nuisance than a serious threat to the security of either nation.

Attempts to disrupt the war effort in both countries were often so amateurish as to border on the comical. In late 1914, the German Foreign Office received intelligence that Japan was deploying troops to Vancouver, so a scheme was hatched to blow up several bridges of the Canadian Pacific Railroad.[15] After learning that the report was untrue, the plan was canceled. The ringleader of the bridge plot, an agent identified only as Captain Böhm, was never informed of the aborted mission and went ahead with the operation to cross into Canada from Maine. Just before they were to leave, seven of his eight recruits backed out at the last minute, so the mission was aborted. The eighth conspirator, a bungling German army reservist named Werner von Horn, had the easiest task: blow up the Vanceboro Bridge just over the Maine border, for which the German government paid him the hefty sum of $700.[16] Thoroughly inept, von Horn arrived late to the rendezvous point, oblivious to the change in plans. Confident of fulfilling his destiny, he and an Irish companion set out to cross the border in frigid temperatures during a snowstorm. Before long, the Irishman got lost, leaving von Horn on his own. He eventually found the bridge, and, in the early-morning hours of February 2, set off several sticks of dynamite before crossing back over the border and into the small town of Vanceboro, Maine, where residents were on alert after having been awakened by the explosion.[17] By daybreak, von Horn was under arrest. It was not difficult to identify the guilty party, as he "was carrying a supply of dynamite and detonators, and spoke poor English with a heavy German accent."[18] For all of von Horn's efforts, he had managed to delay bridge traffic by six hours, and the structure was completely repaired within two days.[19] To describe von Horn's mission as a failure would be an understatement. The

German counsel in New York observed that newspaper publicity surrounding the failed attempt to blow up the bridge only fueled anti-German hostility in America. Von Horn was eventually sentenced to eighteen months in jail and was fined $1,000. But his ineptitude did not end there. He had a propensity to talk too much and claimed to be an officer in the Prussian military. This resulted in his being treated as a prisoner of war; and, in late 1919, he was extradited to Canada and given a ten-year prison term. After concerns had been raised over his mental health, he was deported to Germany in August 1921. British Canadian historian Martin Kitchen writes that while there were several other attempts by Germans to sabotage the Canadian war effort, "they were so unsuccessful that the Canadian authorities were not aware of them."[20] It was a similar story in the United States.

US WAR HYSTERIA RISES AS THE *LUSITANIA* SINKS

The scare over the loyalty of persons of German heritage living in North America intensified on the afternoon of May 7, 1915, when a torpedo fired from a German U-boat lying in wait off the Irish coast slammed into the ocean liner *Lusitania*, killing 1,198 passengers and crew, including 128 Americans.[21] The incident fueled outrage and was widely condemned as a cowardly and ruthless attack on innocent civilians. In reality, the German government had warned of the danger the very day the vessel left Pier Fifty-Four in New York City bound for Liverpool. The German embassy placed ads in several major New York newspapers appearing near notices of the *Lusitania*'s planned voyage, stating that Germany and Great Britain were at war, and they could not guarantee safe passage. It urged passengers to reconsider boarding. The Germans also maintained that the ship had been carrying munitions for the war, a claim supported by recent archeological surveys of the vessel that identified a cache of Remington .303-caliber bullets—the same type used by the British in the war.[22] The anti-German backlash was immediate and swift.

While the overwhelming number of Americans of German heritage were loyal citizens, they were soon widely referred to as "Huns" and "hyphenated Americans" who were looked down upon and viewed with suspicion. As attorney Charles Nagel remarked during the scare: "I do not believe that at this stage any value would be attached to an expression from a citizen of German name."[23] As a result, in the first postwar census taken in 1920, about 900,000 German-born Americans "vanished" by either claiming to have been born in the United States or assuming a different ethnicity.[24] As in Canada, the US government would eventually intern German Americans suspected of disloyalty—about four thousand. Following the cue of their northern neighbors, there were soon calls to rename everything from Germanic-sounding streets and schools to food. A public campaign was mounted to change "sauerkraut" to "Liberty Cabbage."[25] But the hysteria did not end there. Restaurants changed the name of hamburgers to "Liberty Burgers," meatloaf was referred to as "Salisbury Steak" (after a British Lord), while frankfurters and wieners, named after Germanic cities, became known as "hot dogs"—a name that stuck.[26] Luckily, Limburger cheese was given a last-minute reprieve when it was found to have been of Belgian origin. Diseases were not even spared, as some people began referring to Rubella or German measles as "liberty measles."[27] There was even a report in *Life* magazine of people euthanizing dachshunds.[28] In Cincinnati, Ohio, Berlin Street was rechristened Woodrow Street, after President Wilson, while German Street became English Street.[29] In St. Louis, the Kaiser-Huhn Grocery had its delivery wagons pelted with stones. It soon became the Pioneer Grocery Company. In the suburb of St. Charles, the German Evangelical St. John's Church decided in the interests of self-preservation to remove the word *German* from its name. In Chicago, the directors of the Kaiser Friedrich Mutual Aid Society, named after the former German emperor Friedrich III, raised eyebrows when it tried to mask its Germanic origins by becoming the George Washington Benevolent Aid Society. Many residents went so far as to take anglicized names: Müller became

Miller; Schmidt became Smith; and Oachs was changed to Oaks.[30] No German American was above suspicion. Even major league baseball players changed their names to remove any hint of disloyalty. Cleveland Indians pitcher Fritz Coumbe became "Freddie," while Cincinnati Reds third baseman Heinie Groh began calling himself "Henry."[31] When John Fluhrer debuted for the Chicago Cubs in 1915, he went by the British-sounding "William Morris." If the name change was intended to ward off questions of loyalty after his newfound fame, he need not have bothered. His major league career consisted of just six at-bats.[32] Several American towns and cities had the unfortunate distinction of bearing the name of Germany's capital. As a result, Berlin, California, was renamed Genevra; Berlin, Iowa, was re-christened Lincoln; while Berlin, Michigan, became Marne. A number of states had their own Germantown. In Texas, it became Schroeder, to honor Paul Schroeder, the first resident of the community to die in the war; while Germantown, Nebraska, was changed to Garland; and Germantown, Indiana, was renamed Pershing, after General John "Black Jack" Pershing, commander of the American Expeditionary Force on the Western Front.[33] Ironically, his father was of German descent, and the family name was anglicized from Pfoerschin.[34]

There were 10 million German Americans in 1910; about 20 percent were foreign-born.[35] In 1915, one in four high school students studied German; by the end of the war, it was a mere 1 percent.[36] Historian Paul Finkelman observes that during the war, there was a common belief that language was organic to the soul. Hence, if you spoke German, you would start to think like a German, and "you would become a totalitarian in favor of the kaiser."[37] Today, the idea would seem ridiculous. It was a similar picture with German-language newspapers, many of which were forced to survive by unofficially becoming part of the government's propaganda campaign. In Texas, papers that were once vigorously pro-German were suddenly urging their readers to "Buy Liberty Bonds," while the editorial pages of many of these publications carried images of the American flag.[38] In Pennsylvania, the Pittsburgh *Volksblatt und Freiheits-*

freund went to extreme lengths to prove its loyalty, such as publishing images of a bloodied dog with a German emblem, attacking a mother and child.[39] The German press was under careful scrutiny, and by October 1917, Congress passed a law requiring foreign-language papers to provide an English translation of war-related articles and give them to the local postmaster before they were allowed to be mailed. By the end of the war, the number of German-language newspapers had halved, as many businesses withheld their advertising.[40] The German press was in an impossible situation. Historian Alexander Waldenrath observes that "papers were suspect even when they supported the American cause. Consequently, advertising fell off sharply as did circulation. The legislation of 1917 which required translations of the papers to be filed and permits for publication to be secured added heavily to the publisher's burdens."[41]

"SPEAK OF THE DEVIL AND HE IS BOUND TO APPEAR"[42]

Politicians helped to fan the flames of hysteria as social paranoia reached the highest levels of government. While emphasizing that America was at war with the German government, not German Americans, President Woodrow Wilson cultivated a fear of those very people. On June 14, 1917—Flag Day—he issued an ominous warning to Congress that disloyal German Americans "filled our unsuspecting communities with vicious spies and conspirators and sought to corrupt the opinion of our people in their own behalf."[43] Spurred on by fear-mongering politicians and alarmist press reports, citizens were urged to do their patriotic duty by spying on their neighbors. Worried over the government's ability to combat the threat of so many German spies and subversives, Attorney General Thomas Gregory approved a plan to use volunteers to gather information on anyone of German heritage living in the country, especially immigrants. The organization became known as the American Protection League, and it was billed as a group of amateur sleuths who investigated the actions of possible German subversives in their local communities. In reality, it was a hodgepodge of wannabe police officers and private investigators. Members were given a policelike badge identifying them as a "Secret Service" agent of the American government. At one point, their ranks swelled to an astounding 260,000 members.[44] With so many eyes and ears on the lookout for spies, they were soon found to be lurking everywhere. America's ambassador to Germany, James Gerard, proclaimed that "the time has come when every citizen must declare himself American—or traitor!"[45] This "You're either with us or against us" attitude was reflected in the actions of Missouri Governor Frederick Gardner, who declared in April 1918: "A pro-German is no better than a spy." His inflated rhetoric and bombastic warnings are no more evident than in his claim that any pro-German found in Missouri would face a firing squad.[46] During the war, the term "100 percent American" became a popular battle cry among super-patriots on the home front.

Spurred on by groups such as the Anti-German League, there were widespread attempts to ban or burn both books published in German and English works suspected of being subversive and a threat to the nation's youth. One League pamphlet proclaimed: "Any language which produces a people of ruthless conquestadors [sic] such as now exist in Germany, is not a fit language to teach clean and pure American boys and girls."[47] In true, exaggerated moral-panic fashion, it also claimed that Germany was "the most treacherous, brutal and loathsome nation on earth."[48] One educator even asserted that the German language was phonetically difficult to tolerate due to its "unrefined," "uncivilized," and "animalistic" nature. In arguing that German should not be taught in American schools, one American educator claimed that the German philosophy "prides itself in its inhumanity [that] murders children, rapes women, and mutilates the bodies of innocent men."[49] Across the country, organizations controlling local libraries generated lists of unacceptable books that were taken off the shelves and either put in storage or destroyed in rallies culminating in public burnings. In Cincinnati, Ohio, the trustees of the city library voted to remove all 10,000 books written in German. It issued a statement supporting the decision, which read: "English is the language which must become universal in the United States, and the Library should be one of the instruments through which this is to be accomplished." Fortunately, the books escaped the bonfire and were stored in the basement.[50]

Intolerance reared its ugly head in the form of federal and state laws quashing anyone sympathizing with Germany or dissenting against the war, as the government ran roughshod over the First Amendment "guaranteeing" freedom of speech. Passage of the Espionage Act of June 1917 imposed fines and prison terms for engaging in antiwar activities. The following May, the Sedition Act set harsh penalties for anyone found guilty of using "disloyal, profane . . . or abusive language," including insults to the government, the flag, the Constitution, or the military. At least 1,500 people were arrested under these laws as "troublemakers" and dissenters opposing the war.[51] One of the targets of these laws were socialists, who often claimed that the real reason for the war was to boost Wall Street. When New York journalist and prominent socialist Rose Stokes charged that the government was profiteering from the war, she was sentenced to ten years in prison. When the head of the American Socialist Party, Eugene Debs, made similar comments, he was also given ten years. In Texas, the *San Antonio Inquirer* published a letter to the editor criticizing the treatment of black soldiers who had engaged in a violent mutiny in Houston; its editor, G. W. Bouldin, spent the next two years in prison under the Espionage Act. Hysteria began to die down after the war, and Stokes was freed in 1920 when a federal court overturned her conviction, while Debs was pardoned in 1921.[52] Members of pacifist religious groups were also arrested under the new laws because they were viewed with suspicion for their failure to support the war effort; silence and neutrality were often equated with being pro-German.[53] Canada snapped out of the anti-German spell before America. In May 1917, the United States passed the Selective Service Act and tried to draft a variety of pacifist groups. As a result, over 1,500 members of the Mennonites, Hutterites, and Amish sects fled north. The Canadian government aided in their resettlement and even provided them with tracts of farmland. In a similar vein, while both Canada and the United States are experiencing the Islamic refugee panic, Canada has grown more accepting and has agreed to take in many refugees fleeing over its southern border.[54]

Some laws were more symbolic than substantive, like attempts to ban the teaching of the German language in schools. By summer 1918, nearly half of all states had banned or restricted the use of German. Some state legislators went to extremes to counter the threat. In South Dakota, the government's Council of Defense not only ordered a halt to German being taught in schools but also prohibited the speaking of German in telephone conversations.[55] On May 23, 1918, Iowa Governor William Harding signed a proclamation that English must be spoken in public places, prefacing with the extraordinary claim that his decision was *not* in violation of American's right to free speech![56] When the Reverend Henry Prekel of the Immanuel Lutheran Church defied the order, preaching half of his sermons in German, state agents turned up. He soon agreed to comply after he was "generously" allowed to repeat the gospel in German during an "after-meeting." The ban presented a dilemma for one Lutheran pastor in Alta, Iowa, who was not fluent in English. When he refused to take a leave of absence to study English, he was summoned before a military board, after which he promised to behave.[57] As for Governor Harding's call for banning all languages but English, he made the unsubstantiated claim that German "propaganda and plots against the federal government were spread through Iowa by the use of all foreign languages."[58] Despite these hostile sentiments toward the German language, within a decade of the war's end, it was once again being taught in schools across the nation. With hysteria clouding their judgment, it is remarkable to think that many American school boards feared that the teaching of German could undermine American values. It is absurd to think that speaking a foreign language in school somehow made a person less patriotic.[59] Nonetheless, after the war, many American classrooms would again hear the echo of German words, helped by a 1923 US Supreme Court ruling that teaching and learning a foreign language in private and religious schools were protected under the Constitution.[60]

During the scare, residents throughout the country were accused of disloyalty and subjected to harassment based on actions that had little or no legal basis. In Indiana, the alleged crimes of local German Americans included failing to buy Liberty Bonds, displaying the kaiser's picture, failure to salute the flag, calling President Wilson a warmonger, "or uttering any sentiment objected to by whatever patriotic ears might overhear the remark."[61] Those deemed to have been disloyal were sometimes forced to kiss the American flag or sing the national anthem. Some groups used the groundswell of anti-German sentiment to further their agendas. The Anti-Saloon League, an advocate for the prohibition on alcohol consumption, expressed concerns that German brewers based in the United States were funneling their profits back home. Hence, they could make the case that supporters of prohibition were aiding the war effort. This state of affairs prompted one Kansas newspaper to assert: "The two great menaces in the world today are German militarism in Europe and German brewerism in America."[62]

The press further raised fears and inflamed passions. In the lead-up to America's entry into the Great War, the *Washington Post* published no less than thirty articles on the internal threat from spies and saboteurs. One sensational headline proclaimed: "100,000 Spies in Country." The *New York Tribune* also contributed to the dark mood with the scare headline: "Spies Are Everywhere! They Occupy Hundreds of Observation Posts ... They Are in All the Drug and Chemical Laboratories."[63] Hollywood played a role in the scare as a series of silent films appeared highlighting the dangers posed by German spies and infiltrators, who seemed to be lurking everywhere. Fraser Sherman has documented the surge in these films during the war. Notable pictures in the genre include *Fair Pretender* (1915), involving stenographer Madge Kennedy, who stumbles upon a German spy nest. That same year, *Her Country First* was released, in which the daughter of a munitions maker, Vivian Martin, suspects that their butler is a German spy. She eventually learns that everyone on their staff is a spy—with one exception: the butler, who turns out to be an undercover government agent![64] Just as contemporary films are filled with Communists and Muslim evildoers, Sherman found that during this period, Germans were the bad guys. As a 1919 article in *Variety* observed," the villain has to be a German spy—the audience wouldn't feel at home if they were confronted with a villain of any other variety."[65]

Another genre of motion pictures was that of the invasion scare, which contributed to fears of a likely, if not imminent, German attack on the continental United States. This notion was supported by many books and magazine articles depicting the threat. Eric Van Schaack has documented the many films that led to this "new view of reality, an America threatened by a ruthless invader intent on the destruction of all that Americans held dear" and "whipped up the public fear of the brutal 'Hun.'"[66] During the summer of 1915, the patriotic film *The Battle Cry of Peace* was released about a group of enemy agents who work with pacifists to cut defense spending. They then launch a full-scale attack on the country. This film was based on the book *Defenseless America* by Hudson Maxim, who made alarmist claims that America was weak and ill-prepared to protect itself from foreign invaders whom he claimed could land hundreds of thousands of men on American soil within a few weeks.[67] After America had entered World War I in May 1917, the film was reissued under the title *Battle Cry of War*.[68] A second invasion film was also released in 1915: *The Nation's Peril*. Its plot centers around the character Ruth Lyons, the peace-loving granddaughter of a Navy admiral who opposes war, and her efforts to stop the development of a powerful American secret weapon—the aerial torpedo, a remote-controlled flying bomb. She unwittingly gives the plans to a man who turns out to be a foreign spy, endangering the country. While the film has a happy ending, its theme is that America must maintain a strong military and be prepared for war. To underscore the threat, it includes appearances by the Secretary of the Navy and two admirals.[69] In 1916, there were three more invasion pictures: *The Flying Torpedo*, *The Fall of a Nation*, and *America Unprepared*, followed by *Zeppelin Attack on New York* (1917), *Womanhood, the Glory of the Nation* (1917), and *The Kaiser, the Beast of Berlin* (1918). During the war years, the Hollywood film industry, not the government, promoted invasion fears. Big government-sponsored feature films of the period—*America's Answer*, *Under Four Flags*, and *Pershing's Crusaders*—never even hinted at the possibility of a German invasion. Their purpose was to reassure the public and show that the American military was strong.[70] Invasion literature was also popular in the early twentieth century, much of which was anti-German. Many books gained wide exposure due to their tie-ins with popular films, such as Maxim's *Defenseless America*. Another book that created fear over a possible German invasion was *America Fallen! The Sequel to the European War* (1915). In it, Germany launches a successful invasion of an ill-prepared America and agrees to withdraw only after the government pays $12 billion. The book was viewed seriously because the author was the prestigious J. Bernard Walker, editor of *Scientific American*.

VIGILANTE JUSTICE

Rumors of German spies and saboteurs abounded. In Muenster, Texas, there were claims that German Americans had secretly stockpiled an arsenal of rifles and ammunition in the cellar of the Sacred Heart Church. By some accounts, it was to be used in an uprising. Another story held that they were to be sent to Germany to help in the war effort. Authorities scoured the church but turned up nothing.[71] There was widespread persecution and harassment of Americans of German ancestry. In many places local citizens either took the law into their own hands or formed vigilante groups, frustrated at the perceived inaction by law enforcement. In East Alton, Illinois, a German American merchant suspected of being disloyal was forced to kiss the American flag and threatened with hanging. Local police and journalists often turned a blind eye at attempts to dispense small-town justice to those deemed to have German sympathies. In March 1918, an observer in the Midwest wrote: "All over this part of the country men are being tarred and feathered and some are being lynched. . . . These cases do not get into the newspapers nor is an effort ever made to punish the individuals concerned. In fact, as a rule, it has the complete backing of public opinion."[72] Some German Americans were harassed or beaten for not giving enough to war-bond drives.[73]

The most extreme instances of anti-German vigilantism took place in Illinois and Texas. The former case involved German-born coal miner Robert Prager, a baker by trade, who was lynched from a tree in Collinsville, Illinois, after being accused of making disloyal remarks and spying. The incident happened on April 4, 1918. The local mayor and police looked on passively as the events unfolded, and Prager was led by an alcohol-fueled mob to the outskirts of town and hanged from a hackberry tree shortly after midnight. His last request was for his body to be draped in an American flag before burial.[74] It is a testament to the deep feelings of German phobia at the time that a jury acquitted every one of the eleven men who were tried for his murder.[75] After the verdict, there was little remorse. Even the editor of the local newspaper remained stubbornly defiant: "The city does not miss him. The lesson of his death has had a wholesome effect on the Germanists of Collinsville and the rest of the nation."[76] An equally abhorrent episode occurred in Bastrop County, Texas. According to court records at the state archives, a deputy sheriff led a group of vigilantes who tracked down a local farmer who had been uncooperative in the local Liberty Bond fund drive. "On catching up with his mule-drawn wagon, the deputy sheriff held the farmer with one hand while fatally shooting him with the other." They then beat the victim's widow before escorting her home at gunpoint. The local German newspaper, the *Giddings Deutsches Volksblatt*, ironically noted that two of the participants were German Texans.[77] For those accused of disloyalty, it was difficult to regain their reputation. Although not impossible, it took a concerted effort on the part of local residents and government officials to rescue their standing. In 1917, several Gainesville residents accused Marie Deitz of Cooke County, Florida, of committing acts and making statements "that would indicate that she was not loyal to our government." A local official published an article in the local paper affirming that Ms. Deitz was a good citizen, noting that the false accusations were made in part due to her fluency in German. At the end of the article were no less than twenty-eight signatures of her co-workers, vouching for her patriotism.[78]

RUMORS

In the South, long-standing fears of a black revolt merged with rumors of German subversives to create a hybrid narrative: African Americans were being manipulated by German agents to create chaos. Fears of a black uprising flared in 1917. The signs were everywhere. In Greensboro, Tennessee, a citizen wrote an urgent letter to the Justice Department noting that some blacks in the town had refused to yield to whites while walking on the sidewalk. Their actions were interpreted as a blatant display of disloyalty encouraged by outside agitators.[79] During April, the *Tampa Morning Tribune* reported that agents loyal to the kaiser were fanning out throughout the South to form an alliance with blacks. When rumors spread across Bradford County, Florida, that blacks were being offered "political and social equality" in exchange for their aid, police took the stories seriously enough to investigate. In response, armed guards were sent to patrol the Tampa water reservoirs and electricity plant amid "rumors that the Germans had hired Negroes to blow up the plant and poison the water supply."[80] Other Florida papers fueled the social paranoia and kept the population on the lookout for spies. The St. Andrews *Bay News* was one of the worst offenders at fearmongering. While acknowledging that there were many loyal German Americans, it cautioned in April 1917 that some "are but enemies in disguise, who are plotting against us, and even now are committing acts of treason."[81] It asked all patriotic Americans to "search out" these evildoers and report them. With such exhortations, it should come as no surprise that Floridians began turning in neighbors whom they believed were spies. A man in Plant City was arrested, "his baggage searched for vials of typhoid and yellow fever germs which, according to rumor, were to be deposited in the county water supply." That same month, a piano teacher at Florida Female College was fired for un-American acts. Miss Felma Bjerge had reportedly refused to take down a German flag and a picture of the kaiser from her studio. Because Florida is a peninsula with long stretches of coastline, state residents felt vulnerable to an invasion by sea; these fears were reflected in unverified stories of mysterious vessels spotted offshore.[82] On July 21, 1918, anti-German tensions spiked across the country after a German U-boat appeared off the coast of Cape Cod, Massachusetts, and without warning opened fire on a tugboat, the *Perth Amboy*, which was towing several barges. While the vessel sustained heavy damage, there were no fatalities. A few stray shells cratered a marsh near the beach at the town of Orleans, making it the first and only time during the war that any part of the continental United States had been shelled by an enemy. The incident triggered a spate of phantom Zeppelin sightings, while rumors of German plots abounded, including claims that an unfamiliar species of pigeon was spotted flying secret messages over the Canadian border from German agents in the United States.[83]

THE WAR ON GERMAN MUSIC

Moves to ban music and plays of Germanic origin show the depth of fear and ill-feeling during the war. More symbol than substance, these bans had little effect on the war itself. Hostilities even extended to conductors and musicians. Of the nine conductors of major symphony orchestras with German roots, two were considered such threats that they were placed in internment camps: Ernst Kunwald of the Cincinnati Symphony, and Karl Muck of the Boston Symphony. One of the more fortunate conductors was Alfred Hertz, who managed to survive a smear campaign that bordered on the ridiculous. In 1915, the struggling San Francisco Orchestra had hired the accomplished German conductor who had been with the esteemed New York Metropolitan Opera House since 1902. Hertz had the unfortunate distinction of speaking with a thick accent, which did not endear him to some music fans. Before long, residents sent letters to the Justice Department alleging that he was part of a spy ring. Many of the charges made against him were outlandish, such as claims that he had purchased German—not American—butter at a local grocery store, and that he had once left the stage while the orchestra was playing "The Star-Spangled Banner." Authorities could find no evidence to substantiate these claims, and he continued in his post until gaining citizenship in 1917.[84] Other German conductors were not as lucky.

With the declaration of war in 1917, the Boston Symphony, which was composed of no less than nine Germans, was suddenly under great scrutiny. None of its members were scrutinized more than its accomplished conductor, Karl Muck. A Swiss national, Muck was known for his conducting of German arrangements, and he held an honorary German passport. It did not help matters that due to his fame, it had been signed by the kaiser himself. His personality was described as "blunt and tactless," and many of his friends were ardent supporters of the kaiser.[85] A series of unfortunate events would transpire that would result in his losing his job and being imprisoned. One incident involved his summer rental cottage on the Maine coast at Seal Harbor, which was found to have a disassembled radio transmitter. Boston District Attorney Thomas Boynton became concerned that Muck may have been attempting to contact German submarines. In reality, the previous tenant had been a "wireless nut." As a result, Muck was given a stern warning and reminded that German nationals were not allowed to reside or even visit the Maine coast.[86]

The perception of Muck as disloyal and untrustworthy soon grew. It began innocently enough, with a scheduled concert in Providence, Rhode Island, on October 30, 1917. In the lead-up to the appearance, the Boston Symphony had received a telegram from several local civic and patriotic organizations to open the event with the playing of "The Star-Spangled Banner." At the time, it was a common practice for most orchestras to play the composition. The orchestra's manager, Charles Ellis, passed on the request to the orchestra founder, Major Henry Higginson, a stubborn figure who refused to tolerate outside interference. "Does the public think that the symphony orchestra is a military band? No: It is a classical musical organization. To ask us to play *The Star Spangled Banner* is embarrassing. It is almost an insult," Higginson quipped.[87] The trouble was, no one had passed the request onto Muck, who was oblivious to it and was flabbergasted when he first learned about it while riding the train back to Boston. He said that he would have happily obliged the request as a goodwill gesture. Muck would be haunted by the incident for the rest of his life.

The next day, newspapers published a torrent of criticism directed at Muck for his supposed refusal to play the anthem. Newspapers were deluged with angry letters. Many political figures soon entered the fray, including former president Teddy Roosevelt, who declared: "Any man who refuses to play the Star-Spangled in this time of national crisis, should be forced to pack up and return to the country he came from."[88] In Baltimore, where the symphony was scheduled to play, former Maryland Governor Edwin Warfield addressed a rally held to protest the composer's disloyalty, during which could be heard shouts of "Kill Muck! Kill Muck!"[89] Warfield whipped up the crowd and vowed to lead a riot against the concert if it went ahead as planned. He proclaimed: "I told the Police Board members that this man would not be allowed to insult the people of the birthplace of the 'Star-Spangled Banner.' . . . I would gladly lead the mob to prevent the insult to my country and my flag."[90]

A later concert presided over by Muck went ahead at Carnegie Hall, only with a heavy police presence. Public outcry continued to dog Muck for his perceived disloyalty, culminating in his arrest on the night of March 25, 1918. When federal agents combed through his residence, they found nothing that would directly tie him to nefarious activities or indicate disloyalty, but they did find a horde of letters from a love-smitten twenty-year-old socialite from Boston, an aspiring singer named Rosamond Young. A search of her safety deposit box uncovered a series of letters from Muck in which he expressed anti-American sentiments and German sympathies. While he was clearly no spy, he was a German sympathizer who had made insulting comments about his host country. Confronted with the letters, Muck refused to discuss their contents because they were a personal matter involving a lady. He was eventually indicted for the official crime of having violated US postal laws and deemed a potentially dangerous enemy alien. On April 6, he was sent to Fort Oglethorpe, Georgia, where he spent the rest of the war as prisoner number 1357. When the war ended, he was shipped back to Germany in August 1919.[91] That November, the *Boston Post* published a sensational twelve-part series revealing the contents of Muck's letters, in a manner that was intended to enrage patriotic readers. His frustration and anger at America was evident, yet there was no direct evidence that he had been disloyal. On the contrary, in one letter he had stated: "I am doing only my duty and nothing against the holy (even Satan was once holy) laws of the so-called U.S.A."[92] The exposé painted Muck as a cunning, ungrateful spy who went around deflowering young women. Part of the outrage with Muck centered on his perceived immorality: a fifty-eight-year-old man having an affair with a twenty-year-old woman.

Even after the war ended and the peace treaty with Germany was signed, throughout 1919, pressure against German music continued. In January, there were indications that the public mood was beginning to thaw, as several excerpts of Wagnerian music were included in programs conducted by the New York Philharmonic. While some letters of protest were received and four plainclothes police officers were stationed in the hall as a precaution, there were no major incidents. The gradual reincorporation of Germanic music may have taken place without much hubbub, if not for the return of a large number of servicemen who began to disembark in New York City in large numbers during this time. In March, when New York's Lexington Avenue Theater announced plans for several German operettas, patriotic groups like the National Security League and the American Defense Society expressed their usual disapproval, but what could not be ignored was the surge in troops throughout the city. The Navy Club on Fifth Avenue quickly drew up a petition calling for a halt to proceedings, gathered two thousand signatures, and sent a delegation to meet with Mayor John Hylan. It read in part: "We feel that such an undertaking at this time is insulting to our patriotism and to the memory of the brave boys who have given their lives that the world shall be free from German influence."[93] The concerts were postponed indefinitely, amid fears of a full-scale riot. Five hundred sailors marched down Lexington Avenue in a victory parade.

With the signing of the Treaty of Versailles in June 1919, opposition to the playing of German music and the use of Germanic conductors began to wane. On July 3, a *New York Times* editorial called for an end to the witch-hunt: "The crisis is passed now and well passed, and German music can again delight the ear without offending the sensibilities that lie deeper."[94] In October, the Lexington Theater attempted another program with German music, under the "Star Opera Company." There was again immediate opposition by many military organizations. While Mayor Hylan considered closing down the performance, he was unsure of his legal standing and instead sent over two hundred police to guard the theatre and ensure order. The mayor shut the opera down the next day, but they were soon saved by a temporary court injunction, and performances resumed on October 23.[95] By January 1920, opposition to German music and composers subsided. In early January, even the American Legion, heretofore the archenemy of all things Germanic, announced that it was time for a change of heart: "Good music, whether it be by Wagner, Strauss, or Sousa, cannot and should not be killed, and any attempt to suppress it is bound to fail." The organization officially endorsed German opera, "where the spirit, the language and the personnel are truly American."[96]

ISLAMOPHOBIA: THE GERMAN SCARE IN MODERN CULTURAL GUISE

It is remarkable to think that many Americans once thought that listening to German music and learning German in school posed a threat to the United States by corrupting the morals of our youth. In the calm light of day, more than a century removed from the hysteria of World War I, even the most ardent conservative would likely agree that the reaction was extreme and out of proportion to the reality. The exaggerated threat was a tell-tale sign of a social panic. Yet Germanophobia and kindred scares involving periods of intense intolerance of ethnic groups are alive and well. In December 2015, Virginia high school teacher Cheryl LaPorte was overseeing a class on world geography and Islamic culture when she asked her students to practice calligraphy by copying a single sentence in Arabic from the Qur'an. The assignment created such a public furor and deluge of hate mail that the school closed over safety concerns. The Associated Press reported that Riverheads High School received "tens of thousands of e-mails and Facebook posts" from angry citizens, spurred on by a national conservative radio host who highlighted the incident.[97] The school's holiday concert had to be canceled, along with several sporting events. LaPorte, who is not Islamic, asked the students to write a common Muslim prayer—the *shahada*, which proclaims: "There is no god but Allah. Muhammad is the messenger of God." She gave the students the script in Arabic and did not offer a translation—nor were students asked to translate or recite the prayer. The focus of the lesson was not on religion but on the complexity of Arab calligraphy. It is difficult to imagine the same reaction if she had asked them to write a passage in Hebrew letters about Moses from the Torah. As the editorial board of one newspaper retorted: "And the charge that copying an untranslated passage of calligraphy constitutes 'indoctrination' into Islam is as ludicrous as suggesting that American students are 'indoctrinated' by being taught to write words about democracy in French class."[98] It is no small irony that the school closed for fears of safety—fear not of Muslims but after threats of violence and intimidation by American citizens espousing Christian values.

While the German Scare happened over a century ago, there are many parallels with today. Just like members of the Anti-German League in the United States and Canada worked to rid their countries of German influence, anti-Muslim organizations have popped up like mushrooms across North America and Europe today. In Germany, one of the largest is PEGIDA—Patriotic Europeans Against the Islamization of the West. In the United Kingdom, the English Defense League openly advocates against Muslims. In the United States, SIOA—Stop Islamization of America—is one of over a dozen active anti-Muslim hate groups. Just as mysterious fires and industrial accidents were once blamed on the Germans, anything that remotely looks like a terrorist attack is now attributed to Muslims. And just as the number of confirmed acts of German sabotage and espionage were quite small, so too have been the number of Islamist terror attacks in the West. Several so-called terror attacks were later determined to have been the result of mental illness or anger over a work dispute. In 2015, there were 372 mass shootings in America, resulting in 475 deaths. The vast majority of the gunmen were not Muslims.[99] While mass shootings in the United States are a major problem, it is not necessarily a Muslim issue. And just as German Americans were discriminated against and harassed due to their ancestry, many Muslims have experienced verbal harassment and are looked upon as oppressed. Having an Arab-sounding name does not help in applying for jobs, just like many German Americans sought the extreme measure of changing their names in the hope of avoiding discrimination and finding work.

The most remarkable aspect of the German Scare was not its violence, its widespread nature, or even the depth of hostility, but how quickly Americans were able to accept Germans as fellow citizens afterward. Once the fear began to subside and the threat appeared to have passed, the fog of war quickly dissipated, as if a spell had been broken. But for the many German Americans who had to endure this dark chapter in our history, it would take far longer to forgive and forget. For those who changed their names, the scare left a permanent mark on their very identities: a constant reminder of the intolerance of a bygone era, and the lengths that citizens were willing to go to protect themselves and their families.

CHAPTER 6

"BEWARE THE YELLOW PERIL"

THE JAPANESE AMERICAN SCARE

No matter what label is used, the United States govern-
ment, backed by its citizens, identified one group by race,
deemed them dangerous, and ordered them imprisoned
without the benefit of due process as defined in the United
States Constitution. . . . Neither due process nor a trial
were granted to the Japanese who were placed behind
barbed wire.

—Jolie Kelley, "Social Forces Collide:
The Japanese American Internment," 1999

After the bombing of Pearl Harbor in 1941, the mass internment of Japanese Americans that followed is widely believed to have been a sudden, knee-jerk reaction to the attack. In reality, the exaggerated response was based on deeply ingrained, long-standing racist beliefs that began on the West Coast and eventually spread across the country. In the decades leading up to the war, many citizens viewed the Japanese as members of an intellectually and morally impoverished race. American military intelligence had no hard evidence to indicate that people of Japanese ancestry ever posed a threat to the nation's security. The United States was also at war with Italy and Germany, yet those of Italian and German ethnicity were not interred, outside of a small number of enemy combatants such as soldiers who happened to be in the country when the war broke out. The reason for the different treatment is simple: these groups were widely thought to be part of the superior European Nordic race that looked physically similar in appearance and shared common cultural and religious traditions with much of white America. The seeds of discontent with those of Japanese heritage were sown in the late nineteenth century when Asian immigrants began flocking to the West Coast in large numbers to escape food shortages, overcrowding, and political unrest at home. Like the Chinese before them, they came with visions of a better life. Ironically, opportunities existed from the void left by the exclusion laws.[1] At the time, the average wage of a Japanese worker was just fourteen cents a day. In California, they could earn about two dollars. The Japanese newcomers took up many of the same jobs as the Chinese: working the gold mines, laying railroad track, farming, and any occupation that white Americans saw as beneath them.[2]

During much of the nineteenth century, Americans held a favorable view of Japanese immigrants. Many writers portrayed them in glowing terms, often in direct contrast to the Chinese, who had long been despised. They were viewed as cleaner, better educated, of higher intelligence, and more willing to accept Christianity and Western customs. One schoolbook from the period described them as "the most progressive" of the Mongolian racial branches.[3] In fact, early Japanese immigrants to the West Coast stayed away from the local Chinatowns, believing themselves to be a distinct and superior people who were the equals of Anglo Americans.[4] Their positive reception in California would change soon after they began arriving in large numbers.[5] It started with a trickle. By 1885, only a few hundred Japanese immigrants had come to the mainland. By 1900, the number had risen to just over 12,500.[6] With the approach of the new century, the image of Japanese migrants began to erode rapidly as West Coast journalists began depicting them as lazy, ignorant, and dirty. The once curious, exotic strangers from the Orient began to quickly turn menacing over fears that the West Coast would soon be overrun by hordes of cheap workers who would take white jobs.[7] Japanese migrants were easy scapegoats by their dress and distinct physical features, just like the Chinese had been. They were blamed for an array of issues, ranging from crime and vice to low wages.[8] For instance, during June 1892, California union leader Denis Kearney, previously known for the slogan, "The Chinese Must Go!" turned his attention to what was considered the "Oriental menace." On June 17, the *San Francisco Examiner* reported that Kearney had "sounded his old-time slogan 'must go' at the corner of Montgomery Street and Broadway last night to a crowd of about 300 people. He is now urging a crusade against the Japanese." Kearney argued that the Japanese were so fundamentally different from Europeans that assimilation was impossible.[9] San Francisco Mayor James Phelan supported the movement, asserting that people of Chinese and Japanese descent were "not bona fide citizens."[10]

The first major protests against Japanese migration broke out in 1900 after alarming press reports from California that Congress intended to either "water down" or scrap the Chinese Exclusion Act when it came up for renewal in 1902. Suspiciously, that March, Bubonic Plague was "discovered" in the Chinatown district of San Francisco, prompting the mayor and city board to quarantine the Japanese and Chinese sections of the city—but no other locations. The "plague" crisis quickly passed after complaints from business owners that any outbreak would hurt sales and give the city a bad reputation.[11] While some cases of the plague were later identified in California during this period, it was not confined to Chinatown. Despite a complete lack of evidence, and influenced by the racism of the time, many physicians advanced the theory that the plague was spread by Asians.[12] By May 7, the San Francisco Labor Council passed a resolution to include the Japanese under the Chinese exclusion laws.[13] That same month, Stanford University sociologist Edward Ross triggered a firestorm of criticism when he stood in front of an anti-Japanese rally in San Francisco and claimed that cheap Asian labor would soon overwhelm white California. If Ross had stopped there, his speech would have sounded like many other bigoted rants of the period and likely would have gone relatively unnoticed. But he went further, asserting that if the situation grew worse, "it'd be better for us to turn our guns on every vessel bringing Japanese to our shores rather than permit them to land."[14] He had essentially called for the murder of Japanese immigrants and was promptly fired by the university. As more immigrants poured in and were viewed as posing a threat to the white American worker, by the turn of the century, immigrants were depicted as deceitful and menacing.[15] In November 1901, with the Exclusion Act just months from expiring, the San Francisco City Council held a convention to support its renewal. They adopted a resolution recognizing the increasing numbers of Japanese immigrants who posed "a menace to the industrial interests of our people."[16] Some argued that the "Japs" posed a greater danger than the Chinese. One plucky Japanese immigrant stood outside the convention, proclaiming to anyone who would listen that it was OK to exclude Chinese, but the Japanese were a superior race.[17] The mood on the East Coast was very different because there was an overwhelming sentiment in Congress *against* excluding the Japanese, due to the low number of migrants there when compared to the West Coast, and where they were considered less of a threat to jobs and national security. The convention failed to pass its Japanese exclusion resolution.

THE INVASION SCARE

Japan's stunning defeat of Russia in 1905 made it a world power. For Americans on the West Coast, the surprise outcome of the Russo-Japanese War led to heightening fears of a Japanese invasion. That same year, the *San Francisco Chronicle* published a series of inflammatory articles about the threat from Japanese immigrants who had already "infiltrated" the country. Scare headlines included: "The Japanese Invasion—The Problem of the Hour"; "The Yellow Peril—How Japanese Crowd Out the White Race"; "Brown Men an Evil in the Public Schools"; and "Crime and Poverty Go Hand in Hand with Asiatic Labor."[18] Historian Roger Daniels describes the *Chronicle* at the time as, "without doubt, the most influential newspaper on the whole Pacific Coast." As for the motivation, Daniels believes it was its editor John Young's long-standing worry over "the Oriental issue."[19] In March, the Labor Council of San Francisco launched a campaign to boycott any merchants or manufacturers employing Japanese workers. On May 14, labor groups from around the country sent representatives to San Francisco, where they formed what would become the Japanese Exclusion League, and, later, the Asiatic Exclusion League. Their goal was simple: encourage boycotts and lobby lawmakers to restrict Asian migration. They also wanted separate schools for Japanese and European children.[20] Such was the popularity of their message that within three years they would boast 238 branches and 100,000 members.[21] By year's end, California legislators passed a resolution containing nearly all of the *Chronicle*'s main points on stopping Asian immigration.

ANTI-JAPANESE SENTIMENTS SPREAD

Up until 1905, the Japanese exclusionist movement was mostly a California phenomenon, with the concentration of migrants on the West Coast. Anti-Asian sentiments grew as the number of Asian immigrants continued to rise.[22] In October 1906, the San Francisco School Board created a national kerfuffle after voting to separate students of Japanese descent from their white classmates. The resolution was made on racist grounds and stated that it was done "not only for the purpose of relieving the congestion at present prevailing in our schools, but . . . that our children should not be placed in any position where their youthful impressions may be affected by associations with pupils of the Mongolian race."[23] Claims about the need to relieve congestion were farcical. Of the twenty-five thousand students attending city schools, just ninety-three were Japanese, and twenty-five of those were born in the United States.[24] The second part of the resolution, about white students being morally and intellectually polluted by their exposure to those of Mongolian descent, was blatantly racist.[25] The decision was made to appease the state's powerful labor unions and prevent Asian males from comingling with white girls, for fear that they might strike up relationships.[26] Despite stereotypes of the Japanese as lacking in moral aptitude and being prone to crime, Stanford University sociologist Walter Beach would later publish the results of a study of Asian criminal activity in California from 1900 to 1927. Most of those involved were of Japanese and Chinese descent. However, the nature of the crimes were in stark contrast to stereotypes held by many white Californians. Most offenses were traffic violations (27 percent), followed by gambling (16 percent), and intoxication (11 percent). The Japanese were found to have committed the fewest felonies of any racial group.[27] The school board withdrew its segregation order in March 1907 after President Theodore Roosevelt intervened; he promised to take action to reduce the number of Japanese laborers migrating into the country by lobbying the imperial government to restrict the flow. The two governments soon reached a series of informal agreements on the issue.[28]

Even among groups supporting Asian citizenship, there was not a widespread view that Asians were on an equal par with whites, although they were considered to be of better genetic stock than the "lower races" like the "Negro." A prominent nineteenth-century anthropologist, Daniel Brinton, asserted that the Mongolian race—that is, the Japanese and Chinese, were second only to whites, and that they could assimilate with relative ease if given the opportunity.[29] During the early 1900s, there was an attempt by pro-Japanese groups in California to view the Japanese as a distinctly separate race from the Chinese. In their attempt to gain full equality with Anglo Americans, the Japanese American Citizens League would later claim that they shared a similar Mongolian heritage with Native Americans who crossed the land bridge from Asia during the last ice age.[30]

In 1907, the National Socialist League announced its opposition to Asian immigration. While some members cited economic reasons, others were more worried about the threat posed by interbreeding and diluting the "purity" of white America.[31] One of the more curious anti-Japanese organizations at this time was the Anti-Jap Laundry League, which was created in 1908. Centered in San Francisco, its goal was to organize boycotts and pickets of Japanese-owned laundries and to intimidate customers. As a result, several laundries were driven out of business.[32] In August 1908, the issue of Japanese assimilation came to the fore as former San Francisco mayor James Phelan called on the exclusion of all Japanese from the state because they could not assimilate into white society and therefore posed a menace. During 1909, California was plagued by a wave of fear, hysteria, and prejudice that was fanned by racially charged reporting on the exclusion issue. Phelan's anti-Japanese stance led to his soaring popularity. He was soon elected US senator. During that same year, state lawmakers introduced no less than seventeen separate anti-Japanese bills, although little was accomplished because it was realized that any immigration laws would be rescinded by the federal government in Washington, DC.[33] Also in 1909, the secretary of the California Corrections Board, W. Almont Gates, gave a national address in which he made the sensational claim that after the Russo-Japanese War, a wave of former Japanese soldiers, owing their allegiance to the emperor, had migrated to the United States in search of work. He saw them as a grave risk to national security. "It would be easy to marshal an army of fifty thousand Japanese veterans at any point in California in forty-eight hours. . . . These ex-soldiers of Japan did not surrender their allegiance to their emperor. They are today as truly his subjects."[34] Gates noted that when the war with Russia had broken out, many ex-soldiers returned to their homeland to take up arms, and that they would do so against the United States.

Historian Michael Meloy observes that by 1910, "through the persistent efforts of many dedicated white Californians, Japanese-hating became a cottage industry with branches reaching into virtually every corner of California life."[35] The movement to ban all Japanese immigration had an unlikely ally in another group that was struggling for equal rights: white women. The campaign for (white) female equality and voting rights, which gained momentum during the second half of the nineteenth century, served to heighten anti-Asian sentiments by employing racist and anti-migrant themes. One prominent suffragist, Maud Younger, complained that white women were in poor company when it came to those who were not allowed to vote: "In California every adult may vote excepting only Mongolians, Indians, idiots, insane, criminals, and women."[36] She and other feminist leaders believed that Anglo American women were inherently more worthy and capable of being given the right to vote over "inferior" people of color.

A 1920 propaganda pamphlet epitomizes the literature of the period. Produced by newspaper publisher Valentine McClatchy, it pleads for severe restrictions on Japanese immigration. He argues that their prolific ability to breed would result in America becoming a province of Japan by 2080—at which point, the number of ethnic Japanese would have reached an astounding 216 million![37] The exclusion issue had waned during the Great War, with the Japanese fighting on the side of America, but it quickly resurfaced in the early 1920s and would snowball into an unstoppable force, as a who's who of California politicians launched an all-out campaign to halt Japanese immigration. This time they would succeed, first at a state level and then nationally. In 1913, California legislators had passed the Alien Land Law, which prohibited nonresidents who were ineligible for citizenship from owning farmland. At the time, Asians who were not already citizens were barred from obtaining it. The law was a clear attempt to target Japanese migrants and limit the amount of farmland they controlled. There were also fears that Japanese farmers would soon take control of the state's food supply. In contrast, European and African immigrants could obtain citizenship and were unaffected by the law. In 1920, the land law was toughened to prevent a loophole that allowed Japanese migrants to buy farmland under the names of their

American-born children and managing the property themselves.[38] While hailed as a victory for white Californians, it was more psychological than tangible, as the net effect was to cut the percentage of Japanese producing crops from 13 to 9 percent.[39] As it happened with the Chinese, the measure was in blatant disregard of the Fourteenth Amendment, which says that "No state shall deny to any person within its jurisdiction the equal protection of the law" regardless of race, color, or creed.[40]

Four years later, the Fourteenth Amendment would again be trampled on as Congress passed the Immigration Act of 1924. The law prohibited all Japanese immigration and limited European migration to no more than 150,000 persons per year using a quota system, which was "based on the contribution of each nationality to the overall US population in 1890, thereby preserving the racial and ethnic status quo."[41] Historian Russell Bearden writes that passage of the legislation was the culmination of a campaign replete with "dubious statistics that pointed to an 'alien invasion' of agriculture, to the 'peaceful penetration' of America by alien people and to the proliferation of 'yellow babies' in California."[42] Although the action angered the Japanese and violated a gentleman's agreement between the two countries, Congress had deemed the preservation of racial purity to have been more important than maintaining a good relationship with Japan.[43] In the lead-up to passage, the anti-Japanese propaganda campaign was in full swing and took the form of newspaper and magazine articles, books, pamphlets, speeches, and films. One of the most brazen was *Shadows of the West*, released in November 1920. The film reinforced every negative stereotype about the Japanese in America. It depicted Japanese Americans as sexual deviants, spies, wife-beaters, abductors, and would-be murderers, as well as cunning profiteers who were manipulating food prices by dumping fish and vegetables into the ocean.[44] In 1917, the Hearst Corporation had released a fifteen-part anti-Japanese serial that was to be shown in weekly installments under the title of *Patria*. It depicted a plot by Mexico and Japan to invade the southwestern United States, and contained unflattering and inflammatory representations of the Japanese. The serial was so offensive that, by request of President Woodrow Wilson, it had to be reedited and toned down because the United States wanted to maintain some semblance of a relationship with its ally Japan after America entered the war that April.[45]

RACIST IDEOLOGY

During the early twentieth century, California politicians and union leaders led the charge to repel the West Coast "Asian invasion," especially the Japanese; this was a cause that was frequently bolstered on racial grounds by scientists of the day. At the time, it was widely believed that humanity was composed of several distinct races, at the top of which were the Nordic Anglo-Saxons. Such views were common in America and Europe, where one's personal qualities were thought to be fixed by heredity. Whereas today there is a consensus among scientists that nurture is the primary determinant of behavior, back then many prominent scientists believed that nature was the driving force. The Immigration Act of 1924 was driven by scientific racism, where popular opinions were presented as scientific facts. At the time the act was passed, most in Congress had accepted the view that the white Nordic race was superior to all others, and that such a position was supported by science.[46] An influential figure who promoted this view was geneticist Harry Laughlin, who was a paid advisor to the House Committee on Immigration and Naturalization. He had been hired to support the committee's racist views.[47] He and other opponents of Asian immigration were quick to place their objections under the banner of science. Eugenicists of the period asserted that the genetic stock of different races could be improved through selective breeding. The eugenics movement was so influential that some leaders of the Immigration Restriction League even considered changing their name to the Eugenic Immigration League.[48] In reality, eugenics was an unproven science with unproven ideas about superior and inferior races.

A key point of contention in the immigration debate was whether members of the "lesser races," most notably Asians and Southern Europeans, were capable of blending into American society without tainting the white Nordic stock to such an extent that it would be permanently corrupted. These were the proponents of the "melting pot" theory. Opposing them were the restrictionists, exclusionists and isolationists who believed that certain migrants lacked the capacity to assimilate, based solely on their genetics. An enormously influential book at this time was *The Passing of the Great Race*, which had been published in 1916. Its author, Madison Grant, popularized the idea that the United States had been settled by the biologically superior and genetically pure Nordic race, which was thought to be under threat by "impure" immigrants.[49] At the time, the Committee on Selective Immigration supported the Immigration Act of 1924, claiming that it would keep out foreigners with "lower grades of intelligence" and who were contributing excessively "to our feeble-minded, insane, criminal and other socially inadequate classes."[50] Hitler would eventually put Grant's proposals into action by sterilizing "defectives" followed by the eventual extermination of "inferior races" such as the Jews and Roma peoples.[51]

Geneticist Laughlin claimed to have been a dispassionate scientist who considered the immigration issue to be a matter of biology rather than economics, and that he was simply following the facts. At one hearing, he said: "I am here simply as a scientific investigator to present the facts to the gentlemen of the committee, with the hope that the facts and their analysis might be of use."[52] Nothing could have been further from the truth. At the time, the influence of the environment was well-known in scientific circles.[53] Laughlin's argument was based on the controversial new field of eugenics. His first premise, that the "Nordic-Anglo-Saxon" race was inherently superior, was justified on the grounds of social Darwinism and the assumption that one's social and economic standing were a reflection of one's genetic worth. Many eugenicists supported this position by making the dubious claim that immigrant communities were notorious for poverty, crime, illiteracy, and disease. His theory of disharmonious crossings held "that the offspring of a cross between two different strains will always be inferior to both parental strains."[54] It was these arguments that eugenicists were using to support laws aimed at putting a stop to the mixing of the races, and thus diluting the nation's so-called racial purity.

Despite the perception that what Laughlin was doing was scientifically grounded, in reality, it was speculation and a biased interpretation of the data. Laughlin had succeeded in passing off popular opinion as scientific fact.[55] It may be that leading scientists of the day were hesitant to publicly challenge such a respected scientist, given the anti-immigration mood of the times, especially as the tenor of the debate often turned ugly. It was also clear that the committee was biased against the role of the environment because most of the experts invited to testify were supporters of the Nordic superiority claim. When Representative Emanuel Celler, a pro-immigration Jew from New York, cried foul and insisted that the committee call an authority on the other side of the issue, Herbert Spencer Jennings was invited to testify. When he arrived, he was told that his testimony would be limited to only a few minutes due to the supposedly crowded schedule, and he was asked to submit a written report—a report that was highly critical of Laughlin. Celler later called the committee hearings a sham: "We have heard a great deal in the discussions of the subject of races, race types, ethnic strains, heredity . . . and so forth. What efforts were made by the committee to know something of the important phases of the subject?"[56] Instead of listening to the testimony of proponents, Celler asked why it was that prominent physical anthropologist Ales Hrdlicka of the National Museum in Washington, DC, was not called. "Dr. Hrdlicka is well known to the chairman of the committee. . . . No; the committee only wanted those who believed in 'Nordic' superiority; men who deal in buncome [sic]." Laughlin's flawed assertions on the need to keep out undesirable races were widely publicized after the measure was enacted on May 26, 1924. For instance, on June 1, the *New York Times* reported that Laughlin's assumptions (on which passage of the act was based) were not grounded in sound science. Other papers, such as the *Chicago Tribune*, also painted Laughlin's claims as dubious, but the damage was done.[57]

After passage of the act, Laughlin boasted that similar arguments were being considered by politicians in Europe, who were contemplating their own restrictions on immigration. One admirer was Adolf Hitler, who wrote in *Mein Kampf*: "There is today one state in which at least weak beginnings toward a better conception are noticeable. Of course, it is not our model German Republic, but the American Union, in which an effort is made to consult reason at least partially . . . refusing immigration on principle to elements in poor health, by simply excluding certain races from naturalization."[58] In December 1936, the Nazi regime would bestow Laughlin with an honorary doctorate in medicine from Heidelberg University for his work on eugenics and immigration restriction. He was praised as a "successful pioneer of practical eugenics and the far-seeing representative of racial policy in America."[59] The man who had nominated him for the award was Dr. Carl Schneider, professor of racial hygiene at Heidelberg University. Three years later, Schneider would serve as a key scientific advisor to the Nazi euthanasia campaign that resulted in the extermination of thousands of mentally and physically disabled Germans.[60] In 1939, the Nazis expanded their eugenics program to include the extermination of the physically and mentally handicapped.[61] It is noteworthy that the first eugenics laws ever passed were in the US state of Indiana in 1907, when the legislature approved a measure to sterilize mentally handicapped prison inmates. Many other states followed suit. The American model was soon adopted in many European countries, such as Sweden and Denmark, by 1934.[62] During the Nuremberg war crimes trials, Nazi administrators often justified the sterilization of "defectives" by pointing to similar policies in American history—policies that included a preoccupation with racial purity.

INTERRED WITHOUT TRIAL

On February 19, 1942, President Franklin Roosevelt issued Executive Order 9066, which paved the way for the forced removal and internment of an estimated 120,000 Japanese, most of whom were American citizens living on the West Coast. The 1940 census counted nearly 127,000 persons of Japanese birth or heritage on the mainland, 47,000 of whom were not US citizens. They constituted a mere one-tenth of 1 percent of the total population of the forty-eight states of the union.[63] The order did not single out Japanese Americans or any particular group or location but stated in general terms that the War Department had the right to circumvent constitutional freedoms and exclude people from certain areas. It was quickly applied to those Japanese on the Pacific Coast who were deemed to pose a national security risk, given their proximity to crucial war assets there. Military officials argued that they might work to undermine the Allied effort by acting as spies and saboteurs and engaging in fifth column activities, especially in California.[64] In a 1943 newsreel produced by the Office of War Information to explain and justify the relocation, it was noted that many Japanese lived near military installations, shipyards, and oil wells. Furthermore, Japanese fishermen could watch vital ship movements, and farmers could observe the activity on airfields—hence the "necessity" of relocation.[65] In addition to California, EO 9066 applied to the western halves of Washington and Oregon, and a small section of Arizona. Americans of Japanese ancestry living on the East Coast "were left in nervous liberty throughout the war." [66]

There were fifteen assembly centers where people were temporarily held, such as the Santa Anita Racetrack in California, and the Puyallup Fairgrounds in Washington State. They were soon moved to one of ten permanent camps that were in preparation—most in remote western locations such as Gila River in Arizona or Heart Mountain in Wyoming. In the haste and chaos that ensued after being forced to leave on short notice, many Japanese Americans sold their homes, businesses, and belongings for a fraction of the cost. Designations such as "relocation" and "evacuation" were euphemisms for forced removal. Words like *occupants* and *interred* were just another way of saying "prisoner" and "inmate." While the "assembly centers" had schools, it was far from a semblance of normalcy. The camps were dirty and overcrowded, and there was little privacy. Historian Paul Spickard writes: "No one could go outside the barbed wire except for extreme medical emergencies, and then they went under guard. Friends could visit. . . . The guard towers, machine guns, guard dogs, searchlights, and fences reminded them that they were prisoners. The daily regimentation reinforced that awareness. There was a roll call in the mess hall each morning. At night there was a curfew, and the inmates were counted again."[67]

Japanese Americans were taken into custody *en masse* as military authorities believed that it would take too long to conduct investigations into the loyalty of each subject. Writing in June 1945, when emotions were still running high on both sides of the debate, Yale law professor Eugene Rostow called the decision an "unjustified," "unnecessary," and "mistaken" action that constituted "the worst blow our liberties have sustained in many years."[68] Historian Roger Daniels concurred, describing it as "a major blot on the record of American democracy."[69] Ironically, as the war was fought to preserve freedom, one group was singled out—without evidence—to temporarily lose its freedoms. At the time of the action, there were about 1,100,000 foreign nationals from enemy nations living in the United States. Less than 4 percent were Japanese nationals.[70] While the United States was at war with both Germany and Italy as well, the order did not apply to those of German or Italian ancestry, despite the fact that they were the largest foreign-born ethnic groups in the country. The internments can only be understood within the context of the long-standing debate in America over the racial suitability of Japanese Americans to assimilate into mainstream society and fears that they may dilute the Nordic stock. Indeed, after having been fed a steady diet of anti-Japanese propaganda over the previous decades, during the war, American soldiers were more hostile to the Japanese than the Germans. According to testing by military psychologists, near 40 percent agreed with the statement: "I would really like to kill a Japanese soldier."[71] Conversely, under 10 percent indicated that they would like to kill a German soldier. Just imagine if the government had applied the same criteria to German and Italian Americans that they had used to intern Japanese residents. Besides being impractical given the sheer numbers of people (in the millions), Paul Spickard observes that there would have been a public outcry because it would have meant interring the likes of New York Yankees outfielder Joe DiMaggio and the mayor of New York City, Fiorello LaGuardia. He writes: "German Americans, in the minds of most White decision makers, were indistinguishable from Anglo-Americans. There was never any thought of interning German Americans, except for the few aliens who had been identified as probably Axis agents."[72] The same was true of Italian Americans. While a small number were arrested because they were believed to pose a threat, and there was initial concern over the loyalty of some who had neglected to file for citizenship, there was never any serious consideration given to interring citizens of Italian heritage.[73]

The issuing of Executive Order 9066 is a remarkable event in American history because the United States is a nation of laws. The order was passed, over the objection of FBI Director J. Edgar Hoover, who believed it was unnecessary, and Attorney General Francis Biddle, who deemed it unconstitutional. Fear and panic had become the order of the day as anti-Japanese hysteria gripped the nation and threatened to undermine the very foundations of American government. Every society lives by a set of core values. These are the nonnegotiables. In the United States, those tenets are the right to life, liberty, and the pursuit of happiness. Historian Jolie Kelley observes that these rights were temporarily suspended for Japanese Americans, in direct contradiction of the Fifth and Sixth Amendments. The Fifth Amendment states that "no person shall be . . . deprived of life, liberty, or property without due process of law," while the Sixth Amendment guarantees those accused of crimes "the right to a speedy and public trial, by an impartial jury . . . and to be informed of the nature and cause of the accusation." Kelley writes: "No matter what label is used, the United States government, backed by its citizens, identified one group by race, deemed them dangerous, and ordered them imprisoned without the benefit of due process as defined in the United States Constitution. . . . Neither due process nor a trial were granted to the Japanese who were placed behind barbed wire."[74] It is notable in that there was support for Japanese Americans during the war, among some liberal left-wing groups and religious organizations, based on moral grounds. Throughout the 1930s and early 1940s, there were also growing doubts about the accuracy of claims by advocates of eugenics, although the movement still held some influence.

Many of the country's most influential newspapers backed the relocation program either directly or indirectly by questioning the loyalty of Japanese Americans, including the *New York Times*, the *Los Angeles Times*, and the *San Francisco Chronicle*.[75] Several religious publications opposed the internment. While supporting the Allied war effort, Reinhold Niebuhr, publisher of the magazine *Christianity and Crisis*, was critical of the removal policy, likening it to Hitler's Nuremberg Laws, which targeted Jews based solely on racial grounds. He also questioned why those of Japanese descent were being targeted when second-generation German Americans were not. The *Christian Century* viewed the decision as racist and imperialistic. The liberal Catholic weekly the *Commonweal* tried to present a human face by printing photos and biographies of those taken away.[76]

During this period of anti-Japanese hostility, some people referred to Japanese Americans with the denigrating term "American-born Japanese." In February 1942, just weeks before President Roosevelt issued the order to intern those deemed at risk of siding with the motherland, *Los Angeles Times* columnist W. H. Anderson typified the view of the Japanese in America as racially inferior and unable to assimilate. He called for *all* Japanese in America to be interned "while we are at war with their race." "A viper is nonetheless a viper wherever the egg is hatched," he observed.[77]

"So a Japanese-American born of Japanese parents, nurtured upon Japanese traditions . . . living in a transplanted Japanese atmosphere and thoroughly inoculated with Japanese thoughts, Japanese ideas and Japanese ideals . . . almost inevitably and with the rarest exceptions grows up to be a Japanese, not an American, in his thoughts," he wrote. After the bombing, a Japanese American medical student at Creighton University, Kenneth Kurita Jr., was assaulted for his ethnicity. He also noted that Chinese students on campus wore tags that read: "I'm not Jap, I'm Chinese."[78]

Almost immediately after the attack on Pearl Harbor, Japanese Americans were looked upon with suspicion. Rumors questioning the loyalty of the territory's 160,000 residents of Japanese heritage spread across the Hawaii islands. Among the many anti-Japanese rumors to appear in the wake of the attack was the assertion that the body of a downed flier was wearing a ring from local McKinley High School. There were also claims that Japanese residents had poisoned the water supply, and Japanese plantation workers on the island of Oahu had cut stalks of cane sugar in the shape of arrows pointing in the direction of Pearl Harbor, to guide Japanese pilots to their prey. According to another rumor, the day before the attack, local Japanese were tipped off by coded messages appearing in a Honolulu newspaper advertisement. Yet another rumor held that many Japanese residents signaled passing Zero pilots by waving their kimonos at them.[79] Not a single claim was ever verified, yet the stories persisted in the press.

The mistreatment of Japanese Americans during World War II is a testament to the importance of analyzing the root causes underlying modern-day events. The mistreatment of the Japanese—and other so-called Mongolian races in America—was part of a global movement that viewed the world's people through the prism of race. The result was catastrophic: the persecution, scapegoating, and murder of six million European Jews, untold destruction to property, and a race-inspired world war that would leave 60 million people dead. When the Americans dropped the atomic bombs on Hiroshima and Nagasaki that quickly drew World War II to a close, they were putting out a fire of their own creation.[80] The

American eugenics movement led to the legalization and legitimation of race-based immigration restrictions, alienated Japanese leaders, and left a global legacy, especially in Germany. Historian Garland Allen writes that "the race hygiene movement, with its emphasis on racial purity and on the inferiority of Jewish and non-Aryan stocks, provided the ideological foundation for the Holocaust. It is unlikely that the Nazis could have carried out such wide-spread decimation of Jewish people had not the ideology of race-hygiene existed, and claimed a scientific foundation."[81]

Will a mass incarceration based on a person's ethnic background, nationality, or religious beliefs happen again? Sadly, the answer is yes. We need only look to the mass arrests of Latin American migrants at the Mexican border during the spring and summer of 2018, and the strategy of separating children from their families in order to serve as a deterrent. Many of these people were refugees and asylum seekers fleeing violence and political persecution, only to find themselves behind bars and treated like criminals for seeking a better life for their families. There have been several other recent instances in our history when mass incarcerations have nearly happened. During the Cold War, an internal security emergency order was authorized, giving the attorney general the power to detain espionage suspects—most likely Communists—and it even provided for the creation of internment camps, but they were never built. During the Iranian hostage crisis of 1979–1981, President Jimmy Carter tried to collect the names and addresses of all Iranian university students in the country. While these latter two events never led to mass incarcerations and were based on ideological rather than ethnic and racial grounds, it is a reminder that specific groups of people may be targeted in the future.

While it is true that the Japanese internment was unprecedented for the twentieth century, there were similar events during the first half of the nineteenth century when the US government forced tens of thousands of Native Americans to leave their ancestral homelands to live on reservations. The forced removals, often overseen by soldiers with bayonets, resulted in the deaths of an estimated four thousand Cherokee alone between 1838 and 1839, from disease, exhaustion, exposure, and starvation. General Winfield Scott oversaw the exodus as troops were placed throughout Cherokee country, where stockades had been built to hold the Native Americans before their removal. American anthropologist James Mooney describes the heartbreaking scenes that followed:

> From these, squads of troops were sent to search out with rifle and bayonet every small cabin hidden away in the coves or by the sides of mountain streams, to seize and bring in as prisoners all the occupants, however or wherever they might be found. Families at dinner were startled by the sudden gleam of bayonets in the doorway and rose up to be driven with blows and oaths along the weary miles of trail that led to the stockade. Men were seized in their fields or going along the road, women were taken from their wheels and children from their play. In many cases, on turning for one last look as they crossed the ridge, they saw their homes in flames, fired by the lawless rabble that followed on the heels of the soldiers to loot and pillage.[82]

During the Second World War, several high-ranking members of the American military harbored deep prejudices against Japanese Americans. Their views were a reflection of popular attitudes. Even Arizona Senator Henry Ashurst once proclaimed: "Against the Japanese and their civilization I have no evil word, but we are a different race. They will vitiate our population, and once it is vitiated, it is beyond repair."[83] For these officials, the conflict was a race war. After the attack on Pearl Harbor, the commander of the Western Defense Force, General John DeWitt, sent a report to Secretary of War Henry Stimpson, urging the "evacuation" of Japanese from the West Coast. He asserted that it was not necessary to make a distinction between Japanese in Japan and Americans of Japanese ancestry because they both were part of the same race. He wrote: "The Japanese race is an enemy race and while many second and third generation Japanese . . . have become 'Americanized,' the racial strains are undiluted."[84] DeWitt viewed all Americans of Japanese ancestry as potential traitors. In April 1943, he would famously declare: "A Jap's a Jap," noting that even if they have American citizenship, "he is still a Japanese and you can't change him."[85] That he was not immediately dismissed from his command is a testament to just how deep and widespread anti-Japanese sentiments were at this time. Seventy-three years later in 2016, Donald Trump echoed DeWitt's sentiments in claiming that among Muslim immigrants to America, "there's no real assimilation" even for "the second and third generation."[86] This is why the mistreatment of Japanese Americans by their fellow citizens is an important lesson to remember, as it is just as relevant today as it was during World War II. As journalist Katelyn Taira observes, "when America forgets its past disgrace, it is likely to commit the same mistake again."[87] DeWitt's views put the military in an awkward position. Just three months earlier, the War Department had announced the formation of an all-volunteer all-Japanese American military unit. The official name was the 442nd Regimental Combat Team, or "RCT." While much was made about the military trusting Japanese Americans to join in the war effort, the reality was very different. Many of those who signed up would instead be assigned to the Military Intelligence Service.[88]

A government report would later conclude that there is not a single known incidence of a Japanese American having been disloyal.[89] While civil-rights advocates filed lawsuits against the government's action, in 1944 the US Supreme Court ruled that the internments were constitutional because the right to protect the country against espionage outweighed individual rights of any group. In 1980, a special committee was formed to assess the validity of the internments, at the behest of President Jimmy Carter. It culminated in the Civil Liberties Act of 1988, after the committee concluded that the actions were the result of long-standing Asian racism and wartime hysteria, not because they were a legitimate national security threat. Congress offered an official apology and granted each camp survivor $20,000 in compensation for having been interred for up to four years, in bleak camps scattered across the country.[90] In a few instances, overzealous guards shot and killed their captors.

In the wake of Pearl Harbor, the American government released a series of racially charged anti-Japanese propaganda images including pamphlets, films, and posters. Words like *Nip*, *yellow*, and *Jap* came into common usage as Japanese soldiers were depicted as bloodthirsty, slanted-eyed demonic figures devoid of morals.[91] But the most common images of the Japanese were of apes, monkeys, and rats, to emphasize that they were part of the primal Mongolian race that was supposedly lower on the evolutionary scale and a step closer to the animal kingdom.[92] It is the ultimate irony that during the war, Americans and their allies described the Japanese using the same racist imagery that the Germans had reserved for the Jews. There was even concern that the Japanese posed a threat to America's racial purity, just as the Nazis worried about contamination of the Aryan race.[93] While both groups were interred, the major difference between the Nazis and the Americans is that the former had taken their racist beliefs a step further and sought to eliminate, once and for all, those considered inferior.

CHAPTER 7

"THE JEWS ARE SPYING FOR HITLER!"

THE REFUGEE PANIC OF WORLD WAR II

The fault, dear Brutus, lies not in our stars, but in ourselves.

—Shakespeare, *Julius Caesar*

The present-day fear of "killer refugees" from Syria and other Muslim countries, entering the United States to wreak havoc by committing acts of terrorism is an all-too-familiar theme in American history—and well worth recounting. In 1938, the American government closed its doors to the throngs of German Jews who were desperate to seek sanctuary from their Nazi nightmare. For many, it was tantamount to a death sentence. Propaganda minister Joseph Goebbels was fond of pointing out that while his government was more than willing to let them go, few countries would take them.[1] At the time, the Nazis were purging the Reich of Jews by transporting them to nearby countries. While President Franklin Roosevelt had harsh words for Hitler's treatment of Germany's Jewish population, his words alone were little comfort to those who were fighting for their very survival, and that of their families. The United States even put pressure on European countries *not* to take them in, because they supposedly posed an imminent threat to their national security.[2] This tragic episode took place amid great agitation that many Jewish asylum seekers were working for the Nazis and intent on infiltrating the country. Driven by anti-Semitism, bigotry, and a fear of spies, State Department officials

deliberately created piles of bureaucratic red tape to slow the flow of refugees to a trickle. During the entire period that America was at war with
Germany, only 21,000 Jewish refugees were allowed into the country—a
mere 10 percent of the overall quota.[3] Put another way, about 200,000
men, women, and children were turned away in their hour of need,
without any compelling factual evidence—only fear and prejudice. This
dark chapter in our history parallels present-day attempts by the American government to stem the intake of refugees from Muslim countries
over concerns that some may be terrorists in disguise. As with the Jewish
asylum seekers, there is little to substantiate these claims. One study of
terrorist acts by refugees in the United States over the past forty years
places the odds of being murdered by one at roughly one in three and a
half billion (1 to 3,500,000,000).[4] In each era, a decision was made by
government officials to shut out refugees based on emotions instead of
facts, and popular perceptions and stereotypes instead of reality.

America's reaction to the appalling events of Nazi Germany was the
result of several factors that built up during the 1930s to culminate in a
social panic over Jewish refugees. The impact of the Great Depression was
still raw. People had vivid memories of the indignity of soup kitchens and
the humiliation of standing with hat in hand for hours in unemployment
lines. There were concerns that non-Nordic immigrants would take away
jobs and dilute the nation's racial purity. Anti-Semitism was rife. National
opinion polls showed that the public was overwhelmingly against admitting Jewish immigrants. They were seen as Europe's problem. These factors
gave rise to a spy mania that began in 1938 and would persist for the next
four years. The fear of spies and saboteurs was the final nail in the coffin
for refugees hoping that the Roosevelt administration might loosen its
strict immigration policy and let more asylum seekers into the country.

While America was not alone in rejecting the Jews, they were the
leading light of democracy at this crucial time, and almost certainly
could have saved hundreds of thousands of lives. In viewing these events
through the prism of life in the twenty-first century, inaction by the

American government and much of its citizenry may appear incomprehensible. How could the world's wealthiest and most technologically advanced country, with arguably the most sophisticated legal and education systems in the world, allow such a preventable calamity to occur? American officials were well aware of the dire situation for German Jews. Shortly after Hitler took power as chancellor in January 1933, the Nazi regime began a systematic campaign to persecute Jews by passing a series of laws severely impeding their rights. Each year the restrictions grew more severe; and their predicament more desperate. These events were reported in the press for all to see.

THE JEWISH EMERGENCY

Hitler rose to power by blaming the Jews for the harsh terms of the Treaty of Versailles, which officially ended the war with the Allies in June 1919. Having been despised in Europe for centuries, Jews were an ideal target. Since medieval times, when they were blamed for spreading the black death, the Jews had to endure widespread discrimination. Although the Nazis were not the only country discriminating against Jews, what separated them from the rest of Europe and North America were the extreme lengths to which they were willing to go to get rid of them. During the early years of Hitler's chancellery, the American media covered the escalating discrimination and persecution of the Jews in Germany, but rarely on their front pages.[5] It was not until late 1938 that US journalists began to headline the rapidly unfolding events.

In March 1933, the *Chicago Tribune* published a troubling report describing the widespread fear among German Jews after their mistreatment at the hands of the Nazis: "On the nights of March 9 and 10, bands of Nazis throughout Germany carried out wholesale raids to intimidate the opposition, particularly the Jews.... Men and women were insulted, slapped [and] punched in the face, hit over the heads with blackjacks, dragged out of their homes in night clothes and otherwise molested.... Innocent Jews... are taken off to jail and put to work in a concentration camp where you may stay a year without any charge being brought against you."[6] By summer, America's German ambassador, William Dodd, briefed the president on the deteriorating situation, but Roosevelt said he had no intention of meddling in the internal affairs of another country. Despite knowledge of the human tragedy that was unfolding in the heart of Europe, instead of easing immigration laws to help Jews escape, the administration made them stricter. The American public also opposed admitting more German refugees at this time, even if they sympathized with their plight. In 1933, the Nazis organized a boycott of Jewish shops, while across Germany, troops collected and publicly burned tens of thousands of books by Jewish authors. On July 14, a law was passed calling for the forced sterilization of the handicapped. In 1935, the Nuremberg Laws prohibited marriage or sexual relations between "real" Aryan Germans and "inferior" Jewish Germans. Despite these obvious violations of human rights, after a national debate, America still participated in the 1936 Summer Olympics in Berlin. The number of participating countries was forty-nine—the most ever. Not long after, the Nazi campaign against the Jews was ramped up. By 1938, Jewish passports were revoked, Jewish doctors could no longer practice medicine, and Jewish lawyers were forbidden from practicing law. On November 9 and 10, hundreds of synagogues were set alight across the country as German firefighters stood idly by and did nothing; their job was to ensure that no German buildings caught fire. By daybreak on the 10th, nearly one hundred Jews had been killed after being indiscriminately beaten, stabbed, and shot, while thousands of businesses and homes were ransacked or burned by enraged citizens, and Nazi Storm Troopers acting on orders from their leaders. Even Jewish hospitals, schools, and cemeteries were looted. The event would become known as the Night of Broken Glass or *Kristallnacht* (literally "night of crystal") on account of the thousands of Jewish shops that had been ransacked and their windows smashed. Upward of thirty thousand Jewish boys and men were soon rounded up and sent off to concentration camps. Before the year's end, Jews would be forced to hand over all of their business assets.

By late 1938, Germany's Jews were in the midst of the worst humanitarian crisis in history. A slow-motion catastrophe was playing out for the world to read about in the press, and to watch on the newsreels at the local movie theaters. Despite these grim circumstances, the German government was still allowing Jews to leave the country, and in December ten thousand Jewish children were allowed to travel to the relative safety of England in what became known as the *Kindertransport* or "children's transport." There was still time to act. With full knowledge of these and other horrors, the United States steadfastly refused to raise its modest quota of 27,000 immigrants from Germany and Austria, and take in more Jews.[7] It certainly was not because immigrants were pouring into the country, outstripping the capacity to process them. Immigration from eastern Europe was at an all-time low.[8] The Roosevelt administration's anti-refugee intentions were made clear in March 1938, when Germany invaded Austria, generating an additional 190,000 Jewish asylum seekers. Instead of keeping the quotas separate as they had been, the administration chose to combine them into one, eliminating the Austrian allotment.[9] The quota gave the illusion that the Roosevelt administration was doing more than it was, given that 90 percent of the allotment went unfilled during the war years. A poll taken in late November 1938, after the Night of Broken Glass, found an overwhelming 94 percent of Americans expressing sympathy for German Jews. Yet 77 percent were against raising the annual quota and letting more in.[10]

Throughout the 1920s and 1930s, America was a hotbed of racism, be it against Mexicans, Chinese, Japanese, Native Americans, African Americans, or Jews. Similar sentiments were common throughout much of the world as people harbored misguided notions about the effect of race on intelligence and behavior. During this period, heredity was destiny. Like the modern-day gradual acceptance of homosexuality, same-sex marriages, and, most recently, transgender bathrooms, old attitudes would stubbornly persist. By the late 1930s, the eugenics movement—the branch of science devoted to improving the genetic stock of a particular human population, was shifting rapidly away from heredity as the main determinant of a person's life course. Instead, there was an increasing realization that environment was destiny. Led by Columbia University anthropologist Franz Boas, himself a German American, most Western scientists by now had rejected the idea of superior races, but these sentiments stubbornly persisted. It is within this context that the American reaction to the Jewish refugee crisis must be understood. Even though there was no credible evidence for the existence of a large contingent of refugees posing as spies, many Americans were frightened of Jewish asylum seekers. These claims provided a convenient rationale for anti-Semites in the government to shut its gates to the weary and downtrodden of Nazi Germany.[11]

ANTI-SEMITISM AND THE RISE OF EUGENICS

When the Nazis rose to power in the early 1930s, long-standing feelings of anti-Semitism came to the fore as many groups emerged to promote Hitler's views on the Jewish "menace." Foremost among them was the German American Bund or Federation, a group of German-born Americans and German citizens. Members had to pledge that they were of pure Aryan descent and free of any traces of Jewish ancestry.[12] Established in 1936, the group's purpose was to spread the "good news" about the Nazis to America. Their charismatic leader, Fritz Kuhn, openly praised Hitler's extreme racial views. He criticized the president for having too many Jews in his inner circle of advisors, referring to him as "Franklin D. Rosenfeld," and his policies as "the Jew Deal." By 1939, seventy-one local branches were active across the country. Its headquarters were in the German suburb of Yorkville on Manhattan's Upper East Side. The organization's gatherings had all of the trappings of a Nazi party meeting, complete with Hitler salutes and swastikas. At the height of its popularity in 1939, membership approached thirty thousand. The Bund even operated camps similar to those of Hitler Youth. At its peak, its weekly newspaper had a circulation of ten thousand. The group was disbanded in 1941 after America declared war on Germany.[13]

The most influential pro-Nazi group in America at this time was the Christian Front, which was created by Father Charles Coughlin, a Catholic priest who had an enormous following and was one of the most popular public figures of the decade. Coughlin preached Nazi principles to an audience of 15 million during his Sunday-afternoon radio sermons that were heard throughout North America. Fiercely anti-Semitic, he blamed many of America's social problems on the Jews.[14] One historian boiled down his core message to a single sentence: "Jews were evil, money-hungry conspirators who were destroying every value that Christians held sacred."[15] Such was the level of anti-Semitism in the lead-up to the Second World War that in 1937, New York City's exclusive Colony Club excluded the wife of US Treasury Secretary Henry Morgenthau for being Jewish. President Roosevelt's wife, Eleanor, resigned from the club in solidarity.[16] Despite an outpouring of sympathy for the Jews during the 1930s, American anti-Semitism remained strong. Even by 1946, after the horrors of the Holocaust were known, most Americans still singled out the Jews as posing the greatest single menace to the country.[17]

In the decade leading up to the war, prominent American scientists working in the fields of biology and genetics enthusiastically supported the Nazi eugenics program. In his study of the movement, anthropologist Robert Sussman documents the close relationship between American eugenicists and their Nazi counterparts. The two sides frequently corresponded, fraternized at conferences, and took encouragement and inspiration from one another. The Nazi eugenics program had the fingerprints of American scientists all over it. For example, Americans pioneered the concept of sterilizing the physically and socially unfit well before the

Nazis. Throughout the 1930s, many American scientists were cheerleaders of Nazi eugenic policies, even though the Jews were suffering immeasurably as a direct result of it. Sussman writes that "American eugenicists had essentially written Nazi ideology and policy" and that America's legislation on immigration and sterilization had been "used as the model for the new Germany."[18] In 1933, when Germany introduced mandatory sterilization laws, prominent American publications such as the *Journal of the American Medical Association* and the *American Journal of Public Health* applauded the action.[19] In 1935, influential eugenicist Harry Laughlin was still promoting his now-discredited ideas about racial contamination. During the early 1920s, he had testified before congressional committees that the "Mongolian races," such as the Japanese and Chinese, posed an imminent threat to America's racial purity. Laughlin's testimony was instrumental in the passage of the landmark 1924 Immigration Act, which restricted the migration of so-called inferior races. He was now testifying to Congress against allowing German Jews to immigrate to the United States, using similar logic: their interbreeding would pollute the "Nordic race." He even authored a 267-page report justifying his call for restrictions, arguing that if more Jews were allowed into the country to reproduce in significant numbers, it would cause America's downfall.[20] As late as 1939, Laughlin called for reduced immigration quotas for Jews, warning that they represented "human dross" (rubbish) that endangered America's racial stock.[21] The Nazi euthanasia program and its later policy to exterminate Jews were both based on a eugenic theory of racial inferiority that was widely circulated and promoted in America and Europe.

In 1936, an extravagant celebration was to be held in Germany to mark the 550th anniversary of Heidelberg University, a leading light in Nazi eugenics research. Many American eugenicists were in attendance. The *New York Times* called for a boycott and labeled as Nazi propaganda stooges anyone who attended. Despite the warning and years of oppressive laws targeting German Jews, representatives from several major American universities sent delegates, including Harvard, Yale, Columbia,

Cornell, Johns Hopkins, Michigan, and Vassar College. Several weeks later, Virginia physician and staunch eugenicist Walter Plecker traveled to Germany and presented a paper on his state's efforts to stop the "spread of the Mongrel races."[22] Plecker was the state's first registrar of vital statistics, a position he held from 1912 to 1946. Even in 1939, the year that Germany was at war with Poland, Britain, and France, American writer Lothrop Stoddard was allowed to visit the Reich for over four months and was granted an audience with Hitler. Stoddard was the author of the bestselling book *The Rising Tide of Color: The Threat Against White World-Supremacy.* Published in 1920, it advanced the notion that only through eugenics could the white races of the world ensure their future survival against the faster-breeding lower races.[23] During his visit, Stoddard noted that at one gathering, without the subject having been previously breached, someone spontaneously raised a toast and called for the death of the Jews. He later wrote that the Jewish question would soon be resolved "by the physical elimination of the Jews themselves from the Third Reich."[24]

Several American businesses and foundations supported Nazi research into eugenics. The Rockefeller Foundation poured in millions between 1922 and 1936, at which point it cut most funding due to the dire political situation in Germany. Industrialist Henry Ford was a major supporter of Hitler and a virulent anti-Semite who published a series of booklets under the title *International Jew: The World's Foremost Problem.* An admirer and reader of Ford's writings, Hitler kept his picture in his office, and in July 1938, he sent two representatives to Dearborn, Michigan, to present him with a special award. *International Jew* was translated into German and became a bestseller in Nazi Germany.[25] Hitler was mesmerized by Ford's writings to the extent that he plagiarized from them. Several passages in *Mein Kampf* are nearly identical to Ford's newspaper articles.[26] In the American edition of *Mein Kampf* published in 1939, the editors cautioned readers: "These reflections are copied, for the most part, from the *Dearborn Independent*, Mr. Henry Ford's newspaper."[27] The great irony is that an American had essentially written significant tracts of *Mein Kampf*—the Nazi bible—and American scientists were role models for Hitler's sterilization campaign. Both would serve as blueprints for the persecution of the Jews.

TURNING AWAY JEWISH CHILDREN

If there were any lingering doubts as to whether anti-Semitism played a role in the American government turning its back on the plight of Jewish refugees, they were answered in the spring of 1939. That year, a bill was proposed to allow twenty thousand children to escape Nazi Germany and migrate to the United States over two years. It stipulated that the children must be under the age of fourteen.[28] To the astonishment of many, it failed. When Senator Robert Wagner of New York and Representative Edith Rogers of Massachusetts introduced the idea, it won immediate and widespread support from a broad spectrum of Americans: church leaders, academics, the YMCA—even the Boy Scouts. No less than fifty-eight newspapers from thirty-six states wrote positively about the bill, among them were twenty-six from the south where immigration restriction was usually favored.[29] On February 20, the editor of the *Galveston News* in Texas, a state known for restricting immigration, even came out for it: "It is impossible to offer sanctuary in this country to all refugees, however urgent their need. It would dishonor our traditions of humanity and freedom, however, to refuse the small measure of help contemplated by the Wagner resolution."[30] There was no sound rationale for rejecting the bill, save one: anti-Semitism. Those opposing the resolution on the grounds that immigrants would take jobs hardly had a case to object, given the age of the would-be newcomers.

Fear and anti-Semitism eventually killed the bill, as opposition mounted over concerns that its passage would be the first step to the repeal of immigration laws. Public sentiment shifted. A January 1939

Gallup poll found that Americans opposed the children's bill by a margin of two to one.[31] Four months later, a poll by the *Cincinnati Post* asked one thousand women about the issue: nearly eight in ten were opposed.[32] Laura Delano, wife of the immigration commissioner, further enflamed passions by crudely asserting that "20,000 charming children would all too soon grow up into 20,000 ugly adults."[33] Several powerful lobby groups using the battle cry of "America First," including the American Legion and the American Immigration Restrictionist League, pressured Congress into rejecting the bill. Opponents were angry at the lack of non-Jewish children. A writer in the *Nation* argued against the plan because it was "a Jewish bill."[34] Others complained that American children were also in need and should be taken care of first.[35] Ohio Senator Robert Taft made the absurd claim that in taking in the children, the government would be a party to breaking up Jewish families. He concluded that they would be better off staying in Germany![36] The bill died in committee before the summer was out. Ironically, the very next year when the issue of taking in British children was raised to keep them out of harm's way during the bombing of Britain, the Blitz, the administration worked with Congress to quickly approve the acceptance of five thousand. They were promptly shipped over to stay with relatives and host families.[37] Surely, the children of German Jews were in far graver danger. Another revealing event occurred in late 1940 when *Pets* magazine published the photo of a puppy under the heading "I want a home." It asked readers if they would be willing to provide a temporary shelter for a British purebred. Thousands of readers wrote in, offering to help.[38] As the Wagner bill was dying in committee, another drama was playing out just off America's east coast as a cruise ship packed with Jewish refugees sought haven.

NO SAFE HARBOR

In June 1939, the SS *St. Louis* was bound for Cuba with 936 passengers. All but six were Jewish refugees who had bought Cuban landing visas. Since most of the refugees were on waiting lists to enter the United States, they planned to stay in Cuba until being allowed to enter. Their plan was doomed from the start, as Cuban president Federico Laredo Bru signed a decree invalidating the certificates just before the ship left Hamburg. Their documents were now useless, and the passengers were not let off the ship once it reached Havana Harbor.[39] While most newspapers blamed the Cuban government for the crisis, some showed understanding for the Cuban decision because of the country's economic woes. Many American newspaper editors offered possible locations where the refugees could settle. Suggestions included British Guiana, Dutch Guiana, North Rhodesia, the Dominican Republic, and the Philippines.[40] These suggestions were not new. It was well-known that no suitable area and no country existed that was willing to admit Jewish refugees at this point in time. American officials made no attempt to help the refugees that had come agonizingly close to its coast. Their reluctance to act was firmly supported by the American people. Just months earlier, an April 1939 poll found that only 8 percent were willing to expand the quota for European refugees.[41] The saga of the *St. Louis* was used by the Nazis as a propaganda tool to reinforce their claim that the Jews were an inferior race that no one wanted. The *St. Louis* eventually returned to Hamburg. No one knows how many of its passengers later perished in the Holocaust. One small success story was the SS *Quanza*. In September 1940, the Portuguese freighter tried to reach Virginia with eighty-six Jewish refugees on board, after failing to receive permission to dock elsewhere. Only after Eleanor Roosevelt lobbied her husband to intervene were the passengers saved. Franklin Roosevelt circumvented strict visa protocols by issuing an Executive Order allowing the passengers to be admitted into the country, much to the dismay of State Department officials who were incensed by the action.[42]

NEWS OF THE HOLOCAUST EMERGES

In August 1942, an official of the World Jewish Congress in Geneva, Switzerland, received troubling news. Gerhart Riegner had obtained reliable information about a plan by Hitler to exterminate millions of European Jews. His source was a trusted friend who had met with a German businessman who said he had knowledge of the scheme. The confidential source would be identified decades later as industrialist Eduard Schulte. Riegner contacted local law professor Paul Guggenheim, who helped him write an urgent cable to be sent to American and British diplomats in Washington and London.[43] On the morning of August 8, Riegner visited both consulates in Geneva and relayed the information, which was sent by cipher. The original cable to London read as follows: "Received alarming report stating that, in the Fuehrer's Headquarters, a plan has been discussed, and is under consideration, according to which all Jews in countries occupied or controlled by Germany numbering 3 1/2 to 4 millions should, after deportation and concentration in the East, be at one blow exterminated, in order to resolve, once and for all the Jewish question in Europe. Action is reported to be planned for the autumn. Ways of execution are still being discussed including the use of prussic acid." At Guggenheim's urging, the end of the cable was cautiously worded: "We transmit this information with all the necessary reservation, as exactitude cannot be confirmed by us. Our informant is reported to have close connexions with the highest German authorities and his reports are generally reliable. Please inform and consult New York."[44]

Riegner asked that the cable be shared with Rabbi Stephen Wise of the World Jewish Congress in New York, a close confidant of President Roosevelt. But when the US State Department received the cable, they refused to share its contents, citing the "unsubstantiated character of the information."[45] Elbridge Durbrow, the department's assistant chief of eastern European affairs, opposed any move to disclose the information, based on "the fantastic nature of the allegation, and the impossibility of our being of any assistance if such action were taken." Historian Rebecca Erbelding has examined correspondence of State Department officials during this period and observed that they failed to understand "why atrocity information was transmitted, and were such reports true, they believed any assistance to the victims to be impossible."[46] It is clear from their foot-dragging and inaction that key State Department officials were at best apathetic, and almost certainly anti-Semitic. Wise eventually received news of the cable, but not from the Americans; it came from the British Consul. It was not until November 24, 1942, that Wise was given permission to release the information publicly after the US government had become convinced from various sources that the report was true. In reality, one key aspect of the cable was inaccurate: the claim that the mass exterminations were set to begin in autumn 1942. The mass killing of European Jews had been underway for over a year, in a systematic, ongoing process—not as a planned single blow, as stated in the telegram. However, the central premise was correct: the Nazis were intent on exterminating the Jews of Europe.[47]

While the Final Solution was formally approved in January 1942 at a gathering outside of Berlin, the Allies were already aware of the mass slaughter of Jews and other groups that was being perpetrated in Europe. Since summer 1941, and the German invasion of the Soviet Union, intercepts of German radio transmissions detailed "dozens of reports of mass executions" conducted by special mobile death squads of Nazi police and security personnel known as the *SS Einsatzgruppen*.[48] Clearly, by the time of Riegner's cable, the Roosevelt administration was aware that mass atrocities were taking place across Europe at the hands of the Nazis, their only uncertainty was as to the scale.

During 1943, several senior aides to Treasury Secretary Henry Morgenthau uncovered a pattern in the State Department: it became clear that some officials had been blocking efforts to rescue Jews. On January 16, 1944, FDR received a scathing report from the Treasury office, charging that officials in the State Department not only had been apathetic toward Jews but had been working to actively obstruct Jewish refugees from reaching sanctuary in the United States by denying them visas. Several Treasury aides helped to draft the report, which was written by an aid named Josiah DuBois and approved by Morgenthau. As the highest ranking Jew in the Roosevelt administration, Morgenthau's family had migrated from Germany, making him particularly sympathetic. DuBois, who was not Jewish, did not mince words. He began: "One of the greatest crimes in history, the slaughter of the Jewish people in Europe, is continuing unabated."[49] He went on to charge that State Department officials were complicit in the mass murder of Jews. "I am convinced on the basis of the information which is available to me that certain officials in our State Department, which is charged with carrying out this policy, have been guilty not only of gross procrastination and wilful failure to act, but even of wilful attempts to prevent action from being taken to rescue Jews from Hitler."

The report said that the State Department had placed unnecessary restrictions on Jewish refugees who were trying to obtain visas to enter the country, all under the guise of security. It noted that many asylum seekers were denied entry because they had close relatives in Axis-controlled countries, which stoked fears that they may be coerced to act as spies under the threat of harm to family members. Another complaint was the ludicrous amount of red tape that was required for a refugee to be sponsored, including references from two reputable American citizens. Historian David Wyman would later observe that Assistant Secretary of State Breckinridge Long had constructed a "paper wall" of bureaucracy and red tape designed to keep Jewish immigrants out.[50] DuBois wrote tersely: "It is obvious of course that these restrictions are not essential for security reasons. Thus refugees upon arriving in this country could be placed in internment camps similar to those used for the Japanese on the West Coast and released only after a satisfactory investigation. Furthermore, even if we took these refugees and treated them as prisoners of war it would be better than letting them die."[51]

DuBois was blunt and forceful in his criticism of Long, who was in charge of issuing European visas, whom he claimed had given "false and misleading" information about the refugee crisis, and downplayed the mass killing of Jews. DuBois continued: "State Department officials not only have failed to facilitate the obtaining of information concerning Hitler's plans to exterminate the Jews of Europe but in their official capacity have gone so far as to surreptitiously attempt to stop the obtaining of information concerning the murder of the Jewish population in Europe." DuBois remarked that "the evidence supporting this conclusion is so shocking and so tragic that it is difficult to believe."[52] After digesting the report's findings, Roosevelt moved quickly to create the War Refugee Board on January 22, with the goal being the "immediate rescue and relief of the Jews of Europe and other victims of enemy persecution."

THE FIFTH COLUMN SCARE

Historian Bruce Hodge has examined the actions of Breckinridge Long between 1940 and 1944, when he was in charge of the State Department's visa section. Already an enormously powerful position in the best of times, during the war, the role of the assistant secretary of state was even more important; decisions made by the person in this position often determined who lived and died. After analyzing archives and his personal diary, Hodge concludes that Long was a product of his time, and his apathy was a reflection of the prevailing war hysteria and fears of the fifth column infiltrating the country.[53] The term *fifth column* originated in the 1930s during the Spanish Civil War, when General Emilio Mola, who was in charge of four columns of troops heading for Madrid, proclaimed that he had a fifth column of sympathizers inside the city. The term refers to any group in a country at war who are aiding its enemies.[54] As early as 1940, before America had entered the war, Long was advocating for tougher visa restrictions out of fears that enemy agents were already in the country. He wrote that America was harboring "thousands of aliens, some of them known to be active German agents, and many illegally in this country."[55] Fifth column fears were heightened in May 1940, with the Tyler Kent affair. A clerk at the US embassy in London, Kent managed to copy hundreds of sensitive documents before his arrest. Fearing that other embassies may have been compromised, Long concluded that Kent's activities "made it apparent that he may have accomplices and confederates or that there may be other cells . . . of another Government representing their interests in our own offices abroad."[56]

Some Americans were hesitant to raise the issue of Jewish refugees, for fear of being viewed as disloyal and unpatriotic.[57] During the late 1930s and early 1940s, a significant portion of American Jews were noncommittal toward German Jewry, despite the steady stream of news reports detailing the hardships they were facing.[58] Historian Joyce Delgado writes that disagreement and disorder "permeated every aspect of the Jewish community's plans to help the victims of Nazism. Some Jewish organizations championed emigration to the United States while others opposed this, fearful that increased Jewish immigration might result in violent anti-Semitic eruptions . . . 20% of the American Jews polled favoured the absolute exclusionist policy."[59] By summer 1940, a Roper poll found that seven in ten Americans believed that a German fifth column was at work in the country.[60] A Gallup survey conducted at about the same time found that 48 percent of Americans were convinced that *their own communities* had been infiltrated.[61] During summer and fall of 1940, several prominent newspapers each published a series of articles on how the fifth column had gained a foothold in America. These included the *New York Journal-American*, the *New York Post*, the *Pittsburgh Press*, and the *New York World-Telegram*. While FBI Director J. Edgar Hoover had earlier urged Americans to be on guard against the fifth column, he had grown so alarmed by the spy panic that by the following year he was warning against the dangers posed by "vigilantes," "fearmongers," and "hysterical mobs" that were threatening American democracy.[62]

In his study of American immigration policy during the war, historian Saul Friedman concurs with Hodge's assessment that national self-interests were more influential than anti-Semitism in solidifying attitudes against Jewish refugees.[63] Well before the war, conspiracy theorists had spread the notion that Hitler was preparing a network of spies to infiltrate the country.[64] This fear grew into a full-fledged spy mania that lasted from 1938 until 1942. Although the threat was real, it was massively inflated. As Interior Secretary Harold Ickes later observed, many citizens had worked themselves into a panic and viewed "every alien as a possible enemy spy or saboteur."[65] Even President Roosevelt contributed to the scare. On May 26, 1940, he told a national radio audience: "Today's threat to our national security is not a matter of military weapons alone. We know of new methods of attack. The Trojan Horse. The Fifth Column that betrays a nation unprepared for treachery. Spies, saboteurs and traitors are the actors in this new tragedy. With all of this, we must and will deal vigorously."[66] By 1941, the Justice Department and the FBI tried to reassure an anxious public that spies were not lurking in every community. It was true that the Nazis had pro-German spies and groups in America—people who supported the idea of a superior Aryan race and the concept of a European Reich. But these groups never formed a spy network, and they did not pose a threat to the extent that the American public liked to believe and that the press attributed to them. Nevertheless, the idea of an underground movement of Nazi spies made good headlines and drew much attention. The media reported on Nazi groups that pledged allegiance to a foreign power and had militaristic training, leaving the impression that they posed an actual threat to the American people, when they did not.[67]

SPIES EVERYWHERE

The impact of the espionage scare on the refugee issue cannot be understated. In his examination of the fifth column scare in the United States during the Second World War, historian Francis MacDonnell found that despite the commotion and concern, "Axis operations in the United States never amounted to much," and what existed was easily countered by the FBI. Nevertheless, by the time the United States had entered the war in December 1941, he stated that "the Fifth Column scare had deeply penetrated the nation's psyche."[68] In one instance during January 1940, the FBI arrested, with great media fanfare, seventeen members of the pro-Nazi Christian Front and charged them with plotting terrorist acts. Hoover claimed that they had intended to "knock off about a dozen congressmen" and "blow up the goddamned Police Department" [of New York City].[69] When their case went to trial, it was so weak that a jury failed to convict a single member. Some of the material entered as evidence against them was laughable. For instance, two of the confiscated weapons included an 1873 Springfield rifle and an old cavalry sword.[70] Of the few cases that were uncovered, most involved amateurs who were easily captured. Another prominent case involved twenty-eight-year-old Herbert Bahr. In June 1942, the German engineer boarded an ocean liner from Sweden and traveled to New York, where he tried to pass himself off as a refugee. While he may have been a respectable engineer, he was a thoroughly incompetent spy. He was quickly caught after his story unraveled and he admitted to spying for Germany after being given $7,000 by the Gestapo and sent to steal industrial secrets. He drew the attention of authorities after he was found to be carrying the entire wad of money in his pants. After a rushed trial, he was sentenced to thirty years in prison.[71]

The motion-picture industry also fed the flames of hysteria. Between 1940 and 1942 alone, Hollywood released no less than seventy-two films dealing with the fifth column.[72] The result was a refugee spy scare that would grip the nation and cloud judgments on the immigration issue for much of the war. The failure of the US State Department to relax immigration restrictions and accept more Jews was a reflection of the spy mania. *Time* captured the mood, reporting that from Lake George, New York, to Baton Rouge, Louisiana, America had become a nation engulfed by "morbid fears of invisible enemies," as people began to chase "ghosts and phantoms."[73] George Britt's 1940 book, *The Fifth Column Is Here*, further fanned the hysteria, becoming an immediate bestseller. In it he made the sensational claim that over a million enemy agents and subversives were scattered about the country, including Germans, Italians, and Communists.[74] After one fireside chat by Roosevelt about the threat posed from subversives, public anxieties increased to such an extent that FBI offices received nearly three thousand reports of suspicious people in a single day, nearly twice the number for the entire previous year.[75] The rise of the spy mania can be tracked by looking at the number of reports of suspected espionage and subversive acts that were received by the FBI. Between 1933 and 1938, the bureau averaged thirty-five reports per year. In 1939 it shot up to 1,615, and by the following year on a single day in May, an astounding 2,871 complaints were logged. In fact, when the FBI released these figures, J. Edgar Hoover noted that the number of confirmed sabotage cases to that point was "negligible."[76]

HISTORY REPEATS

While America prides itself as a nation of immigrants, it is no small irony that many of the descendants of those who flocked to our shores seeking protection from discrimination and bigotry have shown intolerance toward Islamic and Central American refugees. These hostilities are grounded not in reality but in a fear of the foreign and the unfamiliar. The rise of American Islamophobia and depictions of Muslims as terrorists parallels historical attempts to demonize Catholics as enemies of the state, and Jews as Nazi collaborators. Even before the United States was founded, the Puritans fled religious persecution in England by voyaging to the Massachusetts Bay Colony to worship in freedom. The persecuted soon became the persecutors, as their leaders began arresting and executing those who were different from them, culminating in the infamous Salem witch trials of 1692. The fundamental problem facing Jewish refugees during World War II was that fear and anti-Semitism were driving the government's refugee policy. Throughout the war, there remained a widespread belief that Jews were an inferior Semitic race that posed a threat to America's security. There is no other way to explain the refusal to accept twenty thousand Jewish children, or why America's wartime German refugee quota was only at 10 percent of capacity. Few events in our history compare to the government's treatment of Jewish refugees during the Second World War. It was a preventable, human-created catastrophe that remains one of our greatest failures. In the second decade of the twenty-first century, history is repeating itself as the American government attempts to block the intake of Islamic refugees who are fleeing war and persecution and Central American asylum seekers who are trying to escape poverty and drug and gang violence. Equally disturbing is the realization that America and much of the world have failed to learn from the lessons of the past. If we fail to act again, history will judge us harshly.

CHAPTER 8

"BE WARY OF THE WOLF IN SHEEP'S CLOTHING!"

Muslim Refugees and Immigrants— Just the Latest Fear

For it is clear enough that under certain conditions men respond as powerfully to fictions as they do to realities, and that in many cases they help to create the very fictions to which they respond.
—Walter Lippmann, *Public Opinion*, 1922

Roman statesman Seneca the Elder once wrote that "we are more often frightened than hurt; and we suffer more from imagination than from reality."[1] His words ring as true today as they did over two thousand years ago. As with earlier American moral panics involving ethnic, religious, and political minorities, the same familiar patterns emerge in the Muslim Scare, as threats are exaggerated, statistics are distorted, stereotypes are proliferated, and laws are adopted as authorities rush to address the perceived danger. Catholic Americans were once typified as blindly following orders from Rome, just as today's Muslims are often portrayed as secret supporters or sympathizers of ISIS who are unable to think for themselves. Both have been vilified and lumped into a single simplistic category: religious extremists. As Islamic historian John Esposito notes, the contemporary coverage of Muslims and the Islamic world "assumes the existence of a monolithic Islam in which all Muslims are the same,

182

believing, feeling, thinking, and acting as one."[2] In reality, it is far more complex and diverse, but in the war on terror and the subsequent vilification of Muslim immigrants, perception often passes for reality.

Based on the treatment of the immigration debate by the conservative media and the Trump administration, one could be forgiven for thinking that Islamic refugees and migrants pose a grave and imminent threat to the security of the United States and its citizens. However, the opposite is true. Americans are far more likely to die from falling off ladders, slipping in bathtubs, or being shot by their spouses than they are of being murdered by a Muslim terrorist from overseas. Each year, about twenty people are killed by cows, dozens die from accidents while mowing lawns, and more than five thousand choke to death.[3] While far deadlier than terrorists, lawn mowers, ladders, and chicken sandwiches rarely make headlines. An average of one American dies each year from encounters with sharks—twenty times less than cows, yet few people lie awake at night worrying about being squashed or kicked by large bovines.[4] Shark attacks grab the headlines while more common, mundane causes of death are barely noticed. Take the example of domestic airline safety. Between 2010 and 2017, not a single passenger traveling on a US commercial jet lost their life as a result of an accident. The global statistics are equally impressive. For every seven million flights, there is one fatality.[5] The Islamic immigration hysteria that is gripping America is a textbook example of a moral panic, with the reaction out of proportion to the threat. Americans should be focused on more realistic threats. The lifetime odds of dying in an automobile accident are roughly one in one hundred. Even the odds of being struck and killed by lightning—roughly one in 161,000—are far more likely than dying at the hands of a terrorist on US soil.[6] The threat must be kept in perspective.

A recent study of all terrorist incidents by foreigners on US soil found that the odds of dying in any given year were three and a half million to one (i.e., 3,500,000 to 1)—and this includes the 2,983 people who perished in the terror attacks on September 11, 2001. The threat posed by refugees is in the *billions* to one, while the odds of being murdered by a terrorist who has entered the country illegally is about one in 11 *billion*.[7] Over a recent forty-year period, out of 3.2 million refugees admitted to the United States, only twenty were classified as terrorists. Of these, just three were responsible for murders. None were Muslims. Each case took place during the 1970s and were Cubans assassinating politicians or dissidents who were living in exile.[8]

The reality of the terrorist threat to the United States is very different than what is being portrayed by the Trump administration. In January 2018, the Departments of Justice and Homeland Security issued an alarming report on the danger posed by foreign terrorists. They found that between September 11, 2001, and 2016, 73 percent of those convicted by the United States of engaging in international terrorism, 402 of 549, were born outside the country. In the report, Attorney General Jeff Sessions stated that it "reveals an indisputable sobering reality—our immigration system has undermined our national security and public safety."[9] However, these figures focus exclusively on international terrorism and ignore a more crucial statistic: the number of people killed by terrorists on US soil. Do so, and the statistics flip. Alex Nowrasteh of the Cato Institute has included the most recent figures through 2017, and he found that since 2002, "native-born Americans were responsible for 78 percent of all murders in terrorist attacks committed on U.S. soil while foreign-born terrorists only committed 22 percent." These numbers translate into rare events. Nowrasteh writes that from 2002 through 2017, the odds of dying in a terror attack on US soil by a native-born American was roughly one in 41 million per year. "During the same period, the chance of being murdered by a foreign-born terrorist was about one in 145 million per year. The total chance was about one in 32 million a year."[10] The Trump administration's report that sensationalizes the issue is an attempt to use the machinery of the federal government to manipulate statistics in support of its doom-and-gloom pronouncements about the threat from Muslim immigrants.

ISLAMOPHOBIA

American government policy toward immigrants is too often driven by hysteria and misinformation about the existence of phantom evildoers who are intent on undermining our democracy and destroying our way of life. Attempts by the Trump administration to halt the intake of Syrian refugees over fears that they are likely to commit acts of terror are a thinly veiled form of discrimination that uses a religious test to determine who should be allowed into the country. Parallels to the past are unmistakable. Former Republican presidential candidate Chris Christie has asserted that until vetting rules are tightened, he opposes the entry of *any* Syrian refugees, including "orphans under five."[11] This hardline policy should evoke haunting memories for American Jews and the failure of Congress to accept twenty thousand Jewish children from Nazi Germany. The real reason for turning away these child refugees was anti-Semitism, just as the real reason for trying to stop the flow of Syrian refugees from entering the United States is Islamophobia.

The reluctance to take in Syrian refugees has deeper roots than concerns over vetting. Conservative politicians such as Texas Republican Ted Cruz advocate accepting Christian refugees from Syria but delaying the intake of Muslims until they can be adequately assessed. For some, it appears that no amount of vetting will be satisfactory. Ironically and contrary to popular belief, the vetting of Syrian refugees under Barack Obama was rigorous and typically took between one and two years for approval. It began with an interview by representatives of the United Nations who first decide whether a person qualifies. Before this, many languished in refugee camps for years, hoping for an interview. Only the most vulnerable are considered, who together compose less than 1 percent of the global refugee population. Once referred to the United States for possible resettlement, these few refugees were interviewed by the State Department and required to undergo several background checks on criminal and terrorist databases, and three separate fingerprint checks, before their case was even considered. At this point, they underwent a fraud check, an in-depth interview with Homeland Security, and screening for contagious diseases. Even if they managed to clear each of these hurdles and were approved for resettlement, due to the length of time it took to vet applicants, a final multi-agency security screening was scheduled just before their departure.[12] It is hard to imagine a more rigorous process.

Some conservatives deny that attempts to bar immigrants and refugees from certain Middle Eastern countries amounts to a Muslim ban. The award for the most creative explanation goes to former Republican presidential candidate Mike Huckabee, who argues that Syrian society is so different from America's that their lives "would be completely disrupted" and they would have trouble assimilating. He then raised the issue of climate: "Can you imagine bringing in a bunch of Syrian refugees who've lived in the desert their whole lives that are suddenly thrown into an English speaking community? Where it's maybe in Minnesota . . . 20 degrees below zero? I . . . just I don't understand what we possibly can be thinking."[13] While the resettlement would undoubtedly disrupt their lives, what about the onslaught of suicide bombings, air strikes, kidnappings, rape, torture, and beheadings that they were forced to endure? In comparison, tolerating cold temperatures for a few months of the year would be a minor inconvenience. If he were discussing Christian refugees from Syria, one wonders whether Huckabee, a former ordained minister, would not be breaking out the jackets, blankets, and space heaters? If climate is the real concern, why not resettle them in one of the warmer Southern states or the American desert? Ted Cruz has labeled the acceptance of large numbers of Islamic refugees from Syria as "nothing less than lunacy."[14] However, he has an entirely different view of Syrian Christians: "On the other hand, Christians who are being targeted for genocide, for persecution . . . we should be providing safe haven to them." When asked to justify his reasoning for treating Christians differently, he asserted, "There is no meaningful risk of Christians committing acts of terror."[15] This claim is unfounded. The deadliest act of domestic terrorism in American history occurred in 1995 when white supremacist and self-proclaimed Christian Timothy McVeigh blew up the Oklahoma City Alfred P. Murrah Federal Building, killing 168 people and injuring over 680 others. Tennessee Republican Congressman Glen Casada is even more extreme, calling on the governor to use the National Guard to remove Syrian refugees from his state and halt any further resettlements.[16] The views of these politicians may be popular with their constituents, but they are grounded in fear and fantasy, not reality.

Despite the statistically low threat of terrorism from Islamic refugees and immigrants, the figures are likely even lower than what is being reported. Many attacks that are reported as terrorism are dubious. When twenty-nine-year-old Omar Mateen walked into the Pulse nightclub in Orlando, Florida, on the night of June 12, 2016, and gunned down forty-nine patrons, he was quickly labeled as an Islamic extremist by the FBI. During the ordeal, he even called the police to pledge his allegiance to ISIS.[17] But once investigators delved into his past, they found a man with a history of spousal violence, anger management, hatred of gays, and mental-health issues.[18] The weakest of these factors were ties to a radical Islamic ideology. His attributing the event to ISIS appears to have been an afterthought.[19] Mateen was neither an immigrant nor a refugee: he was an American citizen born in New Hyde Park, New York, to Afghan parents. As a teen, he attended a school for students with behavioral problems and was later kicked out of training as a police cadet for making a gun threat. His first wife said that he would beat her up for not doing the laundry. There is little doubt that Mateen was a troubled, emotionally conflicted person who was battling personal demons. Although he was Islamic, no one who knew him described him as particularly religious.[20] In the case of Sayfullo Saipov, the Uzbekistan-born ISIS-sympathizer who struck and killed eight people with his rented pickup truck in Lower Manhattan on October 31, 2017, authorities believe that he was radicalized *after* arriving in the United States.[21]

While the threat of a terrorist attack is higher in some European countries than it is in America, it is still low. On the evening of July 14, 2016, an Islamic extremist was at the wheel of a nineteen-ton truck that barreled down the Promenade des Anglais in Nice, France, plowing through crowds who were celebrating Bastille Day. Eighty-six people were killed. Over a two-year span beginning in 2015, 247 Europeans died at the hands of terrorists. Most were in France. Although these statistics are appalling, risk analyst Tom Pollock places the attacks in perspective. He calculates the odds of being killed in a terrorist attack in France at less than 0.0002 percent (two ten-thousandths of 1 percent).[22] One week after the Nice attack, an eighteen-year-old Iranian German opened fire on passers-by in a Munich shopping center, killing nine. The mass murderer, David Sonboly, still looked like a schoolboy and had no criminal record. Media outlets assumed that the shooter was a Muslim terrorist, as one witness thought they heard him say the words "*Allahu Akbar!*" ("God is Great," in Arabic). On Facebook and Twitter, people demanded a stop to Muslim immigration. However, not one of the dozens of other witnesses ever verified this claim. Many bystanders clearly heard him shout anti-foreign insults and proclaim: "I am German!" Some of his rantings were even caught on video, but there was no reference to acting in the name of Islam.[23] A police investigation quickly ruled out religion as a motive—unless it was to target Muslims. Authorities said that he had recently spent two months in a psychiatric facility and was subjected to prolonged bullying at school.[24] A search of his family's apartment revealed that he was an admirer of Anders Breivik, a Nazi sympathizer and white supremacist who killed seventy-seven people in a mass shooting in Norway in 2011. The attack in Munich was carried out on the fifth anniversary of Breivik's killing spree.[25] Sonboly had previously expressed pride in sharing the same birthday as Adolf Hitler and had boasted to friends that he was a proud Aryan, claiming that they had originated from what is now present-day Iran. Those who knew him said that he had a seething hatred of Arabs and Turks. The shooter killed himself, so we may never fully understand his motive.[26] This episode is a good example of how people who commit violent acts are often immediately identified as Islamic terrorists when the real trigger is mental illness or other nonreligious factors causing anger and psychological distress.

HISTORICAL ROOTS OF THE ISLAMIC SCARE

Many of America's founding fathers were fierce defenders of religious freedoms. Both Thomas Jefferson and George Washington used Islam as an example of the need to show tolerance for even the most exotic religious beliefs. Jefferson once wrote that "the Jew and the Gentile, the Christian and the Mahometan [Muslim], the Hindoo [Hindu], and infidel of every denomination" were deserving of protection by the government.[27] But as time passed, tolerance faded, and the word *Muslim* became synonymous with the backward and the primitive. Early American travelers to the Middle East portrayed Muslims as superstitious and warlike—a view held by Connecticut explorer John Ledyard after traveling to Egypt, and missionary Eli Smith, who spoke of the "arrogance and blood-thirsty cruelty" of "Mohammedans."[28] Samuel Clemens (Mark Twain) traveled to the Holy Land in 1867 and, after visiting Syria, Palestine, and Egypt, compared Muslims to "primitive" American Indians: "They reminded me much of Indians, did these people. They sat in silence, and with tireless patience watched over every motion with that vile, uncomplaining impoliteness which is so truly Indian, and which makes a white man so nervous and uncomfortable and savage that he wants to exterminate the whole tribe."[29] During the early twentieth century, many Americans learned about Muslims from the popular writings of British archeologist Thomas Lawrence. Better known as Lawrence of Arabia, in his bestselling book *Seven Pillars of Wisdom*, he portrays Arab "Moslems" as simple, "dogmatic people" who were incapable of understanding deep thought. He saw Arabs as an immature race lacking the capacity to question skeptically, and Islam an attractive religion to primitive peoples.[30] President Teddy Roosevelt concurred, writing in 1907 that "it is impossible to expect moral, intellectual and material well-being where Mohammedanism is supreme." [31]

Lothrop Stoddard, the American eugenicist and champion of white supremacy whose influential writings portrayed Asians, Jews, Mexicans, and Native Americans as belonging to an inferior race, also played a role in keeping Muslim immigrants from entering the United States. In his 1921 book, *The New World of Islam*, he observed that the Muslim world would inevitably decline with the collapse of the Ottoman Empire after World War I, as it faced the "superior races" of the West. He describes the West as "overflowing with vitality and striding at the forefront of human progress," while painting a bleak picture of the East as "sunk in lethargy and decrepitude." [32] In 1922, Stoddard testified before Congress that he opposed admitting refugees from Muslim countries such as Turkey, due to their poor "national character" and "racial mixture."[33] He described them as a "very largely parasitic population, living by their wits, by unproductive means of labor, by petty trading, by graft.... Wherever they have gone in great numbers they have exercised a very baneful influence." The chairman of the hearing observed that any Muslims trying to enter the United States were required to denounce polygamy because the law prohibited its preaching and practice.[34] This was seen as a way to keep Muslims from migrating to the United States.

While the events of 9/11 contributed to the widespread perception of Muslims as terrorists, over the previous century, many Americans perceived the Islamic world as uncivilized and barbaric. Films of the early nineteenth century depicted Arabs as warmongering, camel-riding, sword-waving villains. Film historian Rubina Ramji remarks that in recent times, "old stereotypes have been replaced by new ones. The sheik and lusty despot have slowly disappeared, leaving hijackers, kidnappers, and terrorists," while Muslim women have disappeared behind the veil.[35] In 1942, movie theaters across the country showed the popular serial *The Perils of Nyoka*, which depicted Arab warriors waging jihad against "white infidels." Serials were the equivalent of weekly TV shows before the advent of television. Each week, moviegoers would watch the screening of the latest installment before viewing the main feature. Two years later, *The Desert Hawk* aired; this was a serial portraying Arabs as slave traders who relished in rape and torture.[36] In more recent times, one of the most popular TV programs after 9/11 was *24*, which featured CIA agent Jack Bauer hunting down terrorists and radicals, most of them Muslims who were threatening the United States. Capitalizing on the show's success, similar programs followed, complete with sleeper cells in peaceful suburbs, poisoned tap water, and an atomic bomb planted in the center of a major city. One of the more popular of these spin-offs was *Homeland*, which featured Carrie Mathison and her arch enemy, terrorist Abu Nazir—a show where Muslims were presented as terrorists dedicated to destroying Westerners.

HOMELAND INSECURITY

The moral panic over Muslim Americans and immigrants is reminiscent of the American Catholic Scare, the Jewish refugee panic, and the suspicions over the loyalty of German Americans during World War I. Each of these episodes were incubated in a climate of ignorance and fear that led to the victimization of innocent citizens. During the Catholic and German sagas, the shadow of suspicion often fell on teachers who were accused of subverting Protestant values. Today, teachers have faced the wrath of angry parents for simply including lessons on Islam. Events in Tennessee are typical, where the uproar over teaching about Islam in public schools has grown into a major social movement, with worried parents packing board meetings and lobbying their legislators to change the curriculum. In Tennessee, the target of their fear has been sixth- and seventh-grade teachers of world history, where the social studies standards include teaching about the major religions. In trying to combat Islamophobia and introduce students to basic beliefs of the religion, many teachers have been accused of indoctrinating children to accept Islam, or attempting to convert them. Conversely, some parents have claimed that Christianity was being ignored and Christian values denigrated. In classic moral-panic fashion, government agencies and politicians have acted on the complaints, resulting in the Tennessee Department of Education speeding up its review of the social studies curriculum by two full years.[37]

Advocacy groups devoted to stopping the teaching about Islam in schools have popped up across the country. Leading the charge in Tennessee is the American Center for Law and Justice, a right-wing Christian organization created with the explicit purpose to stop what it views as the Islamic indoctrination of public schools. Among their alarmist claims are "reports of innocent school children being taught to pray Islamic prayers, make prayer rugs, and practice other Islamic rituals," while Christian children were "being harassed."[38] In some states, students have allegedly been forced to recite the phrase, "There is no God but Allah, and Muhammad is his messenger"—the Islamic conversion creed—implying that such lessons are thinly veiled attempts to convert them.[39] This episode parallels the Catholic Scare, when rumors circulated that Protestant children enrolled in convent schools were being indoctrinated into accepting a host of Catholic tenets and rituals. In Tennessee, conservative media outlets like Fox News have fanned the flames of anti-Islamic hysteria by airing stories on alleged attempts at conversion.[40] In the Williamson County School District, board member Beth Burgos objected to the teaching of Islamic tenets and urged the use of textbooks that include the notion of jihad in order to highlight the supposedly violent nature of the religion.[41] She also wanted the right to review the material being taught, so as to ensure that it had not been "provided by a terrorist organization, or individuals, groups or countries that support or have links to terrorism."[42]

In White County, Tennessee, a group of concerned residents formed Citizens Against Islamic Indoctrination and placed an ad in the local

Sparta Expositor, warning citizens: "ISLAMIC INDOCTRINATION IS IN SCHOOLS ACROSS OUR STATE AND OUR NATION."[43] It urged people to attend a town hall meeting and was accompanied by a photo of children in Islamic garb brandishing automatic rifles. The caption read: "While your children are learning to tolerate these children, these children are training to kill your children." It is difficult to imagine school administrators in predominantly conservative, white, Christian counties, being a party to converting students to Islam. As Daoud Abudiab, a Muslim parent in Williamson County, observes: "You would think they would go into Davidson County, where they're liberal and there are school teachers who are Muslim. But they're not worried about it there; they're worried about it where there [are] no Muslim teachers. They're worried about it in Columbia, where there isn't, to my knowledge, a single Muslim student, and certainly no teachers."[44]

At Heritage Middle School in tiny Thompson's Station, Tennessee, a twelve-year-old girl reflected popular sentiments by expressing worry over her social studies lessons. "I am being taught in class that Islam is a peaceful religion, yet there are many historical and modern-day examples of violent killings and persecution in the name of Allah and Islam," she said.[45] However, the same could be said for Christianity, which also has a long history of violence and persecution, and its own concept of jihad by another name: Crusade or Holy War. The parallels with Islamic terrorism are unmistakable, from the medieval Crusades and continental European witch-hunts, to the Salem witch trials and the Ku Klux Klan. Throughout history, groups identifying as Christians have used the Bible to justify acts that by any definition of the word would be classified as terrorism. Many Christians complain that anyone engaging in such violent activities are not true Christians. A similar argument has been made by Muslims for decades—most recently with the "Not in My Name" movement.

In Florida, when a parent complained about the teaching of Islamic history in the public school, Fox News reported the case under the caption, "Forcing Faith." The father, Ron Wagner, claimed that "students were instructed to recite this prayer as the first pillar of Islam, off of the board at the teacher's instruction." The phrase, "There is no god, but God. Muhamad is the messenger of God," is known to Muslims as the *shahada* or statement of faith. Wagner's complaint prompted an investigation by the school district, which found that there had been no attempt by the teacher to indoctrinate or convert students, some of whom explicitly said they were not forced to recite the prayer out loud.[46] At La Plata High School in Maryland, a parent became irate when an eleventh-grade student was assigned a three-page essay on the five pillars of Islam, Mohammed, and Mecca. Her father, a former Iraq War veteran, complained so vehemently over the school's ability to "force-feed our kids Islam" that he was banned from school grounds.[47] The teacher required the student to memorize the five pillars and to write and recite the *shahada*. Ibrahim Hooper of the Council on American-Islamic Relations characterized the situation as a "hysterical knee-jerk negative reaction to anything to do with Islam or Muslims in our society."[48] He also noted the absurdity of the concern. "To merely say the *shahada*, the declaration of faith, or to understand what Muslims believe—it in no way converts you to Islam, that's a ridiculous notion. Islam is a belief system. You've got to believe in it or you're not a Muslim." The school defended the action on the grounds that it was part of the world history curriculum.[49]

In New Jersey, a school health handout that included a quote from the Qur'an prompted a fierce backlash from parents.[50] At another Jersey school, a history teacher of Muslim faith filed a lawsuit alleging that she was fired after numerous complaints over her teaching about Islam. Among the concerns was her playing a video featuring Malala Yousafzai, who would later win the Nobel Peace Prize. Her lawsuit stated that the video was shown by another teacher without any complaints, and that she was told "she could not teach current events in the same manner as her non-Arab, non-Palestinian and non-Muslim colleagues."[51] The teacher, Sireen Hashem, said that she followed the same curriculum as other history teachers at her school. To make matters worse, after losing her job, she said that two FBI agents interviewed her after receiving a tip that she had made threats against the school. Prior to her teaching position, she had worked on international relations at the United Nations.[52]

Colleges and universities have also not been immune from the panic over promoting Islam. When in January 2015, Duke University announced its intention to amplify the *adhan* or Muslim call to prayer from the chapel bell tower, it triggered such a social media firestorm that it was reversed within forty-eight hours. In much of the Muslim world, the *adhan* is routinely broadcast five times a day to denote the onset of prayers. Duke officials had intended to amplify the call just once per week to announce the beginning of Friday prayers; Friday is the Muslim holy day, when adherents are expected to worship at a mosque. Previously, as is customary in Islam, a single person is designated to call out the prayer, but without any amplification. It takes about three minutes to complete. The university said its reversal was based more on security concerns than political ones, noting that they had received "a number of credible threats against Muslim students, faculty, and staff" over the issue.[53] However, Duke was also facing a significant economic backlash, as Franklin Graham, son of the famous evangelist Reverend Billy Graham, quickly organized an online protest under the hashtag #boycottduke. On Facebook, Graham called on alumni and donors to withhold their support from the university until the policy was reversed. His plea was shared over 77,000 times.[54] In trying to explain the reaction, religious-diversity expert Issac Weiner observes that "it is easier to close one's eyes than one's ears. . . . Sounds demand our attention more insistently than do sights. When confronted by something we don't want to see, we know that we can just look away. But when we hear something we don't like, we often feel compelled to respond."[55]

In December 2015, a political-science teacher at Wheaton College in Illinois was placed on administrative leave for creating a Facebook post linking Christianity and Islam as sister religions with similar roots. Dr. Larycia Hawkins, who identifies as Christian, had taught at the school for the previous eight years without incident, and at the time of her suspension she was wearing a hijab to school to mark Advent, the period leading up to Christmas day. She did so as an act of solidarity against the intolerance being shown against her sister religion. She wrote: "I stand in religious solidarity with Muslims because they . . . are people of the book. And as Pope Francis stated last week, we worship the same God . . . we are formed of the same primordial clay, descendants of the same cradle of humankind."[56] The links between Christianity and Islam are indisputable; followers of Christianity, Judaism, and Islam all attribute the revelations of the scriptures of their holy books to the God of Abraham. Jesus of Nazareth is even mentioned in the Qur'an as a prophet. Hawkins said that school administrators tried to get her to resign, planned to revoke her tenure, and were particularly concerned about her wearing a hijab to school. She never taught at the school again and eventually took another position elsewhere.[57]

Concerns over the use of Arabic in public parallels the German Scare, when the mere use of the language was sufficient to raise concerns that the speakers were kaiser sympathizers or were acting on his orders. During the present climate of intolerance, there have been several incidents involving Muslim airline passengers being removed from flights over suspicions that they were terrorists, based merely on their appearance, dress, and language. On April 6, 2016, a political-science student at the University of California at Berkeley was removed from a Southwest Airlines flight and interviewed by the FBI after speaking Arabic on his mobile phone as the plane was preparing to take off. An Arabic-speaking passenger thought they overheard him say *shahid*, meaning martyr.[58] Khairuldeen Makhzoomi, a twenty-six-year-old refugee from Iraq, said he was talking to his uncle in Baghdad when an airline employee told him: "Sir, you need to step out of the plane right now."[59] Upon disembarking, he was greeted by three police officers. They called in the FBI, who ushered him into a room. One of the agents reportedly asked: "Okay, you need to be honest with me. Tell us everything you know about martyrdom."

He was eventually released. Ironically, the previous day, he had met and talked with United Nations Secretary General Ban Ki-moon at a lecture in Los Angeles. The airline later told the *Washington Post*, "We regret any less than positive experience a Customer has," but that they were only following procedure. Three months later, a businessman from the United Arab Emirates was arrested at a hotel in Avon, Ohio, when someone mistook him for a member of ISIS. The person phoned local police to report a suspicious man speaking Arabic in the lobby, wearing "a full head dress" and carrying two disposable phones. The caller said that he had pledged himself to ISIS. After police arrived with assault rifles drawn and forced him to the ground, they learned that no one actually heard the man pledge himself to ISIS.[60]

As with the Jewish refugee panic and earlier scares involving Japanese and German subversives, social paranoia has grown to such proportions that law enforcement has been kept busy chasing fanciful tips on suspected extremists. The present atmosphere is also reminiscent of the 1950s Red Scare, when Americans flooded switchboards to turn in their neighbors, fearing they were Communists. The Trump administration has contributed to a similar situation by creating an immigration hotline in April 2017, to report crimes committed by immigrants. A review of the phone logs reveals that hundreds of citizens had used it "to make secret accusations about their immigrant neighbors, coworkers, and ex-friends."[61] American Muslims and immigrants have been falsely accused of everything from starting the California wildfires of October 2017 to making bombs.[62] In one infamous case during September 2015, fourteen-year-old Ahmed Mohamed of Irving, Texas, was arrested by police for bringing a homemade clock to his high school after it was mistaken for a bomb.[63]

The current atmosphere of Islamic intolerance is being fueled by the Trump administration's attempts to portray Muslim Americans as an imminent threat in the form of a Trojan Horse—an enemy within. During 2017, there were 133 incidents involving the targeting of mosques across the country.[64] In Ypsilanti, Michigan, a mosque was burned to the ground. In Bloomington, Minnesota, an explosive device was detonated during morning prayers. A mosque in Tucson, Arizona, was broken into and copies of the Qur'an torn up. For the entirety of 2016, forty-six such incidents were recorded. In January 2018, the Council on American-Islamic Relations filed a civil-rights complaint in Michigan after several Muslim students said they were denied the opportunity to start an Islamic society on the campus of a community college. After submitting the appropriate paperwork, they were shocked to learn that the administration had already formed its own Muslim organization, which was being operated by a school official who was a non-Muslim.[65] This would be akin to an atheist starting a church in order to oversee and control its activities. Just days earlier, two teachers at McKinney Middle School in Texas resigned after tweeting that Islam was an "evil ideology" and a "satanic death cult."[66] During the same month, Trump appointee Carl Higbie was forced to step down after an interview surfaced in which he said, "I just don't like Muslim people."[67]

Any attempt to stop Muslims from entering the United States on the grounds that they pose a security threat solely because of their religious beliefs is doomed to failure. Such actions are not only statistically unsound and incommensurate with the facts, they will sow suspicion and distrust among our allies and inhibit cooperation with Muslim-majority countries. A key point that often gets missed in the war on terror is that globally the overwhelming number of terrorist victims are Muslims. Travel bans only serve to undermine America's moral standing in the world. Such shortsighted policies are created in an atmosphere of ignorance and fear, and they risk infuriating the Islamic world and further encouraging radicalization. The "war" on Islamic extremists is principally an ideological battle that will be won not with bullets and bombs but by winning the hearts and minds of disaffected peoples. Instead of building walls and pushing Muslims away, we need to gain their trust by embracing the peaceful traditions of the overwhelming number of the world's Muslims, and proudly accept them as part of the cultural fabric of American society. Doing so will make us stronger. As Texas Congressman Will Hurd observes, building a wall across our southern border is "a third-century solution to a 21st century problem."[68] Travel bans for Muslim-majority countries would do the same. Instead, reaching out and encouraging the integration of Muslims is the best strategy for making America, and the world, safe from extremists of all religions and creeds. Tolerance is a sign of strength, not weakness.

In combating the war on terror, we would do well to remember the words of English poet Hannah More: "Imagination frames events unknown, In wild, fantastic shapes of hideous ruin, And what it fears, creates."[69] Throughout history, human imagination has led to remarkable architectural achievements, lifesaving vaccines, and breathtaking technological advancements. Albert Einstein was fond of saying, "Imagination is more important than knowledge."[70] But imagination can also be our greatest enemy, magnifying fears by exaggerating threats, and in the process, demonizing those who are different from us. The great irony about the current wave of Islamophobia is that for students of American history, it is a hauntingly familiar story. The names and places may have changed, but the theme remains disturbingly similar: an unjustified fear and scapegoating of foreigners. We must resist calls by the conservative media, politicians, and other merchants of fear, to bar Muslims from the country. There is a difference between hunting legitimate terrorists and witch-hunting Muslims. The latter is driven by fear. Children will someday ask their parents, "What did you do during the Muslim Scare of the early twenty-first century?" Unless we act to change the course of history, the specter of our present treatment of Muslim immigrants and refugees will cast a long and dark shadow over the American legacy for decades to come.

CHAPTER 9

FROM MEXICANS
TO MUSLIMS

STEPPING OUT OF THE SHADOW OF FEAR
AND FACING THE ENEMY WITHIN

In learning about the other, about many 'others,' our conception of humanity is enlarged and enriched. We gain insight into the plasticity of human culture. We begin to see that our way of life is determined not so much by nature but by culture and history. Only then can we see that our way of life is just one of many possible ones.... In studying the other, we begin to learn how to separate fact from fiction ... about humanity itself.
—David Mayberry-Lewis, *Millennium: Tribal Wisdom and the Modern World*, 1992

Throughout its history, America has passed through many periods of intolerance toward outsiders who were believed to pose an imminent threat to the country. Driven by ignorance, bigotry, and a fear of the unfamiliar, foreigners and newcomers have made easy scapegoats for society's ills. At one time in our history, it was widely believed that Roman Catholics were plotting to bring down the government; that German Americans were part of a vast spy network for the kaiser; and hordes of Asians, Jews, Mexicans, and Native Americans were diluting the nation's racial purity. Many of the same fears and prejudices that drove these scares are alive and well today. Donald Trump characterizes Mexican immigrants as teeming with "bad hombres" who are rapists, drug dealers, and gang members, while Middle Easterners are said to be rife with militant jihadists. Yet immigrants and refugees commit far fewer crimes than native-born Americans—regardless of their ethnic background, religious beliefs, or country of origin—and most American terrorists are homegrown.

The unfounded fear of Mexicans, Muslims, and migrants from other ethnic and religious groups has become a reality for many Americans because social panics thrive on public anxieties and uncertainty. As French Cardinal Jean François Paul de Gondi sagely observed over three centuries ago, "fear weakens judgment."[1] There is a fearmongering industry in America that drives the narrative of the menacing outsider: conservative news outlets, publications, blogs, talk shows, and think tanks that are devoted to creating an impression that there is an enemy at our gates, when in fact, the enemy is ourselves. We need to confront our prejudices about foreigners by becoming familiar with America's checkered history of immigration intolerance. Above all, we need to accept the overwhelming consensus of the scientific community that race is a mythical concept. When viewed through the prism of twenty-first-century science, *their* story becomes *our* story. This realization will result in a deepening appreciation of what it means to be human, and different.

CRIMINAL IMMIGRANTS: THE SKY IS NOT FALLING

The American habit of demonizing outsiders shows no signs of abating under the administration of Donald Trump. Today, immigrants are blamed for taking jobs, eroding values, breeding crime, and bleeding the welfare system dry. However, the statistics tell a different story. Most immigrants are law-abiding. Both legal and undocumented migrants are *less likely* to commit crimes than native-born citizens are—and the gap is not even close. This pattern has held true for over a century, irrespective of education level or country of origin.[2] Data from the last four censuses shows that incarceration rates for native-born citizens were two to five times higher than for immigrants.[3] Three separate government inquiries investigated this same question: the Industrial Commission of 1901, the Dillingham Commission of 1911, and the Wickersham Commission of 1931. Each reached the same conclusion: immigrants are far less likely to commit crimes than their native counterparts are.[4]

In recent years the disparity in the number of crimes committed by immigrants and native citizens has been closing, leading some to suggest that an increasing number of foreign criminals and terrorists are managing to slip through the Homeland Security net. This trend is not due to an influx of Muslim terrorists or Central Americans crossing the Mexican border. It is an artificial construct resulting from changes to immigration laws. Unauthorized entry into the country is now a major criminal offense that requires undocumented persons to be incarcerated before being sent back to their home country.[5] One study of undocumented immigrants in state and federal prisons found that 39 percent had been arrested for traffic violations, which then flagged their illegal status, for which they were put behind bars. The vast majority of unlawful migrants in prison were initially caught for nonviolent offenses and posed no threat to public safety.[6]

Immigrants also have a positive impact on the American economy. A long-term study by the National Academies of Sciences found that highly skilled immigrants are vital to the nation's economic growth.[7] The majority of immigrants toil for long hours on low wages in an array of menial jobs that many Americans refuse to do, such as dishwashers, cooks, cleaners, and farm workers.[8] The harm posed by those who have illegally entered the country or overstayed their visa is vastly exaggerated. If every undocumented migrant were deported, it is estimated that the country would lose half a trillion dollars in economic output each year.[9]

Migrants are commonly portrayed as a burden to the welfare system. In 2015, the Center for Immigration Studies reported that over half of all immigrants were receiving welfare benefits including food, housing, medical care, or cash; in contrast, only 30 percent of native households were on government assistance.[10] While this study received considerable attention in the mainstream media, closer examination reveals the findings to be highly misleading, and the Center for Immigration Studies to be a front for the anti-immigration lobby. The report by policy analyst Jason Richwine is part of America's fear industry designed to frighten citizens about foreigners by framing propaganda as fact. It is a case study in how to twist data to support a conclusion. In reality, undocumented immigrants are not eligible to receive most public benefits, and, once their status is legal, there is a five-year waiting period before they can receive such benefits.[11] By counting households instead of people, the report distorts the true picture and gives a false impression that large numbers of immigrants are living off public assistance. Native-born children and spouses of undocumented migrants may receive benefits, but anyone living in the same household who has entered the country without permission is ineligible, except for basic humanitarian needs such as school lunches and emergency medical care.[12] A more accurate comparison of individuals, not households, reveals that native-born Americans are not paying for immigrants who are draining the welfare system—the opposite is true. Undocumented migrants and new immigrants pay into government-assistance programs including Social Security, even though many cannot take advantage of the benefits. Their participation tamps down the costs to all Americans.[13] Economist Tara Watson estimates that this group contributes as much as $12 billion annually in state and local taxes. Instead of draining coffers, undocumented immigrants add to them.[14]

The distorted image of the American immigration picture as portrayed by Richwine is not surprising. In 2009, he advocated granting immigrant visas based on IQ. His alarming assertion that there is a hereditary component between IQ scores and certain ethnic groups, such as Hispanics, resembles writings from the nineteenth century and has no scientific merit.[15] The problem with this model is the misguided assumption that racial and ethnic groups have relatively similar gene pools.

For instance, the racial category referred to as "Hispanics" is a cultural creation that has existed for less than four hundred years and includes descendants of indigenous peoples, Latin Americans, enslaved Africans, and Europeans.[16] "Whites" is another problematic term. IQ is not affected by race per se, because race is a fictional construct; it is affected by one's social and cultural environment. Furthermore, IQ tests are themselves historical and cultural artifacts, as they compare people from vastly different backgrounds and reward their ability to process abstract knowledge. Throughout most of human history, intelligence has been equated with the ability to process practical knowledge for basic survival. As American social and cultural historian Brink Lindsey observes: "To grasp how culturally contingent our current conception of intelligence is, just imagine how well you might do on an IQ test devised by Amazonian hunter-gatherers or medieval European peasants."[17]

LOOKING BEYOND RACE AND RELIGION TO OUR COMMON HUMANITY

In October 1886, ten years after it was gifted to the people of the United States from France, the Statue of Liberty was finally completed. Dignitaries from both countries gathered on Ellis Island to commemorate the accomplishment, accompanied by great pageantry and excitement. It is ironic that this celebration occurred just four years after the Chinese Exclusion Act, amid the fear and suspicion of foreigners. Throughout the ceremony, not a single reference was made to the words that Emma Lazarus had written so eloquently, three years earlier, to raise money for the statue's pedestal. Her words embodied the American ideal "that all men are created equal," and they were held in such high esteem that they were embedded in bronze, seventeen years later, at the base of Lady Liberty, welcoming the huddled masses from faraway lands.[18] Her reference to the statue as the "Mother of Exiles" succeeded in transforming America's most distinguished immigrant into a symbol of hope and tolerance for those seeking refuge from a troubled world. Our government must recognize that as a nation of immigrants, America has a moral duty to fulfill Lady Liberty's promise and recognize that our social, cultural, religious, and political diversities make us stronger. Only a tiny fraction of newcomers commit terrorist acts. Their deeds should not define all immigrants, just as terrorists do not represent the beliefs of an entire religious or ethnic group. When Timothy McVeigh blew up the Alfred P. Murrah Federal Building in Oklahoma City in 1995, his actions did not result in the harassment and widespread stereotyping of Christians as terrorists. Conversely, similar acts committed by persons identifying as Muslims should not be used to reflect on the character of an entire religion.

It is with no small irony that on August 2, 2017, White House senior policy advisor Stephen Miller defended attempts by the Trump administration to reduce the number of legal immigrants by giving priority to high-skilled workers who speak English. Proof of proficiency in basic English is already a requirement for becoming an American citizen, with rare exceptions, such as being over age fifty and having lived in the United States as a permanent resident for twenty years. However, the concern here is the push by the Trump administration to make knowledge of the English language a prerequisite to even pass the first hurdle to enter the country and to give preference to those with a greater proficiency in English. When Donald Trump calls for America to accept only the "best and brightest" immigrants who are highly skilled and educated, it leaves out an entire group of people who, through no fault of their own, have been the victims of social, economic, political, and educational circumstances. If we were to have used in the past the same merit-based system that is currently being pushed by the Trump administration to determine who can and cannot migrate to the United States, then most of our ancestors would never have been allowed in. While Trump has often complained that certain groups, such as Middle Eastern migrants, do not assimilate well into American society, it is important to differentiate between the words "assimilate" and "integrate." *Assimilation* refers to the process whereby an immigrant turns into a person who can hardly be distinguished from the native inhabitants of a country. A more accurate term for what is expected of migrants is *integration*: allowing them to keep their traditions while accepting the laws and conditions of their new country.

When CNN reporter Jim Acosta raised his concerns with Miller over the government's attempt to restrict immigration by giving preference to English speakers, Miller made reference to Emma Lazarus. Acosta asserted: "The Statue of Liberty says, 'Give me your tired, your poor, your huddled masses yearning to breathe free.' It doesn't say anything about speaking English or being a computer programmer."[19] Miller observed that Lazarus's words *did not apply*, because they had been added to the statue years later—as if this diminished their significance. The Thirteenth Amendment abolishing slavery and the Nineteenth Amendment giving women the right to vote were not originally part of the Constitution, either, but that doesn't make these integral amendments any less necessary or meaningful.[20] Likewise, that Lazarus's poem was added later is irrelevant. While the statue was not originally intended to be a symbol of immigration, it quickly took up that mantle as ships carrying immigrants from the far-flung corners of the world passed by her majestic presence on their way to Ellis Island, hoping for a better life. The Statue of Liberty has become an American icon that is synonymous with inclusiveness regardless of skin color, ethnic background, or political affiliation.

The same year that Lazarus's words appeared on Lady Liberty, promising safe haven to the world's persecuted and poor, Congress passed the Immigration Act of 1903. This new law banned immigrants living in extreme poverty. It also gave immigration officers the authority to inquire as to the political views of prospective migrants. The act called for the exclusion and deportation of anyone advocating self-government, even if his or her views were peaceful and he or she agreed to abide by America's laws. In other words, people could be deported solely for their political beliefs. Government officials were given the power to ban anyone "who disbelieves in or who is opposed to all organized government," or who is a member of an organization that advocates such beliefs.[21] This provision was added because of the actions of one man: Leon Czolgosz, a self-proclaimed anarchist who had assassinated President William McKinley two years earlier.[22] In a similar vein, the acts of a small number of Islamic radicals have resulted in attempts by the Trump administration to ban people from entering the United States from several Muslim-majority countries. The year before Lazarus's bronze plaque was laid, in 1902, Congress decreed that all Chinese immigration was to be made permanently illegal.

The history of American immigration policy is epitomized by the treatment of Chinese migrants. In 1850, they were revered as honest, industrious, law-abiding citizens. However, after a decade of competition with more-established Anglo Americans in the California gold fields, they were seen as a threat and despised. Under the 1882 Exclusion Act, Chinese laborers were banned from entering the country. Two decades later, *all* Chinese immigration was prohibited. The tide began to turn during the late 1930s, with the Japanese invasion of China. By the early 1940s, most Americans viewed the Chinese in a positive light. In 1943, the immigration ban was lifted because America and China were working together to fight the Axis powers. A few years later, the Cold War broke out between the United States and Communist countries, resulting in another wave of immigration restrictions on China.

The phrase "the enemy within" refers to people who believe that others are trying to secretly damage or destroy society. It is sometimes used to describe military operatives or "sleeper cells" that have infiltrated a foreign country. At one time or another, each of the groups examined in this study has been viewed as an "enemy within" that must be purged to save American society. This phrase has another meaning, which is the focus of this chapter: the battle with our demons—bigotry, hate, and intolerance that come to the fore during periods of great fear and fuel the search for scapegoats. Philosopher Isaac Berlin once wrote that "passions, prejudices, fears, neuroses, spring from ignorance, and take the form of myths and illusions."[23] As a nation, we must overcome our prejudices and fears to tear down the myths and illusions that hinder America from attaining its promise of justice for all and the belief written in the Declaration of Independence "that all men are created equal." These ideals are symbolized with the Statue of Liberty. They will never be realized until they are put into action by resisting the temptation to exclude certain ethnic groups and religious persuasions. The most prominent of these are the myths of racial and religious superiority.

During social panics, it may seem as if entire segments of society have temporarily lost the power to reason, blinded over the fear of evildoers who are believed to be threatening the very social order. While there may be some truth to the claims, the threat is exaggerated and results in the persecution of marginalized groups based on their ethnic background, political affiliation, and religious convictions. The most tragic example of a social panic in modern times is Nazi Germany, during which the fear of Jews created a powerful backlash of persecution and scapegoating, and the death and suffering of millions. Equally alarming is modern-day persecution and scapegoating in America and around the world, as there remains a reluctance to accept certain groups of refugees, based on fears that they are subversives and terrorists. Parallels with the treatment of Jewish refugees during the Nazi era are unmistakable. We have the opportunity to heed lessons from these events, correct past wrongs, and create a more just and caring future. Today, thousands of refugees have drowned in the Mediterranean Sea, choked on tear gas fired by border guards in Greece and Macedonia, and suffered at the hands of human traffickers. Perhaps, years from now, humanity will look back and realize that our generation failed in its moral duty to assist those in need, just as an earlier generation failed the Jews. The lesson of the Jews is the same lesson to be heeded from our mistreatment of Mexican Americans, Catholic Americans, Chinese Americans, Japanese Americans, German Americans, Native Americans and Islamic Americans. Each of these social panics involved a reaction to "the Other," people who had the misfortune of being trapped on the margins of society and villainized as scapegoats. These scares were driven by erroneous notions of racial and cultural superiority that arose during periods of exaggerated threats, generating great fear as people reverted to antiquated myths and stereotypes about entire groups. While we cannot stop social panics, we can familiarize ourselves with their features, learn to recognize them, and take action to reduce their impact before they spiral out of control. The key to countering these panics is education and familiarity. Perhaps the greatest single act we can undertake to prevent their spread is the realization that there is no Other, that everyone in the world shares a common genetic heritage, and that the concept of race is as mythical as Santa Claus and the Tooth Fairy.

The events in Nazi Germany astonished the world. People were in disbelief that Europe's center of art and culture could allow a campaign to systematically persecute entire groups of people based solely on their race and religious belief. How could their fellow Germans stand by and watch as Jewish literature was burned, Jewish workers were barred from government jobs, Jewish children were banned from public schools, and Jewish neighbors disappeared in the night? It was as if a temporary madness had swept the country. After all, this was the same culture that produced the poetic beauty of Friedrich Schiller and the literary genius of Johann Wolfgang von Goethe, who famously wrote: "There is nothing in the world more shameful than establishing one's self on lies and fables."[24] His words would haunt the German people who had been placed under a spell by Hitler and his notion of an Aryan race. Equally haunting was the inaction by the American government and many of its citizens to the plight of the Jews. Prompted by bigotry, anti-Semitism, and wartime paranoia over Jewish refugees posing as spies, the American government failed to live up to the promise inscribed on the Statue of Liberty. Despite Stephen Miller's recent claims that Emma Lazarus's words ring hollow because they did not originally appear on Lady Liberty, the fact that they were written by an American citizen of Jewish heritage to welcome immigrants from around the world makes them even more special.

CONQUERING THE ENEMY WITHIN

This study highlights the perils of using simplistic labels to make sweeping generalizations about entire groups based on their ethnicity, religious beliefs, political persuasions, physical appearance, and skin color. In doing so, we place people in boxes and reinforce popular stereotypes: "Mexicans are rapists and drug dealers," "Germans are warmongers," "Jews are greedy," "Muslims are terrorists." If we yield to these temptations, we risk dehumanizing those who are different and creating a world of "them" versus "us." Creeds and dogmas are social and cultural creations. The human ethnographic spectrum is breathtaking in its scope and diversity, and confronting to our entrenched beliefs. For instance, in their landmark 1951 study on the patterns of human sexual behavior, anthropologists Clellan Ford and Frank Beach found that from a sample of 185 cultures, in 84 percent men were "permitted by custom to have more than one mate at a time." Such behavior would be deemed a sinful act in most Western societies, and in some cases an arrestable offense under the crime of polygamy.[25] We must learn to accept our differences and cherish our diversity so long as those ideologies and creeds that make the world such an interesting place call for peaceful coexistence.

One of the biggest misconceptions about America's immigration history is that our present reluctance to take in foreigners is an aberration. The truth is, there have been moral panics involving some ethnic group at virtually every point in our history—often several at once. We cannot go back to "the good old days." We have always feared the foreign and the unfamiliar; we have always looked suspiciously upon those who are different from us; and we have always tried to stop people from coming to America, by using arbitrary criteria such as race, color, creed—even physical appearance and sexual orientation. America's fear of Muslims and Central Americans is just the latest chapter in our dark immigration history. It is time to break the cycle of fear and serve as a role model for the world by exhibiting moral leadership.

While moral panics have always been with us, the reaction to them by our political leaders has not always been the same. During the Chinese panic, several prominent senators equated Chinese immigrants with swarms of rats and insects devoid of moral fortitude. Former Speaker of the House of Representatives Maine Senator James Blaine claimed that Chinese and other "Mongolians" reeked of "moral and physical disease."[26] At the height of the German Scare in 1917, President Woodrow Wilson stoked fear and mistrust by warning that German sympathizers "filled our unsuspecting communities with vicious spies and conspirators."[27] In 1950, Senator Joseph McCarthy claimed that there were no less than 205 Communists in the State Department who were working to undermine the foundations of American democracy.[28] His witch-hunt using the House Committee on Un-American Activities triggered a wave of fear and false accusations that would last for four years. More recently, President Trump has disparaged immigrants from Mexico as rapists and drug dealers, and reportedly asked why we should accept people from poverty-stricken "s—hole countries" in the Caribbean, like Haiti, and certain Africa countries.[29] When he learned of a plan to give legal status to the Dreamers—people who were brought to the United States as children by undocumented parents—he reportedly quipped: "Why do we want people from Haiti here?"[30]

Instead of fueling anti-Muslim, anti-immigrant hysteria, some of our leaders have shown us the blueprint to countering the intolerance that such panics bring. Within a week after the traumatic events of September 11, 2001, President George W. Bush, who was known for his conservative Christian values, grew uncomfortable with reports of discrimination against Muslim Americans and visited a mosque. Instead of sowing seeds of division and suspicion, he reminded the country of the inclusiveness of the American dream and went so far as to quote from the Qur'an. He told the audience: "Women who cover their heads in this country must feel comfortable going outside their homes. Moms who wear cover must not be intimidated in America. That's not the America I know. That's not the America I value."[31] He went on to call for tolerance and calm: "I've been told that some . . . don't want to go shopping for their families; some don't want to go about their ordinary daily routines because, by wearing cover, they're afraid they'll be intimidated. That should not and that will not stand in America."[32] Bush's words did much to tamp down the frayed nerves and raw emotions that were prevalent across America immediately after 9/11. Unfortunately, anti-Muslim, anti-immigrant sentiments have resurfaced in recent years and those touting such beliefs have been emboldened by the rhetoric of division and intolerance that has characterized the campaign and election of Donald Trump.

The greatest lesson from America's history of intolerance to immigrants and refugees is the urgent need to address the continuing misuse of the word *race*, and replace it with "ethnic group." *Race* is an archaic, scientifically inaccurate term that has brought nothing but misery and suffering to the world. Past attempts to understand human behavior through a set of racial categories has led to widespread discrimination and exploitation. Scientists estimate that the DNA of any two people taken at random contains about three million different sequences or "letters" that tell our cells how to act. While we each have a unique genetic heritage, we are all part of a single species, *Homo sapiens*, who share a similar ancestry. Humans have been around for at least 300,000 years—not long enough to develop into a separate species.[33] We have evolved differences through mutations as we adapted to different environments. It is easy to see how in the past, the notion of race developed given our visible physical differences. But research on the human genome has shown that no matter how different our outer trappings—be it clothing, piercings, tattoos, adornments, or physical features, humans are far more alike than different. Vast tracts of our genetic code are the same, regardless of what we look like or where we come from. According to the Smithsonian Institution, human DNA is 99.9 percent identical.[34] In fact, there is more variation *within* so-called racial groups than *between* them. In 1950, the United Nations announced that based on the findings of a panel of some of the world's leading scientists in such fields as genetics, psychology, and anthropology, there was an overwhelming accumulation of evidence to support the conclusion that race is a myth. Ever since the United Nation's statement on race, numerous scientific bodies have reaffirmed this position with evidence from their own disciplines, to the point where anthropologist Robert Sussman observes, this assertion is as valid and true today "as the fact that the earth is round and revolves around the sun."[35]

We must spread the message that race has no standing in modern science, and we must challenge pseudoscientific assertions to the contrary. Race is every bit as mythical as the Nazi belief in a "pure" Aryan people. History has shown that there are harsh consequences when we view others through the lens of racial stereotypes. The problem is, race also is a social reality that continues to be used to label people based on the amount of melanin in their skin and their physical features. While it may seem absurd that any group would discriminate against another using something as superficial as, say, nose shape, the Nazis sometimes used this trait to deduce whether or not someone was Jewish—and hence, whether they lived or died. It is time to abolish the antiquated notion of race and refer to people according to their ethnic heritage and country of origin. This still involves labels, but it is a vast improvement over having our children grow up believing in a fictional world divided into racial categories. The use of such labels contributes to the belief that there is a "them" and an "us," when science tells us there is only a "we." When we view the world through the nuanced lens of twenty-first-century science, there is no enemy at our gate. What we have come to fear is nothing more than our own shadow. It is time to shine a light on our fears and put an end to the illusion of race and evoking it when it comes to determining who should be allowed to migrate to the United States. In the words of American animator Walter Kelly, "We have met the enemy and he is us."[36]

NOTES

FOREWORD

1. Erich Goode and Nachman Ben-Yehuda, "The Genealogy and Trajectory of the Moral Panic Concept," in *The Ashgate Research Companion to Moral Panics*, ed. Charles Krinsky (New York: Routledge, 2013), pp. 23–35. See p. 32.

2. Matthew F. Jacobson, *Whiteness of a Different Color: European Immigrants and the Alchemy of Race* (Cambridge, MA: Harvard University Press, 1998).

3. Ibid., p. 56.

4. Irving Goffman, *Stigma: Notes on the Management of Spoiled Identity* (Englewood Cliffs, NJ: Prentice-Hall/Spectrum, 1963), p. 4.

INTRODUCTION: FROM OUT OF THE SHADOWS

1. Jeffrey S. Victor, "The Search for Scapegoat Deviants," *Humanist* 52, no. 5 (1992): 10–13. The term *scapegoat* can be traced back to the Old Testament Book of Leviticus, which states that God ordered the annual sacrifice of two goats. The first was to be killed and its blood sprinkled over the Ark of the Covenant: a wooden chest that supposedly held the Ten Commandments. A priest would place his hands on the second goat and confess the sins of Israel, which were transferred to the animal. The creature was then banished from the community, and, in the process, the people were cleansed of their sins.

2. Julie Gilchrist and Erin Parker, "Racial/Ethnic Disparities in Fatal Unintentional Drowning among Persons Aged ≤ 29 Years—United States, 1999–2010," *Morbidity and Mortality Weekly* (Centers for Disease Control and Prevention) 63, no. 19 (2014): 421–26; Centers for Disease Control and Prevention, "Falls Are Leading Cause of Injury and Death in Older Americans," press release, September 22, 2016.

3. Erich Goode and Nachman Ben-Yehuda, *Moral Panics: The Social Construction of Deviance* (Malden, MA: Wiley-Blackwell, 2010).

4. Jeffrey S. Victor, *Satanic Panic: The Creation of a Contemporary Legend* (Chicago, IL: Open Court, 1992); James Richardson, Joel Best, and David Bromley, eds., *The Satanism Scare* (New York: Aldine de Gruyter, 1993); Robert D. Hicks, "Police Pursuit of Satanic Crime Part II: The Satanic Conspiracy and Urban Legends," *Skeptical Inquirer* 14 (1990): 378–89; Jeffrey

S. Victor, "A Rumor-Panic about a Dangerous Satanic Cult in Western New York," *New York Folklore* 15 (1989): 23–49.

5. Benjamin Radford, "Predator Panic: A Closer Look," *Skeptical Inquirer* 30, no. 5 (2006): 20–21, 69.

6. Ibid., pp. 21 and 69.

7. Clarence Ver Steeg and Richard Hofstadter, *A People and a Nation* (New York: Harper and Row, 1981), p. 287.

8. Ray Allen Billington, "Tentative Bibliography of Anti-Catholic Propaganda in the United States (1800–1860)," *Catholic Historical Review* 18, no. 4 (1933): 492–513.

9. Lewis Hippolytus Joseph Tonna, *Nuns and Nunneries: Sketches Compiled Entirely from Romish Authorities* (London: Seeleys, 1852).

10. William D. Carrigan and Clive Webb, *Forgotten Dead: Mob Violence against Mexicans in the United States, 1848–1928* (New York: Oxford University Press, 2013).

11. "Donald Trump Speech, Debates and Campaign Quotes," *Newsday*, November 9, 2016, http://www.newsday.com/news/nation/donald-trump-speech-debates-and-campaign -quotes-1.11206532.

12. Benjamin Perley Poore, ed., *Message from the President of the United States to the Two Houses of Congress at the Commencement of the First Session of the Forty-Ninth Congress, with the Reports of the Heads of Departments and Selections from Accompanying Documents* (Washington, DC: Government Printing Office, 1885), pp. 898–99.

13. Department of Interior, Office of Indian Affairs, *Rules Governing the Court of Indian Offenses* (Washington, DC: Government Printing Office, March 30, 1883).

14. Francis MacDonnell, *Insidious Foes* (New York: Oxford University Press, 1995), p. 23.

15. See, for example, *Tokio Jokio*, a 1943 propaganda cartoon directed by Norma McCabe for Warner Brothers Pictures. The cartoon can be viewed at https://ia800606.us.archive.org/12/ items/ClassicRareAndCensoredCartoons/051543TokioJokioLt.mp4.

16. Robert Bartholomew, "The Paris Terror Attacks, Mental Health and the Spectre of Fear," *Journal of the Royal Society of Medicine* 109, no. 1 (2016): 4–5.

17. Richard E. Wackrow, "A Skeptic's Guide to the War on Terror," *Skeptic* 20, no. 1 (2015): 32–43. See p. 32.

18. Alex Nowrasteh, *Terrorism and Immigration: A Risk Analysis*, CATO Institute Policy Paper, no. 798 (Washington, DC: CATO Institute, September 13, 2016), p. 1.

19. Michael D. Cusimano and Nadine Parker, "Toppled Television Sets and Head Injuries in the Pediatric Population: A Framework for Prevention," *Journal of Neurosurgery: Pediatrics* 17, no. 1 (2016): 3–12; "The (Mainly) Men Who Have Fallen under the Sway of Drinks Vending Machines," *Guardian*, January 20, 2015.

20. Dick Meyer, "Is the Terrorism Threat Exaggerated?" *Newsday*, September 11, 2015.

21. Nowrasteh, *Terrorism and Immigration*, p. 1; Eric Levenson, "How Many Fatal Terror Attacks Have Refugees Carried Out in the US? None," *New York Times*, January 29, 2017.

22. Meyer, "Is the Terrorism Threat Exaggerated?"

23. Stanley Cohen, *Folk Devils and Moral Panics: The Creation of the Mods and the Rockers* (New York: Routledge, 2002), pp. 26–32.

24. Ibid.

25. See: Paul Boyer and Stephen Nissenbaum, *Salem Possessed: The Social Origins of Witchcraft* (Cambridge: Harvard University Press, 1974), pp. 3, 193–94, 204–206; Peggy Robbins, "The Devil in Salem," *Annual Editions Readings in American History*, vol. 1 (Guilford, CT: Dushkin, 1973), p. 60; Earle Rice Jr., *The Salem Witch Trials* (San Diego, CA: Lucent Books Rice, 1997), pp. 31–32, 193–94.

26. Boyer and Nissenbaum, *Salem Possessed*, p. 3.

27. Paul Boyer and Stephen Nissenbaum, *Salem-Village Witchcraft: A Documentary Record of Local Conflict in Colonial New England* (Boston: Northeastern University Press, 1993), p. 49.

28. Ibid., pp. 155–62.

29. Scott Poynting and George Morgan, *Global Islamophobia: Muslims and Moral Panic in the West* (Burlington, VT: Ashgate, 2012).

30. Mike Jaccarino and Jeremy Walsh, "'Ground Zero Mosque' Opens. No Protests as Exhibit of World's Kids Displayed," *New York Daily News*, September 22, 2011, p. 13.

31. Joel Best and Gerald T. Horiuchi, "The Razor Blade in the Apple: The Social Construction of Urban Legends," *Social Problems* 32, no. 5 (1985): 488–99; Joel Best, "Halloween Sadism: The Evidence" (paper; Newark: University of Delaware, 2015), http://udspace.udel.edu/bitstream/handle/19716/726/DSpace.revised%20thru%2016.pdf?sequence=5 (accessed January 3, 2016).

32. Best, "Halloween Sadism."

33. "Press Finds Halloween Sadism Rare but Warns of Danger," *Editor and Publisher* 106 (March 3, 1973), p. 22.

34. Best and Horiuchi, "Razor Blade," p. 491.

35. Best, "Halloween Sadism."

36. Ronald Smothers, "FBI Finds Bulk Candy Purchase to Be Harmless," *New York Times*, October 23, 2001; See also David Mikkelson, "Terrorist Halloween Candy Purchase," Snopes, October 31, 2009, https://www.snopes.com/fact-check/candy-man/ (accessed June 1, 2018).

37. Madison Grant, *The Passing of the Great Race* (New York: Charles Scribner, 1916), p. 89.

38. Eugene V. Debs, "Foreign Pauper Immigration," *Locomotive Firemen's Magazine* 15, no. 5 (1891): 399–400. See p. 399.

39. Douglas C. Baynton, "Disability and the Justification of Inequality in American History," in *The New Disability History: American Perspectives*, ed. Paul K. Longmore and Lauri Umansky (New York: New York University Press, 2001), pp. 33–57. See p. 50.

40. Barbara Lüthi, "Germs of Anarchy, Crime, Disease, and Degeneracy: Jewish Migration to the United States and the Medicalization of European Borders around 1900," in *Points of Passage: Jewish Migrants from Eastern Europe in Scandinavia, Germany, and Britain 1880–1914*, ed. Tobias Brinkmann (New York: Berghahn, 2013), pp. 27–44. See pp. 30–31.

41. J. G. Wilson. "A Study in Jewish Psychopathology," *Popular Science Monthly* 82, no. 3 (1913): 264–71.

42. Baynton, "Disability," p. 48.

43. Ibid., p. 49.

44. Ibid.

45. Alan M. Kraut, *Silent Travelers: Germs, Genes, and the "Immigrant Menace"* (Baltimore, MD: Johns Hopkins University Press, 1995), p. 55; Gwenyth Swain, *Hope and Tears: Ellis Island Voices* (Honesdale, PA: Calkins Creek, 2012); Baynton, "Disability," p. 49; Wilton S. Tifft, *Ellis Island* (Chicago, IL: Contemporary Books, 1990), p. 86.

46. June G. Alexander, *Daily Life in Immigrant America, 1870–1920* (Westport, CT: Greenwood, 2007), p. 39.

47. Janet B. Pascal, *Jacob Riis: Reporter and Reformer* (New York: Oxford University Press, 2005), p. 19.

48. Douglas C. Baynton, "Defectives in the Land: Disability and American Immigration Policy, 1882–1924," *Journal of American Ethnic History* 24, no. 3 (2005): 31–44. See pp. 37–38.

49. Ibid., p. 38.

50. Ibid.

51. Erika Lee, "The 'Yellow Peril' and Asian Exclusion in the Americas," *Pacific Historical Review* 76, no. 4 (2007): 537–62. See p. 559.

52. Nicholas Von Hoffman, *Citizen Cohn* (New York: Doubleday, 1988), p. 130.

53. David K. Johnson, *The Lavender Scare: The Cold War Persecution of Gays and Lesbians in the Federal Government* (Chicago, IL: University of Chicago Press, 2004).

54. Ibid., p. 16.

55. Ibid., pp. 15–17.

56. Ibid., p. 17.

57. *New York Times*, April 19, 1950; *Washington Times-Herald*, May 9, 1950.

58. Carlos A. Ball, *The First Amendment and LGBT Equality: A Contentious History* (Cambridge, MA: Harvard University Press, 2017), p. 18; Allan Bérubé, *Coming Out Under Fire: The History of Gay Men and Women in World War II* (Chapel Hill: University of North Carolina Press, 2010), p. 269; Susan D. James, "Lavender Scare: US Fired 5,000 Gays in 1953 'Witch Hunt,'" televised report on ABC News, New York, aired on March 5, 2012.

59. John D'Emilio, *Sexual Politics, Sexual Communities* (Chicago, IL: University of Chicago Press, 1998), p. 47; George Haggerty, *Encyclopedia of Gay Histories and Cultures* (New York: Routledge, 2012), p. 910.

60. Carole B. Davies, "Deportable Subjects: US Immigration Laws and the Criminalizing of Communism," *South Atlantic Quarterly* 100, no. 4 (2001): 949–66. See p. 959.

61. Each of these questions were taken verbatim from questioning by inquisitors. The witchcraft question appeared in digitized copies of the original case files for each of those executed in 1692, accessed from "The Salem Witch Trials Documentary Archive and Transcription Project," University of Virginia Library, Charlottesville, Virginia, http://salem.lib

.virginia.edu/contact.html (accessed June 1, 2018); the communist example is taken from Haig Bosmajian, *The Freedom Not to Speak* (New York: New York University Press, 1999), p. 150; the homosexual question appears in Johnson, *Lavender Scare*, p. 168.

62. *Congressional Record: Proceedings and Debates of the . . . Congress* 98, part 13 (Washington, DC: Government Printing Office, 1952), p. 3948.

63. *The Lavender Scare*, directed by Josh Howard (New York: Full Exposure Films, 2017), 77 min.

64. Robert Trager and Donna Dickerson, *Freedom of Expression in the 21st Century* (New York: New York University Press, 1999), p. 64.

65. Jonathan Zimmerman, "Petraeus and the Blackmail Myth," *Los Angeles Times*, November 16, 2012, p. A21.

66. Adam Francoeur, "The Enemy Within: Constructions of US Immigration Law and Policy and the Homoterrorist Threat," *Stanford Journal of Civil Rights and Liberties* (2007): 345–76. See p. 353.

67. Tracy J. Davis, "Opening the Doors of Immigration: Sexual Orientation and Asylum in the United States," *Human Rights Brief* 6, no. 3 (1999): 19–20.

68. Howard, *Lavender Scare*.

69. Baynton, "Disability," p. 37.

70. Chelsea Larson, "The Color of Moral Panic Is Black: Racial Violence and Police Brutality in the Contemporary United States" (master's thesis, New York University, 2016).

71. Claire D. Coles, "Saying 'Goodbye' to the 'Crack Baby,'" *Neurotoxicology and Teratology* 15 (1993): 290–92; Susan Okie, "The Epidemic That Wasn't," *New York Times*, January 27, 2009, p. D9.

72. Quotation from Todd Reed and Sarah Hoye, "Former Crack Baby: 'It's Another Stigma, Another Box to Put Me In,'" *America Tonight*, Al-Jazeera, March 10, 2015, http://america .aljazeera.com/watch/shows/america-tonight/articles/2015/3/10/crack-baby-myth.html (accessed June 4, 2018). For the twenty-year study of "crack babies," refer to L. Betancourt, N. Brodsky, E. Malmud, M. Farah, and H. Hurt, *The Relation of Early Experience with Memory and Language Function in a Cohort of Low SES African American Youth with and Without Gestational Cocaine Exposure (GCE) at Age 20 Years* (platform presentation, Pediatric Academic Societies Annual Meeting, Washington, DC. E-PAS 2205.2, May 2013); L. Betancourt, N. Brodsky, D. Hackman, M. Farah, and H. Hurt, *Stress Reactivity and Problem Behavior in a Cohort of Youth, Half with Gestational Cocaine Exposure (GCE) and Half Without (NCE)* (platform presentation, Pediatric Academic Societies Annual Meeting, Washington, DC, E-PAS 4330.5, May 2013).

73. Mike King, "'The Knockout Game': Moral Panic and the Politics of White Victimhood," *Race & Class* 56, no. 4 (2012): 85–94.

74. Michael Welch, Eric Price, and Nana Yankey, "Moral Panic over Youth Violence: Wilding and the Manufacture of Menace in the Media," *Youth & Society* 34, no. 1 (2002): 3–30.

75. Dora Apel, *Imagery of Lynching: Black Men, White Women, and the Mob* (New Brunswick, NJ: Rutgers University Press, 2004), p. 151.

76. Christopher C. Meyers, "Killing Them by the Wholesale: A Lynching Rampage in South Georgia," *Georgia Historical Quarterly* 90, no. 2 (2006): 214–35. See p. 224.

77. "Accidents or Unintentional Injuries," Centers for Disease Control and Prevention, Atlanta, GA, last updated March 17, 2017, https://www.cdc.gov/nchs/fastats/accidental-injury .htm (accessed June 4, 2018); Awr Hawkins, "Hillary Clinton's Gun Control Ad Swells 'Gun Violence' Number 66 Percent by Including Suicides," Breitbart News Network, November 3, 2015.

78. Edgar Butler, Hiroshi Fukurai, Jo-Ellen Dimitrius, and Richard Krooth, *Anatomy of the McMartin Child Molestation Case* (Lanham, MD: University Press of America, 2001), pp. 13–14.

79. Paul Eberle and Shirley Eberle, *The Abuse of Innocence: The McMartin Preschool Trial* (Amherst, NY: Prometheus Books, 1993), p. 202.

80. Ibid., p. 21.

81. A. Mickalide, K. Rosenthal, and M. Donahue, *Halloween Safety: A National Survey of Parents' Knowledge, Attitudes, and Behaviors* (Washington, DC: Safe Kids Worldwide, 2011), p. 3.

82. Anthony Salvanto, Jennifer De Pinto, Sarah Dutton, and Fred Backus, "Poll: Concerns about Terrorist Attack in US Rise," CBS News, November 23, 2015, http://www.cbsnews.com/ news/poll-concerns-about-terrorist-attack-in-u-s-rise/ (accessed March 12, 2017).

83. Amram Shapiro, Louise Campbell, and Rosalind Wright, *Book of Odds: From Lightning Strikes to Love at First Sight, the Odds of Everyday Life* (New York: William Morrow, 2014), p. 2.

84. Goode and Ben-Yehuda, *Moral Panics*, p. 40.

85. Gregor Bulc, "Kill the Cat Killers: Moral Panic and Juvenile Crime in Slovenia," *Journal of Communication Inquiry* 26, no. 3 (2002): 300–25. See pp. 307–309.

86. Erich Goode and Nachman Ben-Yehuda, *Moral Panics: The Social Construction of Deviance* (Oxford: Blackwell, 1994), pp. 144–84; Erich Goode, *Deviant Behavior* (Upper Saddle River, NJ: Prentice-Hall, 2002), p. 344.

87. David Hernandez, *The Greatest Story Ever Forged (Curse of the Christ Myth)* (Pittsburgh, PA: Red Lead, 2009), p. 119; Mattis Kantor, *The Jewish Timeline Encyclopedia* (Lanham, MD: Rowman and Littlefield, 2004), p. 168; Howard N. Lupovitch, *Jews and Judaism in World History* (New York: Routledge, 2010), p. 92.

88. Donna J. Guy, *Sex and Danger in Buenos Aires: Prostitution, Family and Nation in Argentina* (Lincoln and London: University of Nebraska Press, 1991).

89. Edgar Morin, *Rumour in Orléans* (New York: Pantheon, 1971).

90. Arlette Farge and Jacques Revel, *Logiques de la Foule* [Logic of the Crowd] (Paris: Hachette, 1988).

CHAPTER 1: "THEY'RE PLOTTING TO OVERTHROW THE COUNTRY!"

1. Chris Hughes, "Hundreds of ISIS Sleeper Cells Set Up across Europe—Including Britain," *Daily Mirror* (London), November 16, 2015.

2. "Massive Network of ISIS Sleeper Cells Spanning United States Uncovered—Training Camps And All," *ZeroHedge* (blog), January 8, 2017, http://www.zerohedge.com/news/2017 -01-08/massive-network-isis-sleeper-cells-spanning-united-states-uncovered-%E2%80%93 -training-camps (accessed June 4, 2018).

3. Tyler Anbinder, *Nativism and Slavery: The Northern Know Nothings and the Politics of the 1850s* (New York: Oxford University Press, 1992), pp. 117–18.

4. Ken Thomas and Erica Werner, "Trump Wrongly Blames Fraud for Loss of Popular Vote," Associated Press, January 23, 2017.

5. Justin Levitt, "A Comprehensive Investigation of Voter Impersonation Finds 31 Credible Incidents Out of One Billion Ballots Cast," *Washington Post*, August 6, 2014.

6. William Hogan, *Popery! As It Was and as It Is; Also, Auricular Confession; and Popish Nunneries* (Hartford, CT: Silas Andrus and Son, 1853).

7. Samuel F. Morse, *Foreign Conspiracy against the Liberties of the United States* (1835; New York: American and Foreign Christian Union, 1835), pp. 104–105.

8. Ibid., pp. 13–14. Italics in original.

9. Paul Finkelman, ed., *Religion and American Law: An Encyclopedia* (New York: Routledge, 2013), p. 70.

10. Robert Mackey, "Fox News Apologizes for False Claims of Muslim-Only Areas in England and France," *New York Times,* January 19, 2015.

11. Marie Anne Pagliarini, "The Pure American Woman and the Wicked Catholic Priest: An Analysis of Anti-Catholic Literature in Antebellum America," *Religion and American Culture: A Journal of Interpretation* 9, no. 1 (1999): 97–128; Tim O'Neil, "A Look Back: Irish Immigrants Fight Back in 1854 Nativist Riots," *St. Louis Post-Dispatch*, August 8, 2010.

12. Maureen McCarthy, "The Rescue of True Womanhood: Convents and Anti-Catholicism in 1830s America" (doctoral dissertation, Rutgers University, New Brunswick, NJ, 1996), p. 9.

13. George Godwin, *The Great Revivalists* (London: Watts, 1951), p. 98.

14. Thomas H. O'Connor, *The Hub: Boston Past and Present* (Boston: Northeastern University Press, 2001), p. 34.

15. Ibid.

16. Asa Greene, *The Life and Adventures of Dr. Dodimus Duckworth, A. N. Q.: To Which Is Added, The History of a Steam Doctor*, vol. 1 (New York: Peter Hill, 1833), pp. 163–64.

17. Anbinder, *Nativism and Slavery*, p. 111.

18. Bryan Le Beau, "'Saving the West from the Pope': Anti-Catholic Propaganda and the Settlement of the Mississippi River Valley," *American Studies* 32, no. 1 (1991): 101–14. See p. 103.

19. Joseph Mannard, "Maternity of the Spirit: Nuns and Domesticity in Antebellum America," *US Catholic Historian* 5 (1980): 401–22. See p. 311.

20. Josephine M. Bunkley, *The Testimony of an Escaped Novice from the Sisterhood of St. Joseph* (New York: Harper and Brothers, 1855), p. 319.

21. Thomas Roscoe, "Introductory Essay," pp. vii–xxiii, in *Female Convents: Secrets of Nunneries Disclosed*, ed. Thomas Roscoe (New York: D. Appleton, 1834), p. xxi.

22. Ray Allen Billington, "Tentative Bibliography of Anti-Catholic Propaganda in the United States (1800–1860)," *Catholic Historical Review* 18, no. 4 (1933): 492–513.

23. Jon Gjerde, *Catholicism and the Shaping of Nineteenth-Century America* (New York: Cambridge University Press, 2012), p. 189.

24. Ray Allen Billington, "The Burning of the Charlestown Convent," *New England Quarterly* 10, no. 1 (1937): 4–24. See pp. 4–5.

25. McCarthy, "Rescue of True Womanhood," p. 18.

26. Ibid., p. 43.

27. Thomas H. O'Connor, *Boston Catholics: A History of the Church and Its People* (Boston, MA: Northeastern University Press, 1998), p. 63.

28. McCarthy, "Rescue of True Womanhood," p. 52.

29. Ibid., p. 51.

30. O'Connor, *Boston Catholics*, pp. 63–64.

31. Billington, "Burning of the Charlestown Convent," p. 8.

32. McCarthy, "Rescue of True Womanhood," pp. 55–58.

33. Daniel A. Cohen, "Passing the Torch: Boston Firemen, 'Tea Party' Patriots, and the Burning of the Charlestown Convent," *Journal of the Early Republic* 24 (2004): 527–86.

34. Jeanne Hamilton, "The Nunnery as Menace: The Burning of the Charlestown Convent, 1834," *US Catholic Historian* 14, no. 1 (1996): 35–65. See p. 48.

35. Billington, "Tentative Bibliography."

36. McCarthy, "Rescue of True Womanhood," p. 102.

37. Rebecca Reed, *Six Months in a Convent, or, the Narrative of Rebecca Theresa Reed, Who Was Under the Influence of the Roman Catholics about Two Years, and an Inmate of the Ursuline Convent, on Mount Benedict, Charlestown, Mass., Nearly Six Months, in the Years 1831–32* (Boston, MA: Russell, Odiorne, and Metcalf, 1835).

38. Daniel Cohen, "The Respectability of Rebecca Reed: Genteel Womanhood and Sectarian Conflict in Antebellum America," *Journal of the Early Republic* 16, no. 3 (1996): 419–61. See pp. 434–37.

39. Michael Butler, *Plots, Designs, and Schemes: American Conspiracy Theories from the Puritans to the Present* (Boston: de Gruyter, 2014), pp. 123–24.

40. Nancy Schultz, *Veil of Fear: Nineteenth-Century Convent Tales by Rebecca Reed and Maria Monk* (West Lafayette, IN: NotaBell Books, 1999). pp. vii–xxxiii. See p. vii.

41. McCarthy, "Rescue of True Womanhood," p. 123.

42. Ibid.

43. Mary Anne Ursula Moffatt, *An Answer to Six Months in a Convent, Exposing Its Falsehoods and Manifold Absurdities* (Boston, MA: J. H. Eastburn, 1835).

44. Cohen, "Respectability of Rebecca Reed," p. 437.

45. Ibid., p. 440.

46. Theodore Dwight, John Jay Slocum, and William K. Hoyte, *Awful Disclosures of Maria Monk as Exhibited in a Narrative of Her Suffering during a Residence of Five Years as a Novice, and Two Years as a Black Nun, in the Hotel Dieu Nunnery at Montreal* (London: Richard Groombridge, 1836).

47. McCarthy, "Rescue of True Womanhood," pp. 213–22.

48. Schultz, *Veil of Fear*, p. vii.

49. Dwight et al., *Awful Disclosures*, p. 17.

50. Ibid., pp. 52–53.

51. McCarthy, "Rescue of True Womanhood," p. 236.

52. Dwight et al., *Awful Disclosures*, p. 166.

53. Ibid., p. 165.

54. Ibid., pp. 101–108.

55. William S. Cossen, "Monk in the Middle: The Awful Disclosures of the Hotel Dieu Nunnery and the Making of Catholic Identity," *American Catholic Studies* 125, no. 1 (2014): 25–45. See pp. 29–30.

56. *Encyclopedia Britannica*, s.v. "Maria Monk," last updated May 28, 2018, http://www.britannica.com/biography/Maria-Monk (accessed January 12, 2016).

57. Sandra Frink, "Women, the Family, and the Fate of the Nation in Anti-Catholic Narratives, 1830–1860," *Journal of the History of Sexuality* 18, no. 2 (2009): 237–64.

58. Anonymous, *The True History of Maria Monk* (London: Catholic Truth Society, 1895), pp. 17–18.

59. Robert Blaskiewicz, "Maria Monk's Awful Disclosures: A Classic American Conspiracy Theory," Committee for Skeptical Inquiry, February 27, 2012, http://www.csicop.org/specialarticles/show/maria_monks_awful_disclosures (accessed June 4, 2018).

60. Anonymous, *Evidence Demonstrating the Falsehoods of William L. Stone Concerning the Hotel Dieu Nunnery of Montreal* (New York: no publisher, 1837), p. 3.

61. William L. Stone, *Maria Monk and the Nunnery of the Hotel Dieu: Being an Account of a Visit to the Convents of Montreal and Refutation of the "Awful Disclosures"* (New York: Howe and Bates, 1936), p. 32.

62. Ibid.

63. Maria Monk, *Further Disclosures by Maria Monk, Concerning the Hotel Dieu Nunnery of Montreal; also, Her Visit to Nun's Island, and Disclosures Concerning That Secret Retreat* (New York: J. J. Slocum, 1836).

64. See for example: Harry Hazel, *The Nun of St. Ursula, or the Burning of the Convent: A Romance of Mount Benedict* (Boston: F. Gleason, 1845); Anonymous, *The Escaped Nun; or, Disclosures of Convent Life; and the Confessions of a Sister of Charity* (New York: De Witt and Davenport, 1855).

65. Lucinda Martin Larned, *The American Nun; or, the Effects of Romance* (Boston, MA: Otis, 1836).

66. Susan M. Griffin, "Awful Disclosures: Women's Evidence in the Escaped Nun's Tale," *Publications of the Modern Languages Association* 111, no. 1 (1996): 93–107. See p. 95.

67. Ibid., p. 95.

68. For bibliographic citations, see Billington, "Tentative Bibliography," 1933, and Griffin, "Awful Disclosures."

69. Hogan, *Popery!*

70. Patrick W. Carey, "The Confessional and Ex-Catholic Priests in Nineteenth-Century Protestant America," *US Catholic Historian* 33, no. 3 (2015): 1–26. See p. 14.

71. Ibid., p. 18.

72. Ibid., p. 19.

73. Ibid., p. 1.

74. Anonymous, "The Convent in Aisquith Street—Escape of a Nun—The Doctrine of Celibacy in Popish Priests and Nuns," *Baltimore Literary and Religious Magazine* 6, no. 1 (1840): 1–15. See pp. 1–2. Italics in original except for those words in all capitals.

75. Margaret McGinness, *Called to Serve: A History of Nuns in America* (New York: New York University Press, 2013), p. 60; William R. Sutton, *Journeymen for Jesus: Evangelical Artisans Confront Capitalism in Jacksonian Baltimore* (University Park: Pennsylvania University Press, 1998), p. 188.

76. Robert Curran, *Shaping American Catholicism: Maryland and New York, 1805–1915* (Washington, DC: Catholic University of America Press, 2012), p. 128; McGinness, *Called to Serve*, p. 60.

77. Justin Corfield, "Philadelphia Nativist Riots (1844)," pp. 324–27, in *Revolts, Protests, Demonstrations, and Rebellions in American History: An Encyclopedia*, ed. Steven Danver, vol. 1 (Santa Barbara, CA: ABC-CLIO, 2011); Sandy Hingston, "Bullets and Bigots: Remembering Philadelphia's Anti-Catholic Riots," *Philadelphia Magazine*, December 17, 2015, http://www.phillymag.com/news/2015/12/17/philadelphia-anti-catholic-riots-1844/ (accessed June 4, 2018).

78. Allison Malcom, "Philadelphia Riots and Early Antebellum Nativism," pp. 389–91, in *Anti-Immigration in the United States: A Historical Encyclopedia*, ed. Kathleen Arnold (Santa Barbara, CA: ABC-CLIO, 2012), p. 390.

79. John E. Kleber, *The Kentucky Encyclopedia* (Lexington: University of Kentucky Press, 1992), pp. 88–89.

80. Clyde F. Crews, "Bloody Monday," pp. 108–109, in *Encyclopedia of Religious Controversies in the United States*, ed. Bill J. Leonard and Jill Y. Crainshaw, vol. 1, *A-L* (Santa Barbara, CA: ABC-CLIO, 1997).

81. Ibid.

82. John B. Boles, *Religion in Antebellum Kentucky* (Lexington: University of Kentucky Press, 1995), pp. 78–79.

83. Alex Nowrasteh, *Terrorism and Immigration: A Risk Analysis*, CATO Institute Policy Paper Number 798 (Washington, DC: CATO Institute, September 13, 2016).

84. Daniel Cohen, email message to Robert Bartholomew, January 7, 2016.

85. James Thomas Mann, *Wicked Ypsilanti* (Charleston, SC: History, 2014), pp. 73–75.

CHAPTER 2: "NO DOGS, NO NEGROES, NO MEXICANS"

1. William D. Carrigan and Clive Webb, *Forgotten Dead: Mob Violence against Mexicans in the United States, 1848–1928* (New York: Oxford University Press, 2013), p. 81.

2. William D. Carrigan and Clive Webb, "Mexican Perspectives in Mob Violence in the United States," pp. 53–68, in *Globalizing Lynching History: Vigilantism and Extralegal Punishment from an International Perspective*, ed. Manfred Berg and Simon Wendt (New York: Palgrave Macmillan, 2011), p. 60; Carrigan and Webb, *Forgotten Dead*, p. 82; George R. Nielsen, *Vengeance in a Small Town: The Thorndale Lynching of 1911* (Bloomington, IN: iUniverse, 2011).

3. Carrigan and Webb, *Vengeance in a Small Town*.

4. Juan F. Perea, "A Brief History of Race and the US-Mexican Border: Tracing the Trajectories of Conquest," *UCLA Law Review* 51, no. 1 (2003): 283–311. See p. 292.

5. Ibid., p. 293.

6. James L. Evans, "The Indian Savage, the Mexican Bandit, the Chinese Heathen—Three Popular Stereotypes" (doctoral dissertation, University of Texas at Austin, 1967), pp. 70–72.

7. Laura E. Gomez, *Manifest Destinies: The Making of the Mexican American Race* (New York: New York University Press, 2007), p. 42.

8. Perea, p. 295.

9. David J. Weber, *The Spanish Frontier in North America* (New Haven, CT: Yale University Press, 1992), p. 336.

10. Martha Menchaca, *Recovering History, Constructing Race: The Indian, Black, and White Roots of Mexican Americans* (Austin: University of Texas Press, 2001), p. 16.

11. Lothrop Stoddard, *Re-Forging America: The Story of Our Nationhood* (New York: Charles Scribner's Sons, 1927), p. 259.

12. Ibid., p. 214.

13. Ibid., p. 216. Italics in original.

14. Evans, "Indian Savage," pp. 72–73.

15. Stoddard, *Re-Forging America*, pp. 256–57.

16. Ibid., p. 217.

17. Steven W. Bender, *Greasers and Gringos: Latinos, Law, and the American Imagination* (New York: New York University Press, 2003), pp. 104–105.

18. Ibid., pp. 105–107.

19. United States Postal Service, "Postal Service Honors Legendary Teacher Jaime Escalante Forever Stamp on Sale Today Nationwide," press release, July 13, 2016; "Teacher Delivers Farewell," *Los Angeles Times*, June 19, 1991; "Famed Teacher to Resign. 'Stand and Deliver' Instructor to Drop Out," *Los Angeles Times*, February 22, 1990.

20. "Special Teacher Sets an Example," *Sun-Sentinel* (Broward County, FL), June 20, 1991.

21. Lloyd Dunn, *Bilingual Hispanic Children on the US Mainland: A Review of Research on their Cognitive, Linguistic, and Scholastic Development* (Circle Pines, MN: American Guidance Service, 1987), p. 63. Italics in original.

22. Ibid., p. 64.

23. Bender, *Greasers and Gringos*, p. 110.

24. Anne Anastasi, *Psychological Testing* (New York: Macmillan, 1988), p. 296.

25. Bender, *Greasers and Gringos*, p. 111.

26. Jane Mercer, "Ethnic Differences in IQ Scores: What Do They Mean?" *Hispanic Journal of Behavioral Sciences* 10, no. 3 (1988): 199–218. See p. 200.

27. Carina A. Bandhauer, "A Global Trend in Racism: The Late 20th Century Anti-Immigrant Movement in Southern California" (doctoral dissertation, State University of New York at Binghamton, 2001), p. 66.

28. Michael Calderón-Zaks, "Constructing the 'Mexican Race': Racial Formation and Empire Building, 1884–1940" (doctoral dissertation, State University of New York at Binghamton, 2008), p. 133.

29. Ibid., p. 137.

30. Alexandra M. Stern, *Eugenic Nation: Faults and Frontiers of Better Breeding in Modern America* (Oakland: University of California Press, 2014), p. 63.

31. Miroslava Chavez-Garcia, *States of Delinquency: Race and Science in the Making of California's Juvenile Justice System* (Berkeley: University of California Press, 2012).

32. Roque Planas, "Mexican Americans Sterilized Disproportionately in California Institutions, Study Says," *Huffington Post*, June 9, 2013.

33. Natalie Lira and Alexandra M. Stern, "Mexican Americans and Eugenic Sterilization: Resisting Reproductive Injustice in California, 1920–1950," *Aztlan: A Journal of Chicano Studies* 39, no. 2 (2014): 9–34.

34. Ibid.

35. Ibid., p. 15.

36. Alexandra M. Stern, "Sterilized in the Name of Public Health: Race, Immigration, and Reproductive Control in Modern California," *American Journal of Public Health* 95, no. 7 (2005): 1128–38. See p. 1135.

37. Lira and Stern, "Mexican Americans and Eugenic Sterilization," p. 15.

38. Ibid., pp. 9–11.

39. Ibid., p. 17.

40. Stern, "Sterilized," p. 1135.

41. Eric L. Ray, "Mexican Repatriation and the Possibility for a Federal Cause of Action:

A Comparative Analysis on Reparations," *University of Miami Inter-American Law Review* 37, no. 1 (2005): 171–96. See p. 171.

42. Wendy Gross, "America's Forgotten History of Mexican-American 'Repatriation,'" *Fresh Air*, National Public Radio, September 10, 2015.

43. Ibid.

44. Ibid.

45. Alfreda P. Iglehart and Rosina M. Becerra, *Social Services and the Ethnic Community: History and Analysis* (Long Grove, IL: Waveland, 2011), p. 70; John P. Schmal, "The Latino Vote: An Historical Analysis," *La Prensa San Diego*, October 22, 2004.

46. Jaweed Kaleem, "Election Officials Focus on Whether Voter ID Laws Contributed to Hillary Clinton's Defeat," *Los Angeles Times*, December 17, 2016.

47. Iglehart and Becerra, *Social Services*, p. 71.

48. Philip Bump, "The Series of Choices Faced by Immigrants Fleeing Central America," *Washington Post*, June 19, 2018; Kate Vine, "What's Really Happening When Asylum-Seeking Families Are Separated?" *Texas Monthly*, June 15, 2018.

CHAPTER 3: "THE MONGOLIAN HORDES MUST GO!"

1. "Race in Legislation and Political Economy," *Anthropological Review* 13 (1866): 113–35. See p. 120.

2. Andrew Gyory, *Closing the Gate: Race, Politics, and the Chinese Exclusion Act* (Chapel Hill: University of North Carolina Press, 1998), p. 61.

3. Ryan Dearinger, *The Filth of Progress: Immigrants, Americans, and the Building of Canals and Railroads in the West* (Oakland: University of California Press, 2016), p. 155.

4. Najia Aarim, "Chinese Immigrants, African Americans, and the Problem of Race in the United States, 1848–1882" (doctoral dissertation, Temple University, Philadelphia, 1996), p. 709.

5. Gyory, *Closing the Gate*.

6. Lance D. Muckey, "Nevada's Odd Response to the 'Yellow Peril': Asians and the Western Ineligible Alien Land Laws" (master's thesis, University of Nevada at Las Vegas, 2004), p. 13.

7. Ibid., pp. 9–10.

8. Aarim, "Chinese Immigrants," p. 57.

9. Joyce Kuo, "Excluded, Segregated, and Forgotten: A Historical View of the Discrimination of Chinese Americans in Public Schools," *Asian American Law Journal* 5 (1998): 181–212. See p. 185. Xiaohua Ma, "The Sino-American Alliance during World War II and the Lifting of the Chinese Exclusion Acts," *American Studies International* 38, no. 2 (2000): 39–61. See p. 40.

10. Muckey, "Nevada's Odd Response," pp. 14–15.

11. George A. Peffer, "Forbidden Families: Emigration Experiences of Chinese Women under the Page Law, 1875–1882," *Journal of American Ethnic History* 6, no. 1 (1986): 28–46. See p. 29.

12. William R. Locklear, "The Celestials and the Angels: A Study of the Anti-Chinese Movement in Los Angeles to 1882," *Historical Society of Southern California Quarterly* 42, no. 3 (1960): 239–56. See p. 240.

13. James L. Evans, "The Indian Savage, the Mexican Bandit, the Chinese Heathen—Three Popular Stereotypes" (doctoral dissertation, University of Texas at Austin, 1967), p. 166.

14. Jonathan Rees, *Industrialization and the Transformation of American Life: A Brief Introduction* (Armonk, NY: M. E. Sharpe, 2015), p. 34.

15. Erika Lee, "The Chinese Exclusion Example: Race, Immigration, and American Gate-keeping, 1882–1924," *Journal of American Ethnic History* 21, no. 3 (2002): 36–62. See p. 36.

16. Kermit L. Hall, ed., *The Oxford Guide to United States Supreme Court Decisions* (New York: Oxford University Press, 2000), p. 53.

17. Jeran Pfaelzer, *Driven Out: The Forgotten War against Chinese Americans* (Los Angeles: University of California Press, 2008), p. 5.

18. Aarim, "Chinese Immigrants," p. 222.

19. Ibid.

20. Erika Lee, "At America's Gates: Chinese Immigration during the Exclusion Era, 1882–1943" (doctoral dissertation, University of California at Berkeley, 1998), p. 1.

21. John R. Wunder, "Law and Chinese in Frontier Montana," *Montana: The Magazine of Western History* 30, no. 3 (1980): 18–31. See p. 20.

22. Ibid., p. 21.

23. Stuart Miller, *The Unwelcome Immigrant: The American Image of the Chinese, 1785–1882* (Los Angeles: University of California Press, 1969).

24. Evans, "Indian Savage," pp. 137–38.

25. Ibid., p. 138.

26. Ibid., p. 197.

27. Muckey, "Nevada's Odd Response," pp. 10–11.

28. Massimo Calabresi, "What Donald Trump Knew about Undocumented Workers at His Signature Tower," *Time*, August 25, 2016.

29. Evans, "Indian Savage," pp. 197–98.

30. Ibid., p. 138.

31. Ibid., p. 140.

32. Ibid., p. 141.

33. Ibid., p. 142.

34. Ibid., pp. 164–74.

35. Ibid., pp. 164–66.

36. Muckey, "Nevada's Odd Response," pp. 16 and 161.

37. Evans, "Indian Savage," p. vii.

38. Ibid., p. 144.

39. Ibid., p. 191.

40. Ibid., p. 197.

41. Lee, "America's Gates," p. 39; Judith Gans, Elaine Replogle, and Daniel Tichenor, *Debates on US Immigration* (Thousand Oaks, CA: Sage, 2012).

42. Atwell Whitney, *Almond-Eyed: The Great Agitator; a Story of the Day* (San Francisco, CA: A. L. Bancroft, 1878).

43. William F. Wu, "The Yellow Peril: Chinese Americans in American Fiction, 1850–1940" (doctoral dissertation, University of Michigan at Ann Arbor, 1979), pp. 60–63.

44. Ibid., p. 63.

45. Ibid., p. 69.

46. Ibid., pp. 77–78.

47. Ibid., pp. 64–65.

48. Robert Woltor, *The Taking of California and Oregon by the Chinese in the Year A.D. 1899* (San Francisco, CA: A. L. Bancroft, 1882), p. 77.

49. Oto E. Mundo, *The Recovered Continent: A Tale of the Chinese Invasion* (Columbus, OH: Harper-Osgood, 1898).

50. Shirley Sui Ling Tam, "Images of the Unwelcome Immigrant: Chinese Americans in American Periodicals, 1900–1924" (doctoral dissertation, Case Western Reserve University, Cleveland, OH, 1999), p. 67.

51. Ibid., pp. 114–16.

52. Pfaelzer, *Driven Out*, pp. 13–16.

53. Erika Lee, *The Making of Asian America: A History* (New York: Simon and Schuster, 2015), p. 93.

54. Pfaelzer, *Driven Out*, p. 16.

55. G. Thomas Edwards, *Experiences in a Promised Land: Essays in Pacific History* (Seattle: University of Washington Press, 1986), pp. 186–87; Charles J. McClain, *In Search of Equality: The Chinese Struggle against Discrimination in Nineteenth Century America* (Berkeley: University of California Press, 1994), pp. 173–76; Priscilla Long, "Tacoma Expels the Entire Chinese Community on November 3, 1885," Online Encyclopedia of Washington State History, January 17, 2003, http://www.historylink.org/File/5063 (accessed January 27, 2016); *Report of the Governor of Washington Territory to the Secretary of the Interior* (Washington, DC: Government Printing Office, 1886), pp. 49–52.

56. John Soennichsen, *The Chinese Exclusion Act of 1882* (Santa Barbara, CA: Greenwood Publishing, 2011), p. 33.

57. Sucheng Chan, *This Bittersweet Soil: The Chinese in California Agriculture, 1860–1910* (Berkeley: University of California Press, 1989), pp. 371–73.

58. Gyory, *Closing the Gate*, pp. 3–4.

59. Ibid., p. 5.

60. "Tom Kim Yung's Death Charged to Policeman," *San Francisco Call*, October 6, 1903, p. 2; See also, "Arrest and Death of Tom Kim Yung May Bring International Trouble," *San Francisco Call*, September 15, 1903, p. 3; Tam, "Images of the Unwelcome Immigrant," p. 137.

61. Theodore H. Hittell, *The General Laws of the State of California, from 1850 to 1864*, vol. 1 (San Francisco, CA: H. H. Bancroft, 1870), p. 522.

62. Tam, "Images of the Unwelcome Immigrant," p. 206.

63. Philip Hanson, *This Side of Despair: How the Movies and American Life Intersected during the Great Depression* (Cranbury, NJ: Fairleigh Dickinson University Press, 2008), p. 100.

64. "Ho Ah Kow vs Nunan 12 F. Cas. 252 (C.C.D. Cal. 1879)." Available online from the San Francisco Digital Archive (FoundSF), reproducing the entire text of the court decision, http://www.foundsf.org/index.php?title=Ho_Ah_Kow_v._Nunan (accessed November 16, 2016).

65. Tam, "Images of the Unwelcome Immigrant," p. 208.

66. Kuo, "Excluded, Segregated, and Forgotten," p. 193; Ma, "Sino-American Alliance," p. 40.

67. Iris Chang, *The Chinese in America: A Narrative History* (New York: Penguin, 2004).

68. Tam, "Images of the Unwelcome Immigrant," p. 50; "California Anti-Chinese Legislation, 1852–1878," "The Chinese American Experience, 1857–1892," 1999, http://immigrants.harpweek.com/ChineseAmericans/2KeyIssues/CaliforniaAnti.htm (accessed June 6, 2018).

69. Gabriel J. Chin, "The Plessy Myth: Justice Harlan and the Chinese Cases," *Iowa Law Review* 82 (1996): 151–82. See p. 156.

70. Ma, "Sino-American Alliance," p. 47.

71. Ibid.

72. Ibid., p. 41.

73. Ibid., p. 43.

74. Ibid.

75. Ibid., p. 47.

76. Ibid., pp. 46–52.

77. Ibid., p. 57.

CHAPTER 4: "CHILDLIKE, BARBARIC, AND OTHERWISE INFERIOR"

1. Walter R. Echo-Hawk, *In the Courts of the Conqueror: The Ten Worst Indian Law Cases Ever Decided* (Golden, CO: Fulcrum, 2010), p. 22.

2. *The Addresses and Messages of the Presidents of the United States, Together with the Declaration of Independence and Constitution of the United States* (New York: McLean and Taylor, 1839), p. 466.

3. Nancy Shoemaker, "How Indians Got to Be Red," *American Historical Review* 102, no. 3 (1997): 625–44. See p. 628.

4. Bethany R. Berger, "Red: Racism and the American Indian," *UCLA Law Review* 265 (2009): 591–656. See p. 611–12.

5. Ibid., p. 611.

6. Shoemaker, "How Indians Got to Be Red," p. 626. Shoemaker writes that "the Greek physician Galen's medical philosophy of the four humors must also have served as inspiration, for in the 1758 edition of *Systema Naturae*, Linnaeus attached telltale descriptive labels to each color of people: red people were choleric, white sanguine, yellow melancholic, and black phlegmatic. Thus Linnaeus adapted an existing system of color-based categories to account for differences between the world's peoples."

7. Carol Chiago Lujan and Gordon Adams, "US Colonization of Indian Justice Systems: A Brief History," *Wicazo Sa Review* 19, no. 2 (2004): 9–23. See p. 10.

8. Ibid., p. 11.

9. Russell Hope Robbins, *The Encyclopedia of Witchcraft and Demonology* (London: Spring Books, 1959), p. 158; Erich Goode, *Deviant Behavior* (Upper Saddle River, NJ: Prentice-Hall, 2001), pp. 344–45.

10. Jules Baissac, *Les Grands Jours de la Sorcellerie* (Paris: Klincksieck, 1890), p. 132.

11. Colonialism is usually achieved through aggressive military action by a powerful country against a weaker country, by invaders against native inhabitants of a land. The invaders do so by gaining control of the land, resources, and lives of the native population. This method is called external colonialism. What happened in the early decades of European settlement in North America, however, would be called internal colonialism. This form of colonialism is exercised by a government against a minority within the same country.

12. Lujan and Adams, "US Colonization," p. 11.

13. Ibid., p. 12.

14. Ibid., p. 13.

15. Ibid.

16. Jenna Dawn Gray-Hildenbrand, "Negotiating Authority: The Criminalization of Religious Practice in the United States" (doctoral dissertation, University of California at Santa Barbara, 2012), p. 22.

17. Ibid., p. 17.

18. Ibid.

19. Ibid.

20. Ibid., p. 19.

21. Ibid., p. 22.

22. Lujan and Adams, "US Colonization," p. 15.

23. Clyde Holler, *Black Elk's Religion: The Sun Dance and Lakota Catholicism* (Syracuse, NY: Syracuse University Press, 1995), p. 110.

24. Gray-Hildenbrand, "Negotiating Authority," p. 25.

25. Ibid.

26. Robert N. Clinton, "Code of Indian Offenses," *For the Seventh Generation* (blog), February 24, 2008, http://tribal-law.blogspot.de/2008/02/code-of-indian-offenses.html (accessed December 3, 2016).

27. Robert N. Clinton, "Code of Indian Offenses," *Robert N. Clinton* (blog), February 24, 2008, reading material for non-law students, https://rclinton.wordpress.com/2008/02/24/code-of-indian-offenses/ (accessed February 12, 2016).

28. Ibid.

29. Gray-Hildenbrand, "Negotiating Authority," p. 25.

30. Department of the Interior, Office of Indian Affairs, "Rules Governing the Court of Indian Offenses" (Washington, DC: Government Printing Office, March 30, 1883), https://rclinton.files .wordpress.com/2007/11/code-of-indian-offenses.pdf (accessed December 3, 2016), p. 3.

31. Michael F. Steltenkamp, *Black Elk: Holy Man of the Oglala* (Norman: University of Oklahoma Press, 1993), p. 34.

32. S. E. Wilmer, *Theatre, Society, and the Nation: Staging American Identities* (Cambridge, UK: Cambridge University Press, 2004), p. 35.

33. Gray-Hildenbrand, "Negotiating Authority," p. 4.

34. Clinton, "Code of Indian Offenses," *For the Seventh Generation* (blog); see also Wilmer, *Theatre, Society, and the Nation*, p. 95.

35. Robert K. Utley, *The Last Days of the Sioux Nation* (New Haven and London: Yale University Press, 1963).

36. Serena Nanda and Richard Warms, *Culture Counts: A Concise Introduction to Cultural Anthropology* (Belmont, CA: Wadsworth, 2009), p. 279; Emily A. Schultz and Robert H. Lavenda, *Anthropology: A Perspective on Human Culture* (Mountain View, CA: Mayfield, 1995), p. 545; James Davidson, Pedro Castillo, and Michael Stoff, *The American Nation* (Upper Saddle River, NJ: Prentice-Hall, 2000), pp. 519–20; Paul Boyer, ed., *The Oxford Companion to United States History* (New York: Oxford University Press, 2000), p. 851.

37. David L. Miller, *Introduction to Collective Behavior and Collective Action*, 2nd ed. (Prospect Heights, IL: Waveland, 2000), p. 423.

38. Gray-Hildenbrand, "Negotiating Authority," p. 71.

39. See also Emily A. Schultz and Robert H. Lavenda, *Anthropology: A Perspective on Human Culture* (Mountain View, CA: Mayfield, 1995), p. 545; James Davidson, Pedro Castillo, and Michael Stoff, *The American Nation* (Upper Saddle River, NJ: Prentice-Hall, 2000), pp. 519–20; "Wounded Knee," History.com, 2009, http://www.history.com/topics/native -american-history/wounded-knee (accessed January 3, 2016).

40. Holler, *Black Elk's Religion*, p. 113.

41. Ibid.

42. Ibid., p. 122.

43. Tisa Wenger, "Indian Dances and the Politics of Religious Freedom, 1870–1930," *Journal of the American Academy of Religion* 79, no. 4 (2011): 850–78. See p. 866.

44. Gray-Hildenbrand, "Negotiating Authority," p. 27.

45. Ibid.

46. Ibid., p. 28.

47. Ibid.

48. Ibid., p. 80.

49. Frederick E. Hoxie, "Towards a 'New' North American Indian Legal History," *American Journal of Legal History* 30, no. 4 (1986): 351–57.

50. Ibid., p. 355.

51. Ibid.

52. Jeremiah Gutman, "Constitutional and Legal Aspects of Deprogramming," pp. 208–15, in *Deprogramming: Documenting the Issue*, ed. Herbert W. Richardson (New York: American Civil Liberties Union and Toronto School of Theology, 1977). See pp. 210–11.

CHAPTER 5: "DON'T TRUST THE HUNS!"

1. Chris Richardson, "With Liberty and Justice for All? The Suppression of German-American Culture during World War I," *Missouri Historical Review* 90, no. 1 (1995): 79–89. See p. 87.

2. Richard Rubin, *The Last of the Doughboys: The Forgotten Generation and Their Forgotten World War* (Boston: Houghton Mifflin Harcourt, 2013), p. 254.

3. "Red Cross Bandages Poisoned by Spies," *New York Times*, March 29, 1917.

4. Evans Harrington and Ann J. Abadie, eds., *Faulkner and the Short Story* (Jackson: University of Mississippi Press, 1992), p. 117.

5. Elisabeth Gläser and Hermann Wellenreuther, *Bridging the Atlantic: The Question of American Exceptionalism in Perspective* (Cambridge: University of Cambridge Press, 2002), p. 191; Don Markstein, "The Katzenjammer Kids," Toonopedia, 2009, http://www.toonopedia.com/katzen.htm (accessed July 14, 2018).

6. Francis MacDonnell, *Insidious Foes* (New York: Oxford University Press, 1995); Graeme S. Mount, *Canada's Enemies: Spies and Spying in the Peaceable Kingdom* (Toronto: Dundurn, 1993), p. 25.

7. MacDonnell, *Insidious Foes*, p. 25.

8. William C. Sherman and Playford V. Thorson, eds., *Plains Folk: North Dakota's Ethnic History* (Fargo, ND: North Dakota State University, 1988), p. 89; Wayne Wiegand, *"An Active Instrument for Propaganda": The American Public Library During World War I* (New York: Greenwood, 1989), p. 88.

9. Susan L. Carruthers, *The Media at War* (New York: Palgrave Macmillan, 2011), p. 35; Angela J. Thurstance, "Dehumanizing the Enemy," pp. 466–69, in *The SAGE Encyclopedia of War: Social Science Perspectives*, ed. in Paul Joseph (Thousand Oaks, CA: Sage, 2017).

10. John Higham, *Strangers in the Land: Patterns of American Nativism, 1860–1925* (New Brunswick, NJ: Rutgers University Press, 1955), p. 218.

11. Ralph Young, *Dissent: The History of an American Idea* (New York: New York University Press, 2015), p. 332; Jennifer Keene, *World War I* (Westport, CT: Greenwood, 2006), p. 58.

12. Commission on Wartime Relocation and Internment of Civilians, *Personal Justice Denied: Report of the Commission on Wartime Relocation and Internment of Civilians* (Washington, DC: Civil Liberties Public Education Fund; Seattle: University of Washington Press, 2000), p. 291.

13. Martin Kitchen, "The German Invasion of Canada in the First World War," *International History Review* 7, no. 2 (1985): 245–60, see pp. 245–46; MacDonnell, *Insidious Foes*, p. 40.

14. Desmond Morton, "Sir William Otter and Internment Operations in Canada during the First World War," *Canadian Historical Review* 55, no. 1 (1974): 32–58. See p. 36.

15. Kitchen, "German Invasion," p. 251.

16. Jennifer Crump, *Canada Under Attack: Canadians at War* (Toronto, Canada: Dundurn, 2010), p. 148; Brandon R. Dimmel, *Engaging the Line: How the Great War Shaped the Canada–US Border* (Vancouver: University of British Columbia Press, 2016), p. 104.

17. Kitchen, "German Invasion," pp. 254–55.

18. Ibid., p. 254.

19. Wayne E. Reilly, "Vanceboro Bridge Bombed by German Soldier a Century Ago," *Bangor Daily News*, February 21, 2015; Crump, *Canada Under Attack*, p. 148.

20. Kitchen, "German Invasion," p. 254.

21. Frank Trommler, "The Lusitania Effect: America's Mobilization against Germany in World War I," *German Studies Review* 32, no. 2 (2009): 241–66.

22. Erin Mullally, "From the Trenches: *Lusitania*'s Secret Cargo," *Archaeology: A Publication of the Archeological Institute of America* 62, no. 1 (2009): 9.

23. Katja Wüstenbecker, *Deutsch-Amerikaner im Ersten Weltkrieg: US-Politik und nationale Identitaten im Mittleren Westen* (Stuttgart: Franz Steiner Verlag, 2010), pp. 192–93.

24. Spencer C. Tucker, *World War I: The Definitive Encyclopedia and Document Collection* (Santa Barbara, CA: ABC-CLIO, 2014), p. 651.

25. MacDonnell, *Insidious Foes*, pp. 25–26.

26. Joseph R. Conlin, *The American Past: A Survey of American History*, vol. 2, *Since 1865* (Boston, MA: Wadsworth, 2013), p. 636.

27. Edmund A. Bowles, "Karl Muck and His Compatriots: German Conductors in America during World War I (and How They Coped)," *American Music* 25, no. 4 (2007): 405–40. See p. 406; Dale Maharidge, *Homeland* (New York: Seven Stories, 2004), p. 182.

28. "Songs, Spies, Liberty Pups," *Life* 56, no. 21 (May 22, 1964): 72–73. See p. 72.

29. Tammy M. Proctor, "'Patriotic Enemies': Germans in the Americas, 1914–1920," pp. 213–33, in *Germans as Minorities during the First World War: A Global Comparative Perspective*, ed. Panikos Panayi (Burlington, VT: Ashgate, 2014). See p. 221.

30. Richardson, "Liberty and Justice for All?" p. 88; Jeanie Croasmun, "Heritage Found," *Ancestry Magazine* 24, no. 5 (2006): 40–44. See p. 42.

31. Allan Wood, *Babe Ruth and the 1918 Red Sox* (New York: Writer's Club, 2000), p. 172.

32. Lawrence Baldassaro and Richard A. Johnson, *The American Game: Baseball and Ethnicity* (Carbondale: University of Illinois Press, 2002), p. 42.

33. There were similar efforts in Canada to expunge the names of towns and cities with German names and replace them with Anglo-Saxon ones. The industrial center of Berlin, Ontario, was renamed Kitchener, after Britain's War Minister Horatio Kitchener, who was killed in action. In Saskatchewan Province, the village of Kaiser became Peebles, while the hamlet of Prussia was changed to Leader. Schools and universities even dropped German from their language curriculums, and many teachers were pressured into signing loyalty pledges. Before hostilities ceased in November 1918, over 8,500 German Canadians had been deemed threats to the nation and were placed in internment camps. See Morton, "Sir William Otter," p. 33. See also Craig H. Roell, "Schroeder, TX," *Handbook of Texas Online* (Texas State Historical Association), accessed July 14, 2018, https://tshaonline.org/handbook/online/articles/hls27.

34. Richard O'Connor, *Black Jack Pershing* (New York: Doubleday, 1961), p. 16.

35. MacDonnell, *Insidious Foes*, p. 22.

36. Proctor, "'Patriotic Enemies,'" pp. 213–33. See p. 214; Robert Siegel and Art Silverman, "During World War I, US Government Propaganda Erased German Culture," *All Things Considered*, National Public Radio, April 7, 2017.

37. Siegel and Silverman, "During World War I."

38. Mark Sonntag, "Fighting Everything German in Texas, 1917–1919," *Historian* 56, no. 4 (2007): 655–70. See p. 660.

39. Alexander Waldenrath, "The German Language Newspapers in Pennsylvania during World War I," *Pennsylvania History: A Journal of Mid-Atlantic Studies* 42, no. 1 (1975): 25–41. See p. 38.

40. Sonntag, "Fighting Everything German," pp. 659–60; Waldenrath, "German Language Newspapers," p. 40.

41. Waldenrath, "German Language Newspapers," p. 41.

42. Jon R. Stone, *The Routledge Book of World Proverbs* (New York: Routledge, 2006), p. 421.

43. Arthur Roy Leonard, *War Addresses of Woodrow Wilson with an Introduction and Notes* (London: Forgotten Books, 2013), p. 52.

44. MacDonnell, *Insidious Foes*, pp. 25–26.

45. Robert Torricelli and Andrew Carroll, *In Our Own Words: Extraordinary Speeches of the American Century* (New York: Washington Square, 2000), p. 46.

46. Richardson, "Liberty and Justice for All?" pp. 79–80.

47. Frederick Luebke, *Germans in the New World: Essays in the History of Immigration* (Chicago: University of Illinois Press, 1937), p. 35.

48. Ibid.

49. Ibid., pp. 35–36.

50. Proctor, "'Patriotic Enemies,'" pp. 229–30.

51. Paul S. Boyer, Clifford E. Clark, Karen Halttunen, Joseph Kett, Neal Salisbury, Harvard Sitkoff, Nancy Woloch, and Andrew Rieser, *The Enduring Vision*, vol. 2, *Since 1865* (Boston, MA: Cengage Learning, 2016), p. 638.

52. "Ten-Year Sentence of Mrs. Rose Stokes Overruled by Federal Court in St. Louis," *New York Times*, March 10, 1920, p. 1; Mary Beth Norton, Carol Sheriff, David Katzman, David Blight, Howard Chudacoff, Fredrik Logevall, Beth Bailey, and Debra Michals, *A People and a Nation: A History of the United States*, vol. 2, *Since 1865* (Boston, MA: Wadsworth, 2010), p. 616.

53. William G. Jordan, *Black Newspapers and America's War for Democracy, 1914–1920* (Chapel Hill: University of North Carolina Press, 2001), p. 112.

54. Spencer Tucker, ed., *World War I: Encyclopedia*, vol. 1 (Santa Barbara, CA: ABC-CLIO, 2005), p. 310.

55. Ronald Schaffer, *America in the Great War* (New York: Oxford University Press, 1991), p. 20.

56. Ibid., p. 20; Leola Allen, "Anti-German Sentiment in Iowa During World War I," *Annals of Iowa* 42, no. 6 (1974): 418–29. See p. 419.

57. Allen, "Anti-German Sentiment," pp. 418–20.

58. Ibid., p. 420.

59. Paul Ramsey, "The War against German-American Culture: The Removal of German-Language Instruction from the Indianapolis Schools, 1917–1919," *Indiana Magazine of History* 98 (2002): 285–303. See p. 302.

60. Ramsey, "War against German-American Culture," p. 302.

61. Clark D. Kimball, "Patriotism and the Suppression of Dissent in Indiana during the First World War" (doctoral dissertation, Indiana University, 1971), p. 22.

62. Proctor, "'Patriotic Enemies,'" pp. 226–27.

63. James L. Gilbert, *World War I and the Origins of US Military Intelligence* (Lanham, MD: Scarecrow, 2012), p. 34.

64. Fraser Sherman, *Screen Enemies of the American Way: Political Paranoia about Nazis, Communists, Saboteurs, Terrorists, and Body-Snatching Aliens in Film and Television* (Jefferson, NC: McFarland, 2010), pp. 8–11.

65. Ibid., p. 8.

66. Eric Van Schaack, "The Coming of the Hun! American Fears of a German Invasion, 1918," *Journal of American Culture* 28, no. 3 (2005): 284–92. See p. 291.

67. Hudson Maxim, *Defenseless America* (New York: Hearst's International Library, 1916).

68. Van Schaack, "Coming of the Hun!"

69. John T. Soister and Henry Nicolella, *American Silent Horror, Science Fiction, and Fantasy Feature Films, 1913–1929* (Jefferson, NC: McFarland, 2012), p. 744; Van Schaack, "Coming of the Hun!" p. 288.

70. Van Schaack, "Coming of the Hun!" p. 291.

71. Benjamin Paul Hegi, "German-Americans in Cooke County, Texas, during World War I," *Southwestern Historical Quarterly* 109, no. 2 (2005): 234–57, 248.

72. Schaffer, *America in the Great War*, p. 21; Proctor, "'Patriotic Enemies,'" p. 228.

73. Sherman, *Screen Enemies*, p. 8.

74. Christopher Capozzola, *Uncle Sam Wants You: World War I and the Making of the Modern American Citizen* (New York: Oxford University Press, 2008), p. 117.

75. Proctor, "'Patriotic Enemies,'" p. 228.

76. Siegel and Silverman, "During World War I."

77. Sonntag, "Fighting Everything German," p. 667.

78. Hegi, "German-Americans," pp. 248–49.

79. Theodore Kornweibel Jr., *"Investigate Everything": Federal Efforts to Ensure Black Loyalty during World War I* (Bloomington: Indiana University Press, 2002), p. 43.

80. Peter C. Ripley, "Intervention and Reaction: Florida Newspapers and United States Entry into World War I," *Florida Historical Quarterly* 49, no. 3 (1971): 255–67. See p. 264.

81. Ibid., p. 265.

82. Ibid.

83. Van Schaack, "Coming of the Hun!" p. 291.

84. Bowles, "Karl Muck," pp. 410–11.

85. Ibid., p. 412.

86. Ibid.

87. Ibid., p. 412–13; J. Vacha, "When Wagner Was Verboten: The Campaign against German Music in World War I," *New York History* 64, no. 2 (1983): 171–88. See p. 173.

88. "Send Dr. Muck Back, Roosevelt Advises," *New York Times*, November 3, 1917.

89. Bowles, "Karl Muck," pp. 413–14; Vacha, "When Wagner Was Verboten," p. 178.

90. Marc Ferris, *Star-Spangled Banner: The Unlikely Story of America's National Anthem* (Baltimore, MD: Johns Hopkins University Press, 2014), p. 122.

91. Bowles, "Karl Muck," p. 413.

92. Joseph Horowitz, *Moral Fire: Musical Portraits from America's Fin de Siècle* (Berkeley: University of California Press, 2012), p. 66.

93. Vacha, "When Wagner Was Verboten," p. 183.

94. Ibid.

95. Ibid., p. 184.

96. Ibid., p. 186.

97. Steve Szkotak, "An Islamic Lesson in a Virginia Classroom Creates a Viral Furor and Shutters Schools," Associated Press, December 19, 2015.

98. Editorial Board, "Panic in Augusta County," *Washington Post*, December 23, 2015.

99. "Guns in the US: The Statistics behind the Violence," BBC News, January 5, 2016, http://www.bbc.com/news/world-us-canada-34996604 (accessed July 14, 2018).

NOTES

CHAPTER 6: "BEWARE THE YELLOW PERIL"

1. Raymond Leslie Buell, "The Development of the Anti-Japanese Agitation in the United States," *Political Science Quarterly* 37, no. 4 (1922): 605–38. See p. 606.

2. Herbert P. LePore, "Exclusion by Prejudice: Anti-Japanese Discrimination in California and the Immigration Act of 1924" (doctoral dissertation, Brigham Young University, Provo, UT, 1973), p. 33; Kelley, "Social Forces Collide," p. 10.

3. Lance D. Muckey, "Nevada's Odd Response to the 'Yellow Peril': Asians and the Western Ineligible Alien Land Laws" (master's thesis, University of Nevada at Las Vegas, 2004), pp. 46–47.

4. Michael J. Meloy, "The Long Road to Manzanar: Politics, Land, and Race in the Japanese Exclusion Movement, 1900" (doctoral dissertation, University of California at Davis, 2004), p. 5.

5. Ibid., p. 21.

6. This figure is taken from Yamato Ichihashi, *Japanese Immigration: Its Status in California* (San Francisco, CA: Marshall, 1915), pp. 4–5. These figures should not be confused with the total number of migrants in Hawaii and locations outside of the US mainland.

7. Muckey, "Nevada's Odd Response," p. 48.

8. Ibid., p. 53.

9. Cited in Randa-Noel Johnson, "Women in the Anti-Japanese Movement in California, 1900–1924" (master's thesis, San Jose State University, 2000), p. 8.

10. Roger Daniels, *The Politics of Prejudice: The Anti-Japanese Movement in California and the Struggle for Japanese Exclusion* (Berkeley: University of California Press, 1977), p. 20.

11. Ibid., p. 21.

12. Sarah Wallace, *Not Fit to Stay: Public Health Panics and South Asian Exclusion* (Vancouver, British Columbia: University of Toronto Press, 2017).

13. Buell, "Development of the Anti-Japanese Agitation," pp. 608–609.

14. Ellen M. Eisenberg, *The First to Cry Down Injustice: Western Jews and Japanese Removal during World War II* (Lanham, MD: Lexington, 2008), p. 8; Daniels, *Politics of Prejudice*, pp. 21–22.

15. Meloy, "Long Road to Manzanar," p. 26.

16. Buell, "Development of the Anti-Japanese Agitation," p. 609.

17. Daniels, *Politics of Prejudice*, pp. 22–23.

18. Muckey, "Nevada's Odd Response," p. 53.

19. Daniels, *Politics of Prejudice*, p. 25.

20. Buell, "Development of the Anti-Japanese Agitation," pp. 614–18; Commission on Wartime Relocation and Internment of Civilians, *Personal Justice Denied: Report of the Commission on Wartime Relocation and Internment of Civilians* (Washington, DC: Civil Liberties Public Education Fund; Seattle: University of Washington Press, 1997), p. 32.

21. Commission on Wartime Relocation, *Personal Justice Denied*, pp. 32–33.

22. Daniels, *Politics of Prejudice*, p. 31.

23. Buell, "Development of Anti-Japanese Agitation," p. 623.

24. Elliott Barkan, *From All Points: America's Immigrant West* (Bloomington: Indiana University Press, 2007), p. 131.

25. Buell, "Development of Anti-Japanese Agitation," p. 625.

26. Meloy, "Long Road to Manzanar," p. 5; LePore, "Exclusion by Prejudice," p. 52.

27. LePore, "Exclusion by Prejudice," pp. 132–33.

28. John Powell, *The Encyclopedia of North American Immigration* (New York: Facts on File, 2005), p. 103.

29. Daniel Brinton, *The American Race* (New York: H. C. Hodges, 1891), pp. 39–41.

30. Meloy, "Long Road to Manzanar," p. 10.

31. Daniels, *Politics of Prejudice*, p. 30.

32. Ibid., p. 28.

33. LePore, "Exclusion by Prejudice," pp. 60–62.

34. W. Almont Gates, "Oriental Immigration on the Pacific Coast," address delivered at the National Conference of Charities and Correction (Buffalo, NY) on June 10, 1909. See p. 11.

35. Meloy, "Long Road to Manzanar," p. 33.

36. Johnson, *Women in the Anti-Japanese Movement*, p. 61.

37. Kenneth C. Hough, "Rising Sun over America: Imagining a Japanese Conquest of the United States, 1900–1945" (doctoral dissertation, University of California at Santa Barbara, 2014), pp. 9–10.

38. LePore, "Exclusion by Prejudice," pp. 116–17.

39. Ibid., p. 117.

40. Ibid., p. 118.

41. Peter H. Schuck, *Diversity in America: Keeping Government at a Safe Distance* (Cambridge, MA: Belknap Press of Harvard University Press, 2003), p. 84.

42. Russell E. Bearden, "The Internment of Japanese Americans in Arkansas, 1942–1945" (doctoral dissertation, University of Arkansas, 1986), p. 21.

43. United States Department of State, Office of the Historian, Bureau of Public Affairs, "The Immigration Act of 1924" (Washington, DC: Government Printing Office, 1924), https://history.state.gov/milestones/1921-1936/immigration-act (accessed December 9, 2016).

44. Alan Gevinson, ed., *American Film Institute Catalogue, Within Our Gates: Ethnicity in American Feature Films, 1911–1960* (Berkeley: University of California Press, 1997), p. 908.

45. Stacey Olster, *The Trash Phenomenon: Contemporary Literature, Popular Culture, and the Making of the American Century* (Athens: University of Georgia Press, 2003), p. 34.

46. Kenneth M. Ludmerer, "Genetics, Eugenics, and the Immigration Restriction Act of 1924," *Bulletin of the History of Medicine* 46, no. 1 (1972): 59–81. See p. 77.

47. Hugo Engelhardt and Arthur Caplan, eds., *Scientific Controversies: Case Studies in the Resolution and Closure of Disputes in Science and Technology* (New York: Cambridge University Press, 1989), p. 195.

48. Ludmerer, "Genetics, Eugenics," p. 74.

49. Ibid., p. 64.

50. Douglas Baynton, *Defectives in the Land: Disability and Immigration in the Age of Eugenics* (Chicago: University of Chicago Press, 2016), p. 45.

51. Jonathan Spiro, *Defending the Master Race: Conservation, Eugenics, and the Legacy of Madison Grant* (Lebanon, NH: University of Vermont Press, 2009), p. 377.

52. Ludmerer, "Genetics, Eugenics," p. 68.

53. Ibid.

54. Ibid., p. 67.

55. Quote taken from ibid., p. 68; see also Elazar Barkan, "Progressive Eugenics: Herbert Spencer Jennings and the 1924 Immigration Legislation," *Journal of the History of Biology* 24, no. 1 (1991): 91–112.

56. Ludmerer, "Genetics, Eugenics," pp. 77–78.

57. A. Samaan, *H. H. Laughlin: American Scientist. American Progressive. Nazi Collaborator* (San Diego, CA: A. R. C. Publishing, 2015), p. 112.

58. Ibid., pp. 114–15.

59. Charles P. Patterson, *Eternal Treblinka: Our Treatment of Animals in the Holocaust* (New York: Lantern, 2002), p. 98.

60. Ibid.

61. Richard S. Levy, ed., *Antisemitism: A Historical Encyclopedia of Prejudice and Persecution*, vol. 1, *A-K* (Santa Barbara, CA: ABC-CLIO, 2005), p. 212.

62. Ibid.

63. Roger Daniels, "Incarcerating Japanese Americans: An Atrocity Revisited," *Peace and Change* 23, no. 2 (1998): 117–34. See p. 118.

64. Commission on Wartime Relocation, *Personal Justice Denied*, p. 2.

65. Milton Eisenhower, *Japanese Relocation* (Washington, DC: Office of War, Bureau of Motion Pictures, c. 1943), 9 minutes, 27 seconds.

66. Daniels, "Incarcerating Japanese Americans," p. 122.

67. Paul R. Spickard, *Japanese Americans: The Formation and Transformations of an Ethnic Group* (New Brunswick, NJ: Rutgers University Press, 2009), p. 116.

68. Eugene Rostow, "The Japanese-American Cases—A Disaster," *Yale Law Review* 54, no. 3 (1945): 489–533. See pp. 489–90.

69. Daniels, "Incarcerating Japanese Americans," p. 117.

70. Leslie T. Hatamiya, *Righting a Wrong: Japanese Americans and the Passage of the Civil Liberties Act of 1988* (Stanford: Stanford University Press, 1993), p. 14.

71. Daniels, "Incarcerating Japanese Americans," p. 118.

72. Spickard, *Japanese Americans*, p. 109.

73. Ibid.

74. Kelley, "Social Forces Collide," p. 2.

75. Juan González and Joseph Torres, *News for All the People: The Epic Story of Race and the American Media* (London: Verso, 2011), p. 274.

76. Robert Shaffer, "Cracks in the Consensus: Defending the Rights of Japanese Americans during World War II," *Radical History Review* 72 (1998): 84–120. See pp. 99–100.

77. Meloy, "Long Road to Manzanar," pp. 9–10.

78. Christie C. Armendariz, "Inconspicuous but Estimable Immigrants: The Japanese in El Pasa, 1980–1948" (master's thesis, Department of History, University of Texas at El Paso, 1994), p. 97.

79. Tamotsu Shibutani, *Improvised News: A Sociological Study of Rumor* (New York: Bobbs-Merrill, 1966), p. 133.

80. Garland E. Allen, "The Misuse of Biological Hierarchies: The American Eugenics Movement, 1900–1940," *History and Philosophy of the Life Sciences* 5, no. 2 (1983): 105–28.

81. Ibid., p. 123.

82. James Mooney, *Historical Sketch of the Cherokee* (Chicago, IL: Aldine, 1975), p. 122.

83. Ludmerer, "Genetics, Eugenics," p. 73.

84. Shi-Pu Wang, "Becoming American: Asian Identity Negotiated through the Art of Yasuo Kuniyoshi" (doctoral dissertation, University of California at Santa Barbara, 2006), p. 42.

85. James C. McNaughton, *Nisei Linguists: Japanese Americans in the Military Intelligence Service during World War II* (Washington, DC: Department of the Army, 2007), p. 137.

86. Katelyn Taira, "America's 'Enemy Aliens,'" *Washington University Political Review*, November 3, 2016, http://www.wupr.org/2016/11/03/americas-enemy-aliens/ (accessed March 5, 2017).

87. Ibid.

88. McNaughton, *Nisei Linguists*, pp. 133–37. This quote appears on p. 137.

89. Commission on Wartime Relocation, *Personal Justice Denied*, p. 28.

90. Ibid., p. 2.

91. Alan J. Levine, *The Pacific War: Japan versus the Allies* (Westport, CT: Praeger, 1995), p. 74.

92. John Dower, *War Without Mercy: Race and Power in the Pacific War* (New York: Pantheon, 1986), p. 84.

93. Ben-Ami Shillon, *The Jews and the Japanese: The Successful Outsiders* (Rutland, VT: Charles E. Tuttle, 1991), p. 92.

CHAPTER 7: "THE JEWS ARE SPYING FOR HITLER!"

1. Robert Michael, *A Concise History of American Antisemitism* (New York: Rowman and Littlefield, 2005), p. 182. In reality, a few countries agreed to admit relatively small numbers, but the vast majority of countries refused to accept them.

2. Yoram Kaniuk, *Commander of the Exodus* (New York: Grove, 1999), p. 153.

3. David A. Harris, *In the Trenches: Selected Speeches and Writings of an American Jewish Activist, 1979–1999* (Hoboken, NJ: KTAV, 2000), p. 518.

4. Alex Nowrasteh, *Terrorism and Immigration: A Risk Analysis*, CATO Institute Policy Paper Number 798 (Washington, DC: CATO Institute, September 13, 2016).

5. Susan Welch, "American Opinion towards Jews during the Nazi Era: Results from Quota Sample Polling during the 1930s and 1940s," *Social Science Quarterly* 95, no. 3 (2014): 615–35. See p. 617.

6. Deborah E. Lipstadt, *Beyond Belief: The American Press and the Coming of the Holocaust 1933–1945* (New York: Free Press, 1986), p. 14.

7. Daniel A. Gross, "The US Government Turned Away Thousands of Jewish Refugees, Fearing That They Were Nazi Spies," *Smithsonian Magazine*, November 18, 2015.

8. Roger Daniels, "Immigration Policy in a Time of War: The United States, 1939–1945," *Journal of American Ethnic History* 25, nos. 2/3 (2006): 107–16. See p. 107.

9. Wesley P. Greear, "American Immigration Policies and Public Opinion on European Jews from 1933 to 1945" (master's thesis, East Tennessee State University, 2002), p. 24.

10. Bruce Hodge, "Assistant Secretary of State Breckinridge Long and American Immigration Policy, 1940–1944" (master's thesis, Lamar University, 2012), p. 35.

11. Daniels, "Immigration Policy," p. 109.

12. Joyce A. Delgado, "Official Policy of the Government of the United States of America Regarding Jewish Refugees from Nazi Germany" (master's thesis, Kean College of New Jersey, 1979), p. 11.

13. Ibid.; Tyler Anbinder, *City of Dreams: The 400-Year Epic History of Immigrant New York* (Boston: Houghton Mifflin Harcourt, 2016), p. 493; Thomas Adam, *Germany and the Americas: Culture, Politics, History, a Multidisciplinary Encyclopedia*, vol. 1 (Santa Barbara, CA: ABC-CLIO, 2005), pp. 411–12.

14. Wolfram Kaiser, *Christian Democracy and the Origins of European Union* (New York: Cambridge University Press, 2007), p. 135.

15. Rodger Streitmatter, *Mightier Than the Sword: How the News Media Have Shaped American History* (Boulder, CO: Westview, 2016), p. 106.

16. Monty N. Penkower, "Eleanor Roosevelt and the Plight of World Jewry," *Jewish Social Studies* 49, no. 2 (1987): 125–36. See. p. 125.

17. Robert A. Rockaway, "Review: The Roosevelt Administration, the Holocaust, and the Jewish Refugees," *Reviews in American History* 3, no. 1 (1975): 115.

18. Robert W. Sussman, *The Myth of Race: The Troubling Persistence of an Unscientific Idea* (Cambridge, MA: Harvard University Press, 2014), p. 110.

19. Ibid., p. 133.

20. Ibid., p. 123.

21. Richard S. Levy, ed., *Anti-Semitism: A Historical Encyclopedia of Prejudice and Persecution*, vol. 1 (Santa Barbara, CA: ABC-CLIO, 2005), p. 212.

22. Jonathan Spiro, *Defending the Master Race: Conservation, Eugenics, and the Legacy of Madison Grant* (Burlington: University of Vermont Press, 2009), p. 373.

23. Lothrop Stoddard, *The Rising Tide of Color: The Threat against White World-Supremacy* (New York: Charles Scribner's Sons, 1920).

24. Spiro, *Defending the Master Race*, p. 374.

25. Rudolph Alvarado and Sonya Alvarado, *Drawing Conclusions on Henry Ford* (Ann Arbor: University of Michigan Press, 2001), p. 144.

26. Frederick Schweitzer and Marvin Perry, *Antisemitism: Myth and Hate from Antiquity to the Present* (New York: Palgrave Macmillan, 2002), p. 171; Albert Lee, *Henry Ford and the Jews* (New York: Stein and Day, 1980), p. 59; Anthony C. Sutton, *Wall Street and the Rise of Hitler* (United Kingdom: Clairview, 2010), p. 93; Sussman, *Myth of Race*, p. 137.

27. Adolf Hitler, *Mein Kampf: Complete and Unabridged, Fully Annotated* (New York: Reynal and Hitchcock, 1939), p. 929.

28. Daniels, "Immigration Policy," p. 110.

29. Lipstadt, *Beyond Belief*, p. 113.

30. Ibid., p. 315.

31. Dara Lind, "How America's Rejection of Jews Fleeing Nazi Germany Haunts Our Refugee Policy Today," *Vox*, January 27, 2017.

32. Lipstadt, *Beyond Belief*, p. 115.

33. Daniels, "Immigration Policy," p. 110.

34. Michael Robert Marrus, *Bystanders to the Holocaust* (London: Meckler, 1989), p. 109.

35. Lipstadt, *Beyond Belief*, p. 114.

36. Saul S. Friedman, *No Haven for the Oppressed: United States Policy toward Jewish Refugees, 1938–1945* (Detroit, MI: Wayne State University Press, 1973), p. 155.

37. Angus Calder, *The People's War: Britain 1939–1945* (London: Pimlico, 1992), p. 129; Walter Laqueur, *Generation Exodus: The Fate of Young Jewish Refugees from Nazi Germany* (2004; London: I. B. Tauris, 2008), p. 130.

38. Laqueur, *Generation Exodus*, p. 130.

39. Ibid., p. 116.

40. Ibid., p. 117.

41. Spiro, *Defending the Master Race*, p. 370.

42. Greg Hansard (narrator), *S.S. Quanza: Journey of Refugees from Lisbon to Norfolk*, documentary produced by the Virginia Historical Society, based on a historical society exhibit, Richmond, VA, 2010, 4 minutes, 29 seconds; Matthias Blum and Claudia Rei, "Escaping the Holocaust: Human and Health Capital of Refugees to the US, 1940–42," *Beiträge zur Jahrestagung des Vereins für Socialpolitik 2016: Demographischer Wandel - Session: Economic History*, No. F13-V3 (November 23, 2015): 9–10.

43. Monty P. Penkower, *The Jews Were Expendable: Free World Diplomacy and the Holocaust* (Detroit, MI: Wayne State University Press, 1988), p. 65; Douglas Martin, "Gerhart Riegner, 90, Dies; Disclosed Holocaust Plans," *New York Times*, December 5, 2001.

44. Photograph of the original deciphered cable dated August 10, 1942, sent to the London office (Document 2: FO 371/30917) from the British National Archives, *Britain and the Holocaust* (Washington, DC: National Archives Educational Service), https://nationalarchives. gov.uk/documents/education/britain-and-the-holocaust-prep-pack.pdf (accessed June 12, 2016).

45. Rebecca Erbelding, "About Time: The History of the War Refugee Board" (doctoral dissertation, George Mason University, 2015), p. 30.

46. Ibid., p. 29.

47. "Riegner Cable," Vad Yashem, Shoah Resource Center, International School for Holocaust Studies, http://www.yadvashem.org/odot_pdf/Microsoft%20Word%20-%205827 .pdf (accessed June 20, 2016).

48. Michael J. Cohen, *Britain's Moment in Palestine: Retrospect and Perspectives, 1917– 1948* (New York: Routledge, 2014), p. 339.

49. Rafael Medoff, *Blowing the Whistle on Genocide: Josiah E. DuBois Jr. and the Struggle for a US Response to the Holocaust* (West Lafayette, IN: Purdue University Press, 2009), pp. 40–52. Quotation appears on p. 40. Medoff provides the full text of the "Report to the Secretary on the Acquiescence of This Government in the Murder of the Jews," by Josiah DuBois Jr. for the Foreign Funds Control Unit of the Treasury Department, Washington, DC, January 13, 1944.

50. David S. Wyman, *Paper Walls: America and the Refugee Crisis, 1938–1941* (Amherst: University of Massachusetts Press, 1968).

51. Medoff, *Blowing the Whistle*, p. 44.

52. Ibid., p. 41.

53. Bruce Hodge, "Assistant Secretary of State Breckinridge Long and American Immigration Policy, 1940–1944" (master's thesis, Lamar University, Beaumont, TX, 2012).

54. Angus Stevenson and Maurice Waite, eds., *Concise Oxford Encyclopedia: Luxury Edition* (New York: Oxford University Press, 2011), p. 529.

55. Hodge, "Assistant Secretary," p. 52.

56. Ibid., pp. 53–54.

57. Greear, "American Immigration Policies," p. 29.

58. Friedman, *No Haven for the Oppressed*, p. 44.

59. Delgado, "Official Policy," pp. 28–29.

60. Wyman, *Paper Walls*.

61. Francis MacDonnell, *Insidious Foes: The Axis Fifth Column and the American Home Front* (New York: Oxford University Press, 1995), pp. 7–8. Italics ours.

62. Emily Roxworthy, *The Spectacle of Japanese American Trauma: Racial Performativity and World War II* (Honolulu: University of Hawaii Press, 2008), p. 77; Greear, "American Immigration Policies," p. 31. Quotes are taken from Roxworthy, *Spectacle of Japanese American Trauma*.

63. Friedman, *No Haven for the Oppressed*.

64. Lipstadt, *Beyond Belief*, p. 121.

65. Hodge, "Assistant Secretary," p. 54.

66. Robert Switky, *Wealth of an Empire: The Treasure Shipments That Saved Britain and the World* (Washington, DC: Potomac, 2013), pp. 112–13.

67. Lipstadt, *Beyond Belief*, p. 122.

68. MacDonnell, *Insidious Foes*, p. 3.

69. David M. Kennedy, *The Library of Congress World War II Companion* (New York: Simon and Schuster, 2007), p. 75.

70. Stephen M. Feldman, *Free Expression and Democracy in America: A History* (Chicago, IL: University of Chicago Press, 2008), p. 423.

71. Gross, "US Government Turned Away Thousands"; Jefferson Adams, *Historical Dictionary of German Intelligence* (Lanham, MD: Scarecrow, 2009), p. 18; "FBI Seizes Nazi Spy Attempting US Entry," *Daily Iowan*, July 10, 1942, p. 1; "German-Born Spy Suspect Held without Bail Awaiting Quick Jury Action," *San Bernardino Daily Sun*, July 11, 1942, p. 3.

72. Switky, *Wealth of an Empire*, p. 113.

73. Lynne Olson, *Those Angry Days: Roosevelt, Lindbergh, and America's Fight Over World War II, 1939–1941* (New York: Random House, 2013), p. 106.

74. George Britt, *The Fifth Column Is Here* (New York: W. Funk, 1941).

75. Olson, *Those Angry Days*, p. 106.

76. "Tenfold Gain in Complaints to FBI Told," *San Bernardino Daily Sun*, August 5, 1940, p. 2; MacDonnell, *Insidious Foes*, p. 8; William Dow Boutwell, Pauline Frederick, and Joseph Pratt Harris, *America Prepares for Tomorrow: The Story of Our Total Defense Effort* (New York: Harper and Brothers, 1941), p. 485. This figure of 2,871 is so high that we checked numerous sources to confirm that it is, indeed, correct.

CHAPTER 8: "BE WARY OF THE WOLF IN SHEEP'S CLOTHING!"

1. Bill Girrier, *Fruition: Reflections on a Life Grafted-In* (Bloomington, IN: WestBow, 2011), p. 78.

2. John Esposito, *The Islamic Threat: Myth or Reality?* (New York: Oxford University Press, 1999), p. 227.

3. Centers for Disease Control and Prevention, "Underlying Cause of Death 1999–2015," last reviewed December 20, 2017, https://wonder.cdc.gov/wonder/help/ucd.html# (accessed June 7, 2018); "Choking Prevention and Rescue Tips," National Safety Council, 2018, http://www.nsc.org/learn/safety-knowledge/Pages/safety-at-home-choking.aspx (accessed June 7, 2018).

4. Christopher Ingraham, "Chart: The Animals That Are Most Likely to Kill You This Summer," *Washington Post*, June 16, 2015.

5. Alejandra Reyes-Velarde, "Nobody Died in a US Commercial Jet Crash Last Year—A Trend That Predates Trump," *Los Angeles Times*, January 2, 2018. These figures exclude less-regulated types of aircraft such as ultralights and privately owned flying machines, in addition to government and military planes.

6. "Facts + Statistics: Mortality Risk," Insurance Information Institute, 2018, https://www.iii.org/fact-statistic/facts-statistics-mortality-risk (accessed July 19, 2018).

7. Alex Nowrasteh, *Terrorism and Immigration: A Risk Analysis*, CATO Institute Policy Paper Number 798 (Washington, DC: CATO Institute, September 13, 2016). See p. 1.

8. Ibid., pp. 13–14. While several of the twenty refugees who were classified as terrorists were arrested after 9/11 and were detained on vague charges of aiding or abetting overseas terrorist groups, not a single suspect was ever linked to the 9/11 attacks.

9. United States Department of Justice, Office of the Attorney General, Press Release No. 18-38, January 16, 2018.

10. Alex Nowrasteh, "New Government Terrorism Report Provides Little Useful Information," Cato Institute, January 16, 2018, https://www.cato.org/blog/new-government -terrorism-report-nearly-worthless (accessed July 19, 2018).

11. Gregory Krieg, "Christie on Refugees: Not Even 5-Year-Old Orphans," CNN News, November 17, 2015.

12. Haeyoun Park and Larry Buchanan, "Refugees Entering the US Already Face a Rigorous Vetting Process," *New York Times*, January 29, 2017.

13. Steve Benen, "Huckabee's Anti-Refugee Case Takes an Ugly Turn," MSNBC, November 17, 2015, http://www.msnbc.com/rachel-maddow-show/huckabees-anti-refugee -case-takes-ugly-turn (accessed July 19, 2018).

14. Amy Davidson, "Ted Cruz's Religious Test for Syrian Refugees," *New Yorker*, November 16, 2015.

15. Ibid.

16. Liz Robbins, "Malloy Welcomes a Syrian Family to Connecticut as Christie Shuns Refugees," *New York Times*, November 18, 2015.

17. Ralph Ellis, Ashley Fantz, Faith Karimi, and Eliott McLaughlin, "Orlando Shooting: 49 Killed, Shooter Pledged ISIS Allegiance," CNN, June 13, 2016, http://edition.cnn. com/2016/06/12/us/orlando-nightclub-shooting/ (accessed July 19, 2018).

18. Abigail Pesta, "The Orlando Shooter Was My Ex," *Marie Claire* (October 2016): 147–48.

19. Jay Weaver and David Ovalle, "What Motivated Orlando Killer? It Was More Than Terrorism, Experts Say," *Miami Herald*, June 17, 2016; Adam Goldman, Joby Warrick, and Max Bearak, "'He Was Not a Stable Person': Orlando Shooter Showed Signs of Emotional Trouble," *Washington Post*, June 26, 2016.

20. William Wan and Kevin Sullivan, "Troubled. Quiet. Macho. Angry. The Volatile Life of the Orlando Shooter," *Washington Post*, June 17, 2016.

21. Delvin Barrett, Matt Zapotosky, and Mark Berman, "New York Truck Attack Suspect Charged with Terrorism Offense as Trump Calls for a Death Sentence," *Washington Post*, November 20, 2017.

22. Tom Pollock, "Do You Feel Like You're More Likely Than Ever to Be Hit by a Terror Attack? This Is Why You're Wrong," *Independent* (London), July 16, 2016.

23. Bonnie Malkin, "'I Am German': Munich Gunman in Furious Exchange with Bystander," *Guardian*, July 23, 2016.

24. "Munich Shooting: David Sonboly 'Planned Attack for Year,'" BBC News, July 24, 2016; Umberto Bacchi, "Munich Killer Scouted School Shooting Site, Received Inpatient Psychiatric Treatment," *International Business Times*, July 24, 2016.

25. Rukmini Callimachi and Melissa Eddy, "Munich Killer Was Troubled, but Had No Terrorist Ties, Germany Says," *New York Times*, July 23, 2016; Harriet Alexander, Barney Henderson, Chiara Palazzo, Luke Heighton, James Rothwell, Zia Weise, Camilla Turner, and Justin Huggler, "Munich Shooting: Teenage Killer Ali Sonboly 'Inspired by Far-Right Terrorist Anders Breivik' and 'Used Facebook Offer of Free McDonald's Food to Lure Victims,'" *Telegraph* (London), July 24, 2016; Janek Schmidt and Emma Graham-Harrison, "'Strange and Withdrawn': What Drove Ali Sonboly to Launch Munich Attack?" *Guardian*, July 24, 2016.

26. Kate Connolly, "Munich Gunman Saw Sharing Hitler's Birthday as 'Special Honour,'" *Guardian*, July 27, 2016.

27. Keffrey L. Thomas, *Scapegoating Islam: Intolerance, Security, and the American Muslim* (Santa Barbara, CA: ABC-CLIO, 2015), p. 14.

28. Eli Smith, *Missionary Sermons and Addresses* (New York: Saxton and Miles, 1842), p. 22.

29. Douglas Little, *Us versus Them: The United States, Radical Islam, and the Rise of the Green Threat* (Chapel Hill: University of North Carolina Press, 2016), p. 218.

30. Rashid Shaz, *In Pursuit of Arabia* (New Delhi, India: Milli, 2003), p. 155.

31. Little, *Us versus Them*, p. 217.

32. Lothrop Stoddard, *The New World of Islam* (New York: C. Scribner's Sons, 1921), p. 98.

33. Kathleen M. Moore, *Al-Mughtaribun: American Law and the Transformation of Muslim Life in the United States* (Albany: State University of New York Press, 1995), p. 40.

34. Ibid.

35. Rubina Ramji, "From Navy Seals to the Seige: Getting to Know the Muslim Terrorist, Hollywood Style," *Journal of Religion & Film* 9, no. 2 (2016): 1–40. See p. 3.

36. Little, *Us versus Them*, p. 220.

37. Heater Singmaster, "The Backlash against Teaching about Islam," *Education Week*, January 20, 2018.

38. "Tennessee Reviews Its Social Studies Curriculum," American Center for Law and Justice, https://aclj.org/establishment-clause/tennessee-reviews-its-social-studies-curriculum (accessed July 20, 2018).

39. Ibid.

40. "Parents Object after 7th Graders Write 'Allah Is the Only God' in History Class,'" Fox News, September 8, 2015, http://insider.foxnews.com/2015/09/08/students-write-allah-only-god-tennessee-middle-school-history-class (accessed July 19, 2018).

41. Emma Green, "The Fear of Islam in Tennessee Public Schools," *Atlantic*, December 16, 2016, https://www.theatlantic.com/education/archive/2015/12/fear-islam-tennessee-public-schools/420441/ (accessed July 20, 2018).

42. Melanie Balakit, "Williamson School Board Split on Religious Bias Resolution," *Tennessean*, October 15, 2015.

43. Green, "Fear of Islam."

44. Ibid.

45. Ibid.

46. "9 Investigates: Dad Protests Islamic Lessons at School," WFTV, February 9, 2015, http://www.wftv.com/news/local/9-investigates-dad-protests-islamic-lessons-school/69473209 (accessed January 21, 2018).

47. "Marine Dad Banned from School after Complaining about Islam Assignment," *Fox News Insider*, October 29, 2014, http://insider.foxnews.com/2014/10/29/marine-dad-banned-school-after-complaining-about-islam-assignment (accessed January 21, 2018).

48. Emma Brown, "This Marine Vet Was Banned from His Kid's School after Objecting to Islam Lessons," *Washington Post*, February 23, 2016.

49. Ibid.

50. "School Health Handout Quotes Quran," *Asbury Park Press* (Asbury Park, NJ), September 18, 2016, p. A3.

51. Abby Haglage and Kelly Weill, "Muslim Teacher Fired after Showing Malala Video," *Daily Beast* (New York), December 17, 2015.

52. Ibid.

53. Samantha Laine, "Duke 'Call to Prayer' No More: Why the University Reversed Itself," *Christian Science Monitor*, January 16, 2015.

54. Ibid.

55. Susan Syrluga, "Muslim Call to Prayer at Duke Resonates with a Scholar Who Studies Sound in Religious Life," *Washington Post*, January 20, 2015.

56. Phoebe Weston, "Illinois Teacher Suspended after Claiming Muslims and Christians Worship the Same God," *Independent* (London), December 17, 2015.

57. Christine Hauser, "Wheaton College and Professor to 'Part Ways' after Her Remarks on Muslims," *New York Times*, February 8, 2016.

58. "'Flying While Muslim': Profiling Fears after Arabic Speaker Removed from Plane," *All Things Considered*, National Public Radio, April 20, 2016, https://www.npr.org/2016/04/20/475015239/flying-while-muslim-profiling-fears-after-arabic-speaker-removed-from-plane (accessed January 23, 2018). The program interviewed Zahra Billoo of the Council on American-Islamic Relations, which was providing Mr. Makhzoomi with legal assistance.

59. Yanan Yang, "UC Berkeley Student Removed from Southwest Flight after Speaking Arabic on Plane," *Washington Post*, April 18, 2016.

60. Jeff D. Gorman, "Emirati Man Sues Marriott over Islamic State Accusation," *Courthouse News Service* (Pasadena, CA), May 25, 2017, https://www.courthousenews.com/emirati-man-sues-marriott-isis-pledge-accusation/ (accessed July 20, 2018).

61. Matt Ford, "Trump Is Distorting Statistics to Demonize Immigrants," *New Republic*, January 17, 2018, https://newrepublic.com/article/146634/trump-distorting-statistics-demonize-immigrants (accessed January 23, 2018).

62. Nirja Chokshi, "How the California Wildfire Was Falsely Pinned on an Immigrant," *New York Times*, October 20, 2017.

63. Manny Fernandez and Christine Hauser, "Handcuffed for Making Clock, Gets Time with Obama," *New York Times*, September 17, 2015, p. A1.

64. Zainab Arain, Council on American-Islamic Relations, Washington, DC, Coordinator, Department to Monitor and Combat Islamophobia, telephone interview conducted on January 26, 2017.

65. Council on American-Islamic Relations, "CAIR-MI Files Michigan Department of Civil Rights Complaint against Wayne County Community College District," press release, January 24, 2018.

66. Council on American-Islamic Relations, "CAIR-DFW Welcomes Resignation of Two McKinney ISD Middle School Teachers after Islamophobic, Hateful Tweets," press release, January 20, 2018.

67. Eli Rosenberg, "'I Just Don't Like Muslim People': Trump Appointee Resigns after Racist, Sexist, and Anti-Gay Remarks," *Washington Post*, January 18, 2018.

68. Office of US House of Representatives, 23rd District of Texas, "Hurd Calls Trump's Wall 'A Third-Century Solution to a 21st-Century Problem,'" press release, January 30, 2017, https://hurd.house.gov/media-center/in-the-news/hurd-calls-trumps-wall-third-century -solution-21st-century-problem (accessed January 21, 2018).

69. Henry George Bohn, *A Dictionary of Quotations from the English Poets* (London, privately printed, 1867), p. 276.

70. Larry Chang, *Wisdom for the Soul* (Washington, DC: Gnosophia, 2006), p. 385.

CHAPTER 9: FROM MEXICANS TO MUSLIMS

1. Jean François Paul de Gondi de Retz, *Memoirs of the Cardinal de Retz: Containing the Particulars of His Own Life with the Most Secret Transactions of the French Court and the Civil Wars*, vol. 1 (London: Printed for T. Becket, T. Cadell, and T. Evans, 1774), p. 224.

2. Michelangelo Landgrave and Alex Nowrasteh, *Criminal Immigrants: Their Numbers, Demographics, and Countries of Origin* (Immigration Research and Policy Brief; Washington, DC: CATO Institute, March 15, 2017); Walter Ewing, Daniel E. Martínez, and Rubén G. Rumbaut, *The Criminalization of Immigration in the United States* (Washington, DC: American Immigration Council, July 13, 2015), pp. 1, 6.

3. Ewing et al., *Criminalization of Immigration*, p. 1.

4. Ibid., p. 6.

5. Ibid., p. 8.

6. US Government Accountability Office, *Criminal Alien Statistics: Information on Incarcerations, Arrest, and Costs*, GAO-11-187 (Washington, DC: Government Printing Office, March 2011), p. 20, cited by Ewing et al., *Criminalization of Immigration*.

7. The National Academies of Sciences, Engineering, and Medicine, *The Economic and Fiscal Consequences of Immigration* (Washington, DC: National Academies, 2016).

8. Jed Kolko, "How the Jobs That Immigrants Do Are Changing," *Indeed* (blog), January 19, 2017, http://blog.indeed.com/2017/01/19/how-jobs-immigrants-do-are-changing/ (accessed July 20, 2018). Kolko is the chief economist at Indeed.com and holds a doctorate in economics from Harvard University. His analysis is based on data from I-PUMS, the world's largest individual-level population database consisting of US and international records.

9. George J. Borjas, "The Labor Supply of Undocumented Immigrants" (working paper no. 22102, National Bureau of Economic Research, Cambridge, MA, March 2016).

10. Jason Richwine, *The Cost of Welfare Use by Immigrant and Native Households* (Washington, DC: Center for Immigration Studies, May, 2016).

11. Ben Rosen, "Do Immigrants Receive More Welfare Money Than Natural Born US Citizens?" *Christian Science Monitor* (Boston, MA), May 9, 2016.

12. Alex Nowrasteh, "Center for Immigration Studies Report Exaggerates Immigrant Welfare Use," Cato Institute, September 2, 2016, https://www.cato.org/blog/center-immigration-studies-exaggerates-immigrant-welfare-use (accessed July 20, 2018); Tara Watson, *Do Undocumented Immigrants Overuse Government Benefits?* (Medford, MA: Edward R. Murrow Center for a Digital World, Tufts University, 2017).

13. Laura Reston, "Where Trump Gets His Fuzzy Border Math," *New Republic*, March 11, 2017.

14. Watson, *Do Undocumented Immigrants*.

15. Jason Richwine, "IQ and Immigration Policy" (doctoral dissertation, Harvard University, Cambridge, MA, May 1, 2009), p. 66. For an excellent critique of Richwine's claims, see Elspeth Reeve, "The Heritage Foundation's Immigration Guru Wasn't Just Racist—He's Wrong," *Atlantic*, May 8, 2013, https://www.theatlantic.com/politics/archive/2013/05/heritage-foundation-jason-richwine/315481/ (accessed July 20, 2018).

16. Elizabeth Chin, "What Jason Richwine Should Have Heard from His PhD Committee," *Anthropology Now*, May 29, 2013, http://anthronow.com/online-articles/what-jason-richwine-should-have-heard-from-his-phd-committee (accessed June 8, 2018).

17. Brink Lindsey, "Why People Keep Misunderstanding the 'Connection' between Race and IQ," *Atlantic*, May 15, 2013, https://www.theatlantic.com/national/archive/2013/05/why-people-keep-misunderstanding-the-connection-between-race-and-iq/275876/ (accessed June 8, 2018).

18. Bette Roth Young, *Emma Lazarus in Her World: Life and Letters* (Philadelphia, PA: Jewish Publication Society, 1995), p. 3.

19. Liz Stark, "White House Policy Adviser Downplays Statue of Liberty's Famous Poem," CNN Politics, August 3, 2017. http://edition.cnn.com/2017/08/02/politics/emma-lazarus-poem-statue-of-liberty/index.html (accessed July 20, 2018).

20. Ibid.

21. Hyung-Chan Kim, *Asian Americans and the Supreme Court: A Documentary History* (Westport, CT: Greenwood, 1992), p. 110.

22. Regin Schmidt, *Red Scare: FBI and the Origins of Anticommunism in the United States, 1919–1943* (Copenhagen, Denmark: Museum Tusculanum, 2000), p. 55.

23. Isaiah Berlin, *The Proper Study of Mankind* (London: Vintage, 2013), p. 213.

24. Wood, James, *The Dictionary of Quotations from Ancient and Modern English and Foreign Sources* (London: Frederick Warne, 1893), p. 475.

25. Clellan Ford and Frank Beach, *Patterns of Sexual Behavior* (New York: Harper and Row, 1951), p. 108.

26. Andrew Gyory, *Closing the Gate: Race, Politics, and the Chinese Exclusion Act* (Chapel Hill: University of North Carolina Press, 1998), pp. 3–4.

27. Arthur Roy Leonard, *War Addresses of Woodrow Wilson with an Introduction and Notes* (London: Forgotten Books, 2013), p. 52.

28. Robert Torricelli and Andrew Carroll, eds., *Extraordinary Speeches of the American Century: In Our Own Words* (New York: Kodansha International, 1999), p. 174.

29. Julie Davis, Sheryl Stolberg, and Thomas Kaplan, "Trump Alarms Lawmakers with Disparaging Words for Haiti and Africa," *New York Times*, January 11, 2018.

30. Josh Dawsey, "Trump Derides Protections for Immigrants from 'Shithole' Countries," *Washington Post*, January 12, 2018.

31. George W. Bush, "Islam Is Peace," Office of the Press Secretary, September 17, 2001, remarks given by the president at the Islamic Center of Washington, DC, White House Archives.

32. Ibid.

33. Bern Guarino, "*Homo Sapiens*, We Keep Getting Older," *Washington Post*, June 8, 2017, p. A3.

34. "One Species, Living Worldwide," Smithsonian Institution National Museum of Natural History, last updated July 19, 2018, http://humanorigins.si.edu/evidence/genetics/one -species-living-worldwide (accessed July 20, 2018).

35. Robert Sussman, *The Myth of Race: The Troubling Persistence of an Unscientific Idea* (Cambridge, MA: Harvard University Press, 2014), p. 1.

36. Ralph Keyes and David Mayberry-Lewis, *The Quote Verifier: Who Said What, Where, and When* (New York: St. Martin's Griffin, 2006), p. 57.

INDEX

equated with insects and
animals, 81, 94
from public menace to model
minority, 98–100
Tom Kim Yung affair, 95
Christian Century (magazine), 155
Christianity and Crisis (magazine),
155
Christie, Chris, 185
chronic constipation, odds of
dying from, 38
Chronicles of Mount Benedict, The
(1837), 59
Cincinnati, Ohio, 120, 123
Cincinnati Post (newspaper), 171
Cincinnati Reds (baseball team),
33, 121
Cincinnati Symphony Orchestra,
132
Citizens Committee to Repeal
Chinese Exclusion and Place
Immigration on a Quota Basis,
99–100
Civil Liberties Act of 1988, 159
Civil War (Spanish), 176
Civil War (United States), 18, 44,
63, 107
Clark, Hugh, 62
Cleveland Indians (baseball team),
121
Clinton, Hillary, 36–37, 78
Clinton, Robert, 109

Coal Creek, Washington, 93
Code of Indian Offenses, 19, 101,
109, 114
Cohen, Daniel, 51, 56
Cohen, Stanley, 9–10, 22, 24
Collinsville, Illinois, 129
colonialism
Catholic scare, 18, 47
Mexicans, 66–72
Native Americans, 19, 102–14
Puritans, 47
Committee on Public Informa-
tion, 117
Committee on Selective Immigra-
tion, 149
Commonweal (magazine), 155
Communist "Red Scare," 31–33,
39, 41, 69, 127, 157, 180, 197,
207, 211
Constitution (US). *See* Amend-
ments to the US Constitution
Continental European witch scare,
39
*Convent's Doom; A Tale of Charles-
ton in 1834, The* (1854), 59
Cooke County, Florida, 130
Coumbe, Fritz, 121
Courts of Indian Offenses, 112
cows, threat from, 183
"crack babies" scare, 35
Creighton University, 156
crossers, 104–105